Press, Politics and Society: Uttar Pradesh, 1885-1914

KIRTI NARAIN

Foreword by
RAVINDER KUMAR

MANOHAR
2025

First published 1998
Reprinted 2023, 2024, 2025

ISBN 978-81-7304-223-2

Published by
Ajay Kumar Jain for
Manohar Publishers & Distributors
4753/23 Ansari Road, Daryaganj
New Delhi 110 002

Printed at
Replika Press Pvt. Ltd.

To

SWAMI SHYAM

Contents

Tables and Figure

TABLES

FIGURE

Foreword

It gives me great pleasure to say a few words about this valuable work of scholarship, entitled *Press, Politics and Society: Uttar Pradesh, 1885-1914,* which stems from the intellectual labour of Dr. Kirti Narain, a young scholar of promise, who has addressed herself to issues relating to the growth of nationalism among the popular classes in north India over a seminal phase.

As the title indicates, there are some distinctive features of the book under consideration which need to be highlighted for the benefit of its readers. It deals with nationalism as a social and intellectual phenomenon, in its formative stage, prior to the outbreak of World War I. Further, it is in its essence a regional study—the region in question being the State of Uttar Pradesh—and, therefore, offers a relatively cohesive cultural area as the base for historical exploration. Finally, it relies substantially on nationalist phenomena as seen in the *Language Press,* i.e. in newspapers published in Hindi and Urdu. The use of such sources enables us to gain access to the world-views and mentalities of the popular classes in north Indian society.

In view of the issues which Dr. Kirti Narain seeks to explore in this book, and the sources which she has utilised, her insights are of great value to historical scholarship. I hope, therefore, that her book will have the wide readership it deserves.

Teen Murti Bhawan
New Delhi

RAVINDER KUMAR

Acknowledgements

A work of this magnitude requires the support of many people at various stages of study and compilation. I place on record my gratitude and thanks to Dr. S.P. Dube and the late Dr. K.C. Srivastava of the Lucknow University; the Directors and Staff of the National Archives, New Delhi and the State Archives, Lucknow; and Professor Ravinder Kumar, the Director of the Nehru Memorial Museum and Library, Teen Murti, New Delhi. The Central Secretariat and the UP Secretariat libraries and the Information Department of the Government of UP provided me with adequate material.

This book would not have been possible without the unstinted support of my family—my husband Amitabh, my brother Mr. Y.S. Das, and my niece Namita—and the cooperation and understanding of my daughters, Aparajita and Arohini. I thank them all.

KIRTI NARAIN

Abbreviations

CC	Chief Commissioner
COMMR.	Commissioner
DEPT.	Department
EC	Education Commission
GAD	General Administration Department
LT.-GOVERNOR	Lieutenant-Governor
MEMO	Memorandum
NAI	National Archives of India, New Delhi
NWP & O	North-West Provinces and Oudh
PSC	Public Service Commission
RAD	Revenue Administration Department
RDPI	Report of the Director of Public Instruction
REV	Revenue
SEC	Secretary
THE UP	The United Province of Agra and Avadh
UP	Uttar Pradesh
UPSA	Uttar Pradesh State Archives, Lucknow
VNR	Vernacular Newspaper Reports

The Lieutenant-Governors of the United Provinces 1877-1914

	From
Sir George Couper Bart, KCSI, CB	15 February 1877
Sir Alfred Comyns Lyall, KCB	17 April 1882
Sir Auckland Colvin	21 November 1887
Sir Charles Hawkes Todd Crosthwaite, KCSI	28 November 1892
Mr. Alan Cadell, CSI	9 January 1895
Sir Anthony Patrick MacDonnell, KCSI & GCSI	6 November 1895 6 November 1898
Sir James John Digges LaTouche, KCSI	14 November 1901
Sir John Hewett	December 1906
Sir Leslie Porter	Acting Lt.-Governor
Sir James Scorgie Meston	1912-18

Introduction

Having lived in Uttar Pradesh all my life, I was interested in understanding the factors that had gone into the making of this great province. To my amazement, I found a total lack of material documenting its evolutionary processes, its travails and turmoils, and more so its contribution to the historical processes that changed the destiny of the country.

I therefore turned to newspapers of the late nineteenth and early twentieth centuries as sources which help us in defining and evaluating historical processes. In the hundred years prior to Independence, when colonial control was at its peak, the voice of Indians could be heard only through the Indian-language newspapers of the time—in fact many editors were also leaders of the people. With the preponderance of government-backed English newspapers, the language press, despite its limitations and insecurities, proved an efficacious voice of the political, social and economic phenomena distinctive of the Province.

As language journalism developed, the newspapers became reflective of the changes occurring in the Province which they highlighted with impunity. The political developments here and elsewhere in the country necessitated the growth of a more vocal press. Soon the newspapers started posing a threat to the well-entrenched colonial power as they became representative of the views of the people on a variety of issues and with the growing awareness, became more analytical and critical. It is difficult to separate the national movement from the social and cultural movements of the time. The social inequalities, the economic malaise, the cultural and educational discrepancies and the growing national and communal consciousness, all became intertwined and interdependent. The colonial government reacted strongly as it saw a connection between these ostensibly unrelated facets, which if ignored could develop into an opposition of alarming proportions.

With experience the language newspapers became more and more adept at exposing the colonialism and imperialism of the administration and its attempt to subvert the society, culture, politics and the economy of the Province. Social control was practised by evincing a desire to rid the social evils that plagued society. Educational policies, especially the introduction of English education, were formulated to enable social and political control by churning out a band of loyalists. This control was most visible in the economic policies of the government wherein it tried to maintain a balance between the tillers of the soil and the landowners. The latter were seen as the 'natural leaders of the people' and had to be fostered so that a permanently loyalist block could be created. The government could use this group to curb any discontent whether it be associated with land revenue, or with epidemics or even with communal complexes. Colonial control however, disturbed irrevocably the socio-economic-cultural equations in UP. Divisiveness, predominantly communal, but also in other spheres, became a potent colonial creation.

The threat to the colonial and imperialistic attitudes of the British posed by the language newspapers resulted in punitive measures being taken against them. While they could not always meet the standards of objective journalism and eschewed bias and partisan reporting, yet it is a measure of their relevance to the contemporary political and social milieu that in spite of heavy odds, they survived and continued to put forth and shape public opinion. As language journalism became increasingly popular, more and more educated people participated in it. Soon, different newspapers became representative of the different socio-political permutations. They reflected a variety of interest groups who were also influenced by them to a large extent.

Interestingly what becomes clear is that contemporary issues which are creating such a furore today, all had their roots somewhere in the nineteenth-century India. Ayodhya was being claimed as a sanctified spot by both Hindus and Muslims. Cow-slaughter which raises so much dust today was even in those days a contentious issue. The ills of the dowry system were regularly highlighted. Illicit liquor was a malady even then and the grievances of the minorities were ever present. Caste and communal discords seem to have defied the passage of time as has the sycophancy of some newspapers *vis-a-vis* the government, in the hope of getting adequate recompense for services rendered. This was looked upon with contempt by other newspapers. The parallels are mind-boggling and leaves one wondering whether the basic issues will ever be solved.

My entire study is based on the reports of the language newspapers of the years 1885-1915. Very few original newspapers are available as most of them have been destroyed or are lost. In the absence of these, I have to rely upon the important extracts of newspapers available in bound volumes in the UP State Archives, Lucknow and the National Archives, New Delhi. These extracts were compiled by the Government Reporter every month for the perusal of the Lieutenant-Governor. The government of the day, was itself keen to get an accurate picture of the entire scenario in the province, so naturally could not overlook any laxity on the part of the Reporter who was always asked to provide authentic information. So one can assume that the extracts are fairly extensive and relevant.

The methods adopted by the language newspapers of the day were not very different from those followed today. Theirs was not only an insipid reporting of topical issues. They had the capacity to analyse, deduce, condemn and also applaud. As is true of today's newspapers, even then newspaper reporting was never free of bias, intentional or unintentional. Rather than seeing it as a drawback, I have viewed it as a marker of the preoccupation of the times. This has retained the spirit of a bygone era imparting a certain amount of liveliness and sustainable interest to the enterprise.

Primary sources in the form of government records have been used extensively. These lend authenticity to the reporting of the language newspapers. These form a firm base on which theories, deductions and narrations rest. The secondary sources complete the triangle. They lend substance and provide believable paradigms to the book, preventing it from becoming too ponderous.

There are certain aspects of the book that I have to clarify. I have avoided using old spellings and terms as far as possible, except when absolutely necessary. For example old names like'Banaras' have been used only where 'Varanasi' seemed incongruous. Similarly 'Awadh' is seldom written as 'Oudh' except where primary sources have been referred to Indians have never been referred to as 'natives' except in a few places where I have emphasized upon the racial superiority practised by the British. To show that the term 'native' was used in a pejorative way, I have put it in inverted commas. English language newspapers are those papers which were published in India in English, majority of the cases had Indian editors. English newspapers were those which were published in England. The term 'vernacular' for the language press has been used only in the references as most of the records refer to the language press as the vernacular press.

During the period that the book covers (1885-1914) the initial name of Uttar Pradesh was the North-West Provinces and Awadh, which was rechristened the United Provinces of Agra and Awadh in 1902. I have used these names keeping chronology in mind and also to retain the flavour of the day. These provinces have been called Uttar Pradesh only when some aspect which is not time specific is being referred to.

PART I

The Relevance of the Language Press

1. Hindi and Urdu Newspapers in Uttar Pradesh

The growth of the Hindi and Urdu Press had a special significance as it indicated the emergence of a new variety of politics in India and the emergence of new classes as active elements in this political activity. The language press enables one to study the development of national consciousness amongst the intelligentsia as it became increasingly aware of the economic and social anomalies in the British form of governance. The language press had, in the second half of the nineteenth century, developed sufficiently to take on the role of an oppositional force to the British Indian government, which could not be held in check by any institutional organ at that time. Though nascent the press did not fail to critically evaluate government policies, thus becoming an integral part of the growing national consciousness.

HISTORY

The first Hindi newspaper, *Udant Martand*, appeared in Calcutta in 1826 and closed down in 1827. The first weekly paper to be published from a Hindi-speaking province was *Benaras Akhar*, in a mixture of Urdu and Hindi. The *Buddhiprakash* appeared in Agra in 1852, and the *Sarvahitkarak*, a weekly in Hindi and Urdu, also of Agra, in 1855. During 1857 the press was quiet, as in North-West Provinces the few organs that existed leaned heavily on government support and were under the dual control of subsidy and censorship.

Lord Canning, the Governor-General, promulgated the Press Act of India in 1857. Popularly known as 'the Gagging Act', it drove a wedge between English-owned and Indian newspapers and created a distinction between the English language and Indian language journals. Though the Act was directed at both European and Indian newspapers, Canning made no bones about the fact that this legislation was meant to curb the provocative Indian newspapers.

Indian language newspapers nevertheless grew, albeit slowly. The Urdu press flourished and the majority of the Urdu newspapers in

NWP were owned by Hindus in 1861. The progress of Hindi journalism was slow, but several newspapers were published in Hindi. The newspaper that created waves was the *Kavi-Vachan-Sudha*, a Hindi weekly published by Bharatendu Harishchandra in Varanasi. Its discussions of political matters were spirited and created a furore in government circles. It gained immense popularity but accused of instigating revolution, had to close down in 1885. In 1876 the *Kashi Patrika* came out as a weekly under the patronage of Bharatendu. Its success can be gauged from the fact that it was later used as a part of the school curriculum. We may mention also *Arya Darpan* from Shahjahanpur, a famous Arya Samaj paper.

Gradually a flow of literary journals came into existence, most of them short-lived. The more notable were Balkrishna Bhatt's *Hindi Pradip*, strongly political, the *Bharat Mitra*, and Ram Krishan Varma's *Bharat Jiwan*. In 1878 the first caste newspaper came out in Allahabad, the *Kayastha Samachar*. The *Dinkar Prakash* was a monthly issued by Babu Ramdas Verma in Lucknow. In 1879, the *Bharat Sudash Apravartak* was circulated by the Arya Samaj from Farrukhabad. These papers attacked the prevalent social ills and by their virulent criticisms influenced the government to an extent.

The Urdu press, in the latter half of the nineteenth century, was revived, and a great part of the credit for this goes to Sir Syed Ahmad. Urdu journalists objected to the growing Hindi journalism and a number of Urdu journals came out in Delhi, Meerut, Agra, Lucknow, Aligarh and Lahore, mostly weeklies or fortnightlies. Generally moderate in political and religious matters, these journals did not hesitate to comment on racial discrimination and the manifestations of anti-Indian bias in the administration. The main Urdu journals of the time were the *Oudh Akhbar, Bharat Patrika, Kankub-i-Hind, Maraqqa-i-Tehzib, Akhbar-i-Tamannai, Anwar-ul-Akhbar, Oudh Punch, Mashir-i-Qaisar* of Lucknow. Circulating from Meerut, there were the *Akhbar-i-Alam, Najm-ul-Akhbar, Lawrence Gazette* and *Shahana-i-Hind*. These papers, however, contained very little original matter; they borrowed from English newspapers, and could not be considered reliable.

The Vernacular Press Act of Lytton in 1878, was thoroughly criticized as it completely fettered the Indian press, and was repealed by Ripon in 1881. The office of the Press Commissioner was abolished,[1] and his work delegated to the Home Department. The work of supervizing the Indian language press was now relegated to the provincial government. Ripon tried to meet the expectations of the language press, much to the apprehension of the publishers of English papers—the gulf between them forever widening. The Vernacular Press Act triggered off the ire of the Indians, and eventually the Bengali press, of which the *Amrit Bazar Patrika* was the foremost newspaper, expressed resentment against differentiation between Indians and Englishmen. Lord Ripon's tenure was thus a time of national awakening which gradually spread from the educated Bengali to the rest of India.

In the NWP and Awadh several vocal newspapers came up. Deserving mention are *Prayag Samachar* of Allahabad, *Kashi Samachar* and *Brahman* of Kanpur. But 1884 marked a very important development in newspaper publication, when Raja Rampal Singh of Kalakankar got out the *Hindustan*, a daily in English and Hindi, in London and in 1885 in Kalakankar. The other important newspapers to appear were the *Hindustani* in Lucknow, an Urdu weekly started by Babu Ganga Prasad Verma, and the *Bharat Jiwan*, a Varanasi weekly.

1885 symbolized the birth of the Congress, and in the words of Pat Lovett, 'The real development of the art and business of journalism, as it is understood in the West, dates in India from the birth of the Indian National Congress in 1885.'[2]

Though the language newspapers were still in their incipient stage as far as their effectiveness, and independent criticism were concerned, they had come a long way and the prospect of the formulation of a healthy public opinion was not a remote possibility. With Lord Dufferin as the Viceroy, the Indian press was encouraged. In a communication to Babu Ganga Prasad Verma, editor of the *Hindustani*, Dufferin expressed his friendship and support of the language press. He professed to regard it as essential to the welfare and progress of the nation, and thought that it might render invaluable aid to the government and people.[3] Alfred Lyall, the Lt.-Governor of NWP and Awadh, also acknowledged that the language press had made progress in 'intellectual power' and 'civilized feeling'. The newspapers hoped that he would see that justice was meted out impartially to them.[4]

The reason for this growth of journalistic enterprise was that certain developments had taken place during the last quarter of the nineteenth century. Several initiations in transport and communications—the introduction of the railway and the telegraph—saw the first illustrated journals coming out and some regional newspapers acquired national status. The national movement gained impetus and the press became more vocal and discriminating. The rise of the great educationist, Sir Syed Ahmad Khan and the growth of the Aligarh School, made journalism meaningful, even if in later years Muslim bias was to seep into the Muslim press. Improvement in the education system, and the growing number of educated Indians provided a reading public and better journalists. There was a large number of students passing out and jobs were few. Many became school teachers but in the hope of a more remunerative career, some joined the press.[5] Meanwhile the social reforms initiated by the British made the orthodox elements among the newspapers more articulate, as they saw in them a threat to their established religious practices.[6]

However, as Gokhale remarked as late as 1903, 'Nowhere is the press so weak in influence, as it is with us.'[7] Yet press repression was practised through legislation. The Copyright Bill introduced in 1885 prohibited the republication of a telegram by one newspaper from another until twenty-four hours had elapsed since its first appearance. The government felt that telegraphic messages obtained at great expense from foreign countries, either directly or through such agencies as Reuters, were copied with impunity by all papers, and that this form of piracy discouraged honest journalistic enterprise.[8]

The local language journalists were furious, as they felt that this would be beneficial to the handful of well-to-do English language newspapers, which had arrangements for receiving telegrams. Some papers even accused the government of wanting to stop the publication of 'native' newspapers, which, owing to their unsatisfactory finances, depended on their English language contemporaries for the news.[9]

Journalists became wary of Dufferin and advised their colleagues moderation for fear of government gagging.[10] Lyall was accused of doing nothing to encourage the 'native' press. Sir Auckland Colvin, too, stated that the 'vernacular' newspapers of the NWP and Awadh were in the hands of poor, indigent men, whose object was to extort money from noblemen by threats. The fact of the matter was that towards the close of the nineteeth century, the Indian press was becoming an important vehicle of expression. It vigorously criticized the measures and policies of the government, thus seeking to check the abuses of the bureaucracy and administration.[11] Thus press legislation was meant mainly to curb and punish the press for 'seditious' writings. The English language press was encouraged and its opinions heeded, but the government completely ignored the opinions of the 'native' newspapers.[12] The English language newspapers and the government accused the language newspapers of seditious utterances.[13]

The Official Secrets Act of 1889 aimed at preventing state employees selling information on government plans, models, etc., to foreign governments. Any government servant who disclosed an official secret would be liable to imprisonment for a year. Government servants would be chary about supplying any information whatever to the press. The decision whether a document was secret or not rested with the government, which enabled it to favour certain newspapers, and injure the ones it disapproved of. The obvious targets would be the local language newspapers, and they protested vehemently.[14] The Act was criticized in the Indian-owned newspapers as a way of abolishing the most important source of information to the Indian press, and calling the language editor a 'thief and receiver of stolen goods'.[15]

Crosthwaite, the new Lt.-Governor, reiterated the old refrain that 'native' editors talked without thinking.[16] There was a rumour afloat that the Press Act was going to be revived. An interesting cartoon was published in which the 'native' press was represented as a woman standing with her legs chained and her mouth gagged.[17] The English newspapers were accused of lending credence to this rumour, by trying to make the government believe that the Hindi and Urdu papers were inciting Hindus and Muslims against it.[18]

Even a liberal Lt.-Governor like Anthony MacDonnell, who saw the 'native' press as temperate and non-inflammatory,[19] was not in favour of giving it too much importance. He was struck with the 'growing license and disregard for reasonable restraints of truth and moderation' of the language newspapers. He perused a mass of extracts from 'native' papers and felt that they were disloyal, covertly insinuating, and openly incited sedition. He felt that there was no workable law of seditious libel, and the press was too free. The respectable classes of Indians would be grateful to the government if it could effectively curb the language newspapers that directed venom and oppression upon these Indians.[20]

A new law on sedition was passed in 1898, which would give power to District Magistrates, to hear sedition cases, which need not go to the High Courts. All papers were against this Act. Many of them cryptically remarked that besides the press losing its freedom, '. . . the government will be a still greater loser (in being deprived thereby of the means of knowing the true feelings of its Indian subjects'.[21]

The Official Secrets Act of 1889 had prevented the publication of secret information relating to naval and military matters. The Indian Official Secrets' (Amendment) Act extended the scope of the Act to information connected with the civil administration. The language papers felt this was evidence of the retrogression and repression of Lord Curzon's policy. The usefulness and independence of the press, both English and Indian, would be sufficiently curbed and '. . . it will have the sure effect of transforming each official, from the Governor-General to a Sub-Deputy Magistrate, into a Czar'.[22]

The partition of Bengal in 1905 created a turmoil in the country, and, with the growth of extremism in politics, the language press too became more vociferous. Whether extremist or moderate, Hindu or Muslim—whatever political or communal leanings the newspapers may have had—their writings were considered instigatory enough for the government to take further repressive measures. Hewett, the Lt.-Governor of the United Provinces, was convinced of the spread of sedition there and blamed editors for inciting the people. The Government of India passed the Seditious Meeting Act in 1907. By this, the Local Government was empowered by the Governor-General in Council 'to institute prosecution in consultation with their legal advisers in all cases where the law has been wilfully infringed'.[23] The Government of India sent another directive to the Local Government that postal articles and telegraphic messages should be censored, to avoid excesses being made by newspapers.[24] This Act was extended to the UP only in 1910. The newspapers disapproved of it: it was considered necessary for disturbed areas and the UP was hardly that![25]

In June 1908, two repressive bills were hastily passed by Lord Minto's government which considerably fettered the language newspapers. These were the Explosives Act and the Newspapers Act VII—incitement to violence. These gave considerable powers to the Local Government to take action against erring persons and errant newspapers. The Local Government became all powerful, because the same District Magistrate who could report a defaulting newspaper in his capacity as a district officer, and could sit as a magistrate and order its confiscation. Following this, the extremist newspapers of Bengal, *Jugantar, Bande Mataram* and *Sandhya*, were suppressed, and by the end of 1908, the situation, as far as the government was concerned, had improved.[26]

This was only a temporary reprieve for the government. In UP, extremist papers, though not ultra-violent as in Bengal, were adopting a sterner tone. The *Swarajya, Karmayogi* and *Hindi Pradip* are striking examples. Fearless journalists could not be curbed, and the *Swarajya* editor, Ram Das Ram, wrote, 'Those who have in their hearts love for their country, do not care about the punishment (inflicted on them) by foreigners.'[27] Hewett feared that unless the government did something to curb 'seditious tendencies of the press' in some parts of the country, it would have to 'face with consequences of a most serious character'. Newspapers, if not blatantly seditious, were 'instigated by a feeling of overt hostility to government and calculated to have a harmful effect on the relations between the government and the people'.[28] The only way left to the government was 'to disarm dishonest and disloyal journalism and that by a vigorous press law'.[29] The existing law enforced only made the offending paper more popular and its editor a martyr. The Local Government had to be invested with more power and redressal of grievances by the courts had to be limited.

A series of deportations and press prosecutions followed, and the radical press was repeatedly threatened with fresh government action. The Legislative Assembly had already passed another repressive measure in December 1908: the Criminal Law Amendment Act. Despite this, fearless journalists expressed their opinions without mincing words, and government took recourse to drastic measures, the culmination of which was the Press Act of 1910. This Act was considered a 'serious contraction of popular liberties' even by the moderate press. Its provisions gave immense power to the Local Government. Editors could not take recourse to the law. The system of licenses and registrations was made more stringent. Repeated misdemeanours by a newspaper entailed the intensive hounding of persistent editors, who could either 'reform themselves' or had to close down their papers.[30]

Several extremist newspapers thus closed down, and some moderate newspapers too were warned about hints at something that was considered incendiary. Minto boasted that when he left in 1911, he had successfully repressed 'incipient anarchy'. His successor, Hardinge, was, however, less pompous and rather uncertain when he declared, 'I had a very uncomfortable legacy from my predecessor in the Seditious Meetings Act which had to be passed and which met with almost universal condemnation.'[31]

The year 1911 saw the rapid growth of Pan-Islamic trends with the Italian invasion of Tripoli, the Moroccan crisis, the Balkan wars of 1912-13 and finally the First World War in 1914 in which Great Britain was arraigned against Turkey. This shocked the Indian Muslims out of their belief in the goodwill of the British government, which was regarded as a potential aggressor against even Mecca and Medina. The Muslim press became pungent in its condemnation of British designs. The rise of politico-religious newspapers like Muhammad Ali's *Comrade* and *Hamdard*, Abul Kalam Azad's *Al Hilal* and Zafar Ali Khan's *Zamindar*, preached anti-British dictums, and Indian Muslims were convinced of their religion being in danger. This development enhanced the effectiveness of the press in general. Sensationalism became the order of the day, and though several language newspapers resorted to mud-slinging, their effect on the public mind was undeniable. For example, the young party among the Muslims began to regard Muhammad Ali as their leader. 'No paper has so much influence with the students as the *Comrade*, and no individual has the authority over them which is exercised by Muhammad Ali.'[32]

The government resorted to more persecution, this time mostly directed against the vocal section of the Muslim press. Hardinge passed the Criminal Law Amendment Act in 1913. The internationalization of the press and the outbreak of the First World War created turmoil within the British government, which heard rumours, substantiated and otherwise, of a widespread conspiracy threatening its very existence. The Government of India passed the Press and Sea Customs Act in 1914 proscribing pamphlets bearing the inflammatory titles of *Al Jehad* or 'holy war'. Instigatory literature like the German and Turkish newspapers or pamphlets, which were being imported into India, were also proscribed.[33] The Naval and Military News (Emergency) Ordinance was passed in August 1914, which created a virtual military censorship. The Defence of India Act of 1915 was used to restrain the liberties of all who were encouraging sedition among Muslims against the government.

These Acts did curb the spontaneity of the 'native' press; and with lack of authentic news during the War, the newspapers did feel stifled; but they did not allow themselves to be fettered, and gradually grew in number as well as in circulation and eventually proved effective in influencing the public mind. Deported or imprisoned press men like Tilak, when released, resumed their activities. Both the Hindu and the Muslim press became a potent force in channelizing and highlighting the national movement that picked up strength with the coming of Mahatma Gandhi.

This discussion of the development of the press would be incomplete without enumerating the names of the important language newspapers of UP during this period. I have picked out those newspapers which were in publication for more than nine years. A few of them functioned over the entire period of study. The actual number of language newspapers was much more, but then many were either inconsequential or short-lived. Financial constraints were many and sometimes newspaper proprietors found it extremely difficult to publish their particular papers. For example, out of 101 newspapers published in 1890, only 82 remained in circulation at the end of the year. In 1896 out of 123, only 95 remained on the register. In 1900, out of a total of 109 newspapers, only 89 were reported at the end of the year.[34]

Hindi journalism seemed to have picked up as the years progressed; circulation rose. This could have been because of the growth of religious papers as can be deduced from Table 1.1.[35] The Arya Samaj had almost ten newspapers forwarding its cause; there were about six that espoused the cause of the Hindu religion and opposed the Arya Samaj and other reform movements. Some newspapers propounded the cause of the Muslim religion, regardless of Shia or Sunni affiliation. There was an upsurge of caste papers. Probably those espousing the cause of the Kayasthas (about twelve) were more than the others. The Khattris had papers like the *Khattri Hitkari* of Agra, to plead their cause. The *Devanagari Gazette* of Meerut took up the cause of the Devanagari alphabet, the *Godharm Prakash* of Lucknow wanted social reforms among the Kurmis, and the *Rajput* of Agra was supported by the rajas.[36]

Besides all these, there were several papers which the Government Reporter did not take up in his weekly reports on the language newspapers of NWP and Awadh. For example, in 1905, about twenty-six 'native' newspapers were not reported.[37]

THE TECHNIQUE OF NEWS REPORTING

The Government Reporter

The Government Reporter was stationed at Allahabad, to consolidate important news in the local newspapers into a weekly report for the information of the Local Government. This role became especially

TABLE 1.1: LIST OF LANGUAGE NEWSPAPERS THAT REMAINED IN PUBLICATION FOR MORE THAN FIVE YEARS BETWEEN 1885 AND 1914: PERIODICITY, RELATIONSHIP BETWEEN PROPRIETORS/PUBLISHERS/EDITORS, FINANCIAL AND SOCIAL STATUS AND LEANINGS

Name	*Periodicity*	*Language*	*Circulation*	*Place*	*Proprietor/Publisher*	*Editor*	*Leanings & Contents*
1. *Abhyudaya****	Weekly	Hindi	2000	Allahabad		Pt. Krishna Kant Malviya	
2. *Advocate****	Bi-weekly	English	1000	Lucknow	Babu Ganga Prasad Verma	Babu Ganga Prasad Verma	A great supporter of the Indian National Congress criticises government measures. Is hostile to Europeans and to officials and sometimes to Muslims.
3. *Agra Akhbar*****	Weekly	Urdu	200-500	Agra	Yusuf Ali	Yusuf Ali, Professor	Little influence and not original.
4. *Akhbar-i-Inamia*****	Twice a month	Urdu	250-325	Lucknow	Mir Abid Ali a bigotted Shia	Mir Abid Ali	Religious subjects peculiar to Shias.
5. *Aligarh Institute Gazette*****	Bi-weekly later becomes a weekly	Urdu English	350-900 (almost half taken by government)	Aligarh	Nawab Mohsin-ul-Mulk. Sect of Muhammadan Anglo-Oriental College, Pensioner of Rs. 800 a month	(a) Sir Syed Ahmad, Member of Provincial Council. (b) Nawab Haji Muhammad Ishaq Khan (1914) (c) Muhammad Mumtaz ud-din (1907-8) (d) Muhammad Mukhtada Khan (1911)	Loyal to government no hold on people, anti-Congress.

6. *Almora-Akhbar*****	Weekly between 1905-11, Bi-monthly 1912-13	Hindi	106-55	Almora	3 Hindu servicemen educated & respectable Munshi Sadananda Sonwal (1900-14) Badri Dat Pande (1915)	Lala Nand Joshi—a clerk and one of the proprietors.	Local matters in a temperate zone, intelligent, later anti-government.
7. *Al-Bashir*****	Weekly	Urdu	677-950	Etawah	Muhammad Bashir-ud-din, former editor *Najmu-l-Akhbar*	Muhammad Bashir-ud-din	Contains translations copies and extracts from other papers. Original articles too Pro-Muslim loyal Anti-Congress.
8. *Allahabad Law Journal***	Bi-Monthly	English	600-2000	Allahabad	(i) Satish Chandra Banerji, M.A., L.L.B. Bengali Brahman (ii) Dr. Tej Bahadur Sapru, M.A., L.L.D., Kashmiri Brahman		Deals with legal matters. Ably conducted.
9. *Anand****	Weekly	Hindi	100-200	Lucknow	Pt. Shiv Nath	Pt. Shiv Nath	
10. *An-Nadwah****	Monthly	Urdu	450	Lucknow	Abdul Hai	Maulvi Shibli Nomani and Maulvi Habib-ur-Rahman	Contains miscellaneous articles chiefly on points connected with the Muslim religion.

Name	Periodicity	Language	Circulation	Place	Proprietor/Publisher	Editor	Leanings & Contents
11. *An-Najm****	Weekly	Urdu	400-900	Lucknow	Maulvi Abdus Shakur	Maulvi Abdus Shakur	Generally deals with the Muslim religion.
12. *An-Nasir****	Weekly	Urdu	225-400	Lucknow	Muhammad Shahid Hussain	Wasi-ul-Hasan Ulvi and Zafar ul-mulk Ulvi	Aims at exalting the Muslim faith and lowering the Arya Samaj.
13. *Anjuman-i-Hind*	Weekly	Urdu	100-200	Lucknow	3 Taluqdars of Awadh	Kunwar Harnam Singh	Devoted to only Awadh Taluqdars. Pro-govt.
14. *Arya Mitra****	Weekly	Hindi	1400	Agra	Hukam Singh	Pt. Sarvanand	An Arya Samaj Paper. Supports the Gorakshini Sabha.
15. *Arya Pataka****	Monthly later Weekly	Urdu	850-2500	Bareilly	Pt. Puran Mal	Shambhu Sahai Joshi	Deals with Arya Samaj affairs.
16. *Arya Samachar****	Monthly	Urdu	500	Kanpur	Babu Anand Swarup—good status	Babu Anand Swarup	Arya Samaj Paper. Little consequence. Pro-swadeshi.
17. *Azad**	Weekly	Urdu	150-82	Lucknow	Ahmad Ali friend of Sir Sayed. Sajjad Hussain of *Oudh Punch*	Ahmad Ali	Intelligent, loyal and anti-Congress.

18. *Bharat Jiwan*****	Weekly	Hindi	1500-1700	Varanasi	(i) Ram Krishna Khattri, Educa-ted but of low origin. (ii) Babu Sri Krishna Verma	Ram Krishna Babu Sri Krishna Verma	Sometimes attacks govt. policy but supports too. Pro-Congress, harmless.
19. *Bharat Sudasha Pravartak* ***	Monthly later weekly	Hindi	350-1000	Farrukhabad	Pandit Ganesh Prasad Sharma tutor to the proprietor.	Pandit Ganesh Prasad Sharma	Arya Samaj Journal religious matters only. Inoffensive tone.
20. *Brahman Sarvasva* ***	Monthly	Hindi	600-800	Etawah	Pandit Bhimsen Sharma	Pandit Bhimsen Sharma	Sanatan Dharma paper.
21. *Cawnpore Gazatte* (was there earlier too)***	Weekly	Hindi	400-500	Kanpur	Harnam Singh. No social standing.	Harnam Singh but actually edited by Congressmen Later Babu Brij Narayan.	Pro-Congress. Anti-British.
22. *Colonel* (was there earlier too)***	Weekly	Urdu	200-500	Morababad	(i) Pt. Banwari Lal educated, fair social standing. Also Proprietor *Sitara-i-Hind* (ii) Muhammad Ismail	Pt.Banwari Lal	Illustrated satirical paper. Moderate. Contains poems considered obscene by the government
23. *Dabdaba-i-Sikandari* ****	Weekly	Urdu	300-425	Rampur	(i) Muhammad Husain Khan (ii) Muham-mad Faruk Khan	(i) Muhammad Husain Khan & Brothers Middle Class Muslims (ii) Faruk Khan	Ordinary and mild.

Name	*Periodicity*	*Language*	*Circulation*	*Place*	*Proprietor/Publisher*	*Editor*	*Leanings & Contents*
24. *Dabdaba-i-Qaisari* *	Weekly	Urdu	200-50	Bareilly	Thakur Prasad Member Municipal Board, Respectable	Thakur Prasad	Politics, current affairs, temperate later bigotted pro-Congress, anti-Muslim and anti-government
25. *Fitnah* (was there earlier too)***	Weekly	Urdu	392-400	Gorakhpur	Hakim Abdul Karim Khan, editor of *Sulahkul* Anti-Congress	Mirza Abdullah Hasrati, notorious for blackmail and libel	Small paper as a supplement to *Riaz-ul-Akhbar*
26. *Hindi Pradip* (till 1910)**	Monthly	Hindi	140-220	Allahabad	Balkrishna Bhatt—Sanskrit scholar, not any position	Balakrishna Bhatt	Critical of government sometimes uses strong language.
27. *Hindustan***	Daily	Hindi	165-470	Kalakankar	Rampal Singh Taluqdar of Pratapgarh	Rampal Singh. He carried on his own publication at his own press. The printer was his servant.	Intelligent, moderate liberal, pro-Congress later anti-Congress loyal to government
28. *Hindustani*****	Weekly	Urdu	300 till 1905 1300 (1907) 1700 (1914)	Lucknow	Babu Ganga Prasad Verma No position Later he is called able & edcuated and of good conduct	Ganga Prasad Verma	Anti-government pro-Congress

29. *Hindustan Review******	Monthly	English	1500	Allahabad	Munshi Shadi Lal	Sachchidanand Sinha Barrister at Law	Well-written, Politics, History, moderate, intelligent, pro-Congress.
30. *Jami-i-Jamshed****	Weekly	Urdu	125-200	Moradabad	Qazi Jamshed Ali Mukhtar	Qazi Jamshed Ali Mukhtar	Ordinary, Irregularly published. Anti-government.
31. *Jasus******	Monthly	Hindi	300-500	Gahmar, Ghazipur	Gopal Ram Bania—No social status	Gopal Ram Bania	Inoffensive, publishes detective series.
32. *Kanya Kubja Hitkari******	Monthly	Hindi	800-1500	Cawnpore	Manohar Lal Misra	Manohar Lal Misra	Brahmin Caste paper.
33. *Karnamah***	Weekly	Hindi-Urdu	115-265	Lucknow	Maulvi Muhammad Yakub	Maulvi Muhammad Yakub	Ordinary
34. *Kashi Patrika***	Weekly	Hindi-Urdu	560 including 344 copies to govt.	Varanasi	Pt. Lakshmi Shanker Misra, Inspector of Schools.	Pt. Lakshmi Shanker Misra	Scientific and literary matter for school boys.
35. *Kayastha Hitkari******	Weekly	Urdu	400	Agra	Ahmad Husain (1907)	Kamta Prasad Kayastha	Caste paper.
36. *Khichri Samachar****	Weekly	Hindi	150	Mirzapur	Madho Prasad—Policeman and rascal	Madho Prasad	Disreputable and anti-government Inconsequential.

Name	*Periodicity*	*Language*	*Circulation*	*Place*	*Proprietor/Publisher*	*Editor*	*Leanings & Contents*
37. *Mihr-i-Nimroj* replaced by *Urojin* 1900**	Weekly	Urdu	240-300	Bijnor	Hafiz Karim Ullah—former government employee, educated but low position.	Maulvi Riaz-ud-din a man owning little land—average position	Ordinary and moderate
38. *Mufid-i-Am* (was there later too)**	Tri-monthly	Urdu	100-200	Agra	Ahmad Khan Sufi—esteemed	Ahmad Khan	General topics, orthodox Muslim views, subsidized by Rampur.
39. *Mukhbir-i-Alam* ***	Weekly	Urdu	300	Moradabad	Qazi Abdul Ali low status	Qazi Abdul Ali	Moderate, political and social news.
40. *Musafir* ***	Weekly	Urdu	800	Agra	Pandit Bhoj Datt	Pandit Bhoj Datt	Arya paper, attacks Muslims sometimes
41. *Nagri Pracharak****	Monthly	Hindi	300	Lucknow	Babu Gopal Lal (1907)	Uma Charan Banerji (1914)	
42. *Naiyar-i-Azam*****	Monthly later Weekly	Urdu	200-450	Moradabad	Sheikh Amjad Ali—former teacher	Sheikh Amjad Ali later Syed Ibn-i-Ali	Ordinary
43. *Najm-ul-Akhbar**	Weekly	Urdu	120-275	Etawah	Family of a Muslim Tehsildar	Relative of Proprietor	Intelligent, loyal, though criticizes government policies. Anti-Congress.

44. *Nasim-i-Agra*****	Weekly later bi-weekly	Urdu	225-300	Agra	Jamnadas Biswas Pleader—member of Municipal Board. Bireshwar Sanyal Bengali Brahmin	Jamnadas Biswas, Bireshwar Sanyal	Independent and important paper of Agra.
45. *Nizam-ul-Mulk* ****	Weekly	Urdu	100-400	Moradabad	Amin in Survey Deptt.—educated and respectable.	Amin in Survey Deptt.	Local Rampur affairs
46. *Nur-ul-Anwar* *	Weekly	Urdu	Not available	Kanpur	Abdul Rehman—respected and good social standing	Abdul Hamid Khan, respectable man.	General topics and unobjectionable subscribed to by native princes. Royal.
47. *Oudh Akhbar* ****	Daily	Urdu	300-700	Lucknow	Munshi Nawal Kishore wealthy	Jalpa Prasad Kayastha	Moderate, loyal, anti-Congress, edited with care and intelligence.
48. *Oudh Punch* (was there later too) **	Weekly	Urdu	300-75	Lucknow	Sajjad Hussain—educated and respected	Sajjad Husain	Illustrated paper. Contains cartoons. Freely critical of government Pro-Congress.
49. *Prayag Samachar* (till 1910) **	Weekly	Hindi	500-600 by 1910 had gone down to 250	Allahabad	Pt. Dewaki Nandan, teacher not a high position in society. Jagan Nath Vaid Ram Gopal Pande (called Sharma too)	Pt. Dewaki Nandan Ram Gopal (1905)	Pro-Congress. Local events.
50. *Rafi-ul-Akhbar**	Weekly	Urdu	250-400	Varanasi	Ghulam Husain	Sharaful-Din	Small, ordinary and temperate.

Name	*Periodicity*	*Language*	*Circulation*	*Place*	*Proprietor/Publisher*	*Editor*	*Leanings & Contents*
51. *Rahbar* ****		Urdu	100-500	Moradabad	Pratap Krishna Aga. No standing, pro-Congress, pro-Hindu, later Brij Lal Bania.	Pratap Krishna Aga from 1910	Anti-government Offensive.
52. *Riaz-ul-Akhbar* **	Weekly later bi-Weekly	Urdu	392-400	Gorakhpur	(i) Hafiz Nizam Ahmad (ii) Saiyad Riyaz Ahmad —well to do	(i) Hafiz Nizam but his brother behind it libeller and blackmailer. (ii) Hakim Abdul Karim Khan	Anti-government Miscellaneous news.
53. *Rohilkhund Punch**	Weekly	Urdu	100-35	Moradabad	Owner of *Jam-in-Jamshed*	Owner of *Jam-in-Jamshed*	Comic paper.
54. *Rohilkhund Gazette* ****	Weekly	Urdu	250-500	Bareilly	Abdul Aziz, Low social position	Abdul Aziz	Anti-Congress, Pro-Muslim.
55. *Sahifa* ***	Weekly	Urdu	350-400	Bijnor	(i) Munshi Faiz-ul-Hasan (ii) Maulvi Nur-ul-Hasan (1907)	Maulvi Majid Hasan (1914)	Local news, Muhammadan, anti-government seditious tone
56. *Sandhyop-karak* ***	Monthly	Hindi	400-600	Agra	Shanker Lal Brahman (1906-10) Braj Vallabh Misra (1911) Lachhmi Narayan Dube (1913)	Shanker Lal Brahman Braj Vallabh Misra Lachhmi Narayan Dube	Brahman paper, sometimes seditious.
57. *Sanatan Dharam Patrika****	Monthly	Hindi	1300-1900	Moradabad	Pt. Ram Sarup—Brahman Influential	Pt. Ram Sarup	Very popular as a typical Hindi paper

58. *Saraswati****	Monthly	Hindi	1600-4000	Allahabad	Babu Chintamani Ghose— Clerk good character	Pt. Mahabir Prasad Dwivedi	Very popular. Literary Nagri magazine. Harmless
59. *Satopkari****	Monthly	Urdu	1600	Bareilly	Bareilly Satopkari Sabha	Lala Ramdhan Das Khattri	Affairs of charitable society
60. *Sitara-i-Hind***	Weekly	Urdu	5-160	Moradabad	Pt. Banwari Lal	A teacher	Anti-government but moderate
61. *Surma-i-Rozgar*****	Weekly	Urdu	100-250	Agra	Munshi Itrat Husain, prints at any press. No property No employment	Munshi Itrat Husain	Sycophant of government like *Nasim-i-Agra* in tone but not so respectable. Venal and abusive.
62. *Tafrih*	Weekly	Urdu	400-1000	Lucknow	(i) Ramji Das Bhargava (ii) Ahmad Ali Kamil (1908)	(i) Ramshankar Prasad Kayastha, probably 1909-13 (ii) Pearey Lal	Miscellaneous and fiction. Moderate
63. *Theosophy in India****	Monthly	English	5000-500	Varanasi	Theosophical Society, Banaras	Jehangir Sorabji Parsi (Theosophist) Babu Bhagwan Das Vaishya (Theosophist) Pt. Ikbal Narayan Gurtu, Kashmiri Brahmin (Theosophist)	Basically a Theosophist paper probably the editorship was by rotation.
64. *Tofah-i-Hind****	Weekly	Urdu	300-400	Bijnor	Munshi Jairaj Singh, Vakil, shady but influential Hindu	(i) Jairaj Singh (up to 1910) (ii) Sajjad Husain Shaikh	Pro-Congress, and malicious.

Name	*Periodicity*	*Language*	*Circulation*	*Place*	*Proprietor/Publisher*	*Editor*	*Leanings & Contents*
65. *Zamanah*, was there earlier too***	Monthly	Urdu	300-600 earlier from 700 in 1907 to 1700 in 1914	Kanpur	(i) Safdar Hasan Khan, respectful Zamindar (ii) Kanhaiya Lal, Vakil, Kayastha, man of standing	(i) Safdar Hasan Khan (ii) Babu Daya Narayan Nigam, Kayastha	Loyal, unoriginal, anti-Congress, political, social and literary matters but no pronounced view. Pro-Swadeshi.
66. *Zia-ul-Islam* ***	Monthly	Urdu	450-550	Moradabad	Mushtaq Husain	Syed Fazl Husain Bismal	Muslim theology, and literature.
67. *Zul-Qarnain* ***	Weekly	Urdu	300-800	Badaun	(i) Maqbul-ur-Rahman (ii) Faizul Hasan	Nizam-ud-din Hasan	

Source: VNR of NWP&O between 1885 and 1914 and the Press Memorandum for Upper India between 1885 and 1914—according to availability. All subsequent deductions would mostly be based on this table.

Key:

* Papers in publication 1885-96
** Papers in publication 1885-1905
*** Papers in publication 1906-14
**** Papers in publication 1885-1914

important in times of crisis as few men in the government could read Hindi or Urdu.

The language newspapers hated this dependence of the government on the Government Reporter. They felt that this Indian was generally not highly educated, and, being indigent and not very able, was also dishonest and biased. They alleged that, on the one hand, he tried to please the government by hiding anti-government articles; on the other he tried to twist the arm of any newspaper that did not toe the line.[38] This was because the government preferred to include in their Press Memorandum only those newspapers which contained translations of English language newspapers and lacked originality and free criticism. The papers were sore about being placed under a Government Reporter while there was no reporter to oversee English newspapers.[39]

These accusations against the Government Reporter do not seem convincing. For a good many years Priya Das, who was an M.A., remained the Reporter for the NWP and Awadh. Religious bias did not seem to be predominant in his mind, as he freely reported the growing communal tension—as the subsequent chapters will show. The government seemed as concerned about receiving the necessary news as the newspapers themselves. The Government of India, on more than one occasion, asked the Local Government to ascertain that adequate news be supplied to the Reporter, so that the weekly selections would contain authentic news.[40] All this shows that the government never condoned negligence. Besides, it would have definitely liked to get all the contents of the language newspapers so that it could feel the pulse of the people. The newspapers not reported were generally the inconsequential ones, on poetry, or about literary, philosophical, scientific, commercial, historical, caste or religious matters. Generally harmless and vague, these closed down after a short duration.[41] The Reporter hence was justified when he vehemently declared in 1902, 'Copies of these Selections have lately been supplied to all District Magistrates. It is almost needless to say that all important articles in newspapers are noticed in the selection.'[42] The accusation about the lack of reporting on the English language press did not make sense as any British official could read English papers. To attribute ulterior motives to the government appears to be an over-reaction on the part of the local language newspapers.

Supply of Government News to the Indian Press

Hindi and Urdu newspapers could either subscribe to Reuters for official news or depend on the government which distributed the Gazette of India. Very few Indian journals could afford the former, so most were keen on getting free copies of the Gazette.

The government floundered in this and in 1886 only nineteen local-language newspapers were receiving the Gazette free, and even these were sent only that information which the government concerned important.[43] However, though agents or correspondents of these chosen papers could apply personally for information to the officers of the various departments, the whole system was operationally uncertain.[44] The Indian newspapers had perforce to depend on news published in the English papers which received government patronage. There were several examples of the language press making mistakes in evaluating and reporting government measures and acts. There were instances too of government officers leaking out valuable information to the press.[45] This engendered the reporting of unsubstantiated news and encouraged corruption.

On its part the government was apprehensive about giving too much authentic news to all the several newspapers. Consider this communication from an Englishman to the Private Secretary to the Viceroy: 'I unhesitatingly assert that the native journalist will find a new and effective weapon of attack against constituted authority in the "official information" which he will be supplied.'[46] The idea of a revival of the Press Commissionership for disseminating news was toyed with, and given up. The papers, it was felt, would still not be satisfied as they would feel that government was still giving valuable information to its favourite newspapers, while supplying only the 'husk' to the Press Commissioner. The government felt that reviving this would foster the inferior newspapers at the cost of the better ones, who took so much trouble in procuring authentic news.[47]

However, it was acknowledged that some sort of official news agency was needed. Curzon suggested the establishment of a Press Room with various departments. Selected newspapers would be supplied the news by different departments, according to the integrity of a particular newspaper and its declared interests. The government felt that this would curb 'perversion and rabidness' on the part of the editors. This measure, however, fell through as the language newspapers in general feared that the government would arbitrarily select those papers upon which it had bestowed its favours.

After 1905, the government remained suspicious of newer newspapers which had cropped up and displayed a heightened nationalistic fervour. Most of them were run by young people who could not be trusted. For example, in 1905 223 new papers had appeared in the country, of which 23 were published by men under 25. In 1907 the government of India sent a directive to the Local Government that postal articles and telegraphic messages were to be censored. This over-caution was more evident when war broke out in 1914. The government got wind of some conspiracies brewing abroad which would endanger national security, and became more stringent about supplying war news to Indian editors. It felt that the press should not discuss the war news at all and should only involve itself with literary, industrial and educational matters. The Naval and Military News Ordinance in August 1914 created military censorship.

The local language journalists could not be expected to be happy about this. People stopped taking an interest in their papers because they seldom published correct or reliable news. The government revealed only those facts that it wanted the editors to know. Besides, the government had instituted a Provincial Press Bureau which issued daily war bulletins which were posted at Post Offices and other public places. This satisfied the people and they thought it unnecessary to buy papers. Actually the news supplied by the Secretary of State for India to the Viceroy was nothing but a summary of Reuters' messages. No Indian-owned paper was rich enough to send its own correspondent to the front for authentic war news. The result was that false war rumours reached those places where news was in any case difficult to send.[48]

COLONIAL CONTROL OVER THE LANGUAGE PRESS

Controlling the press had become imperative for the colonial government. The liberty of the press had to be curbed as it threatened to create a socio-political upheaval in the provinces. One method of control that was adopted by the government was to hold the bait of patronage to such papers who would support the administration. These papers, however, soon lost their popularity with the public. Their fellow editors too protested against favours shown to them.

For example, the *Aligarh Institute Gazette* had nearly half of its copies purchased by the government. In return it gave its unstinted support. It lost its popularity and only its association with the wealthy

Muslim aristocracy could ensure its survival.[49] Sir Syed Ahmad, its proprietor and editor, left no stone unturned to glorify British rule. In 1897, he went to the extent of equating the British rule with that of Naushervan, whom even the Prophet admired. Everything about British rule was good, even the escalating taxes, as these ensured a large British army to defend the country.[50] His favourite line was,

> When the general public is so backward in education, the publication of complaints against the British officers in language newspapers is simply calculated to do mischief in the country. . . . The utterances of a newspaper should be well-weighed and not be allowed to degenerate into the ravings of a maniac . . . .'[51]

In every matter he supported the British and hence his rigid anti-Congress stance.

The newspapers were unhappy about annual government subsidies to chosen papers like the *Aligarh Institute Gazette,* the *Oudh Akhbar* of Lucknow and the *Kashi Patrika* of Varanasi, newspapers which blindly supported government measures and proceedings in utter disregard of the interests of the people. The payment of such subsidies was 'subversive of the freedom of the press'. Even if they were supplied to schools it was wrong, and the headmasters should have been allowed to choose. *The Aligarh Institute Gazette* was filled with effusions of the Principal of the Aligarh School, Mr. Beck, republished from the *Pioneer,* and with other extracts from that in which 'natives' had been abused.[52]

Reports of anti-Congress meetings by Munshi Newal Kishore, C.I.E., proprietor of *Oudh Akhbar,* were given by the language newspapers.[53] The government returned favour for favour! The director of Agriculture and Commerce obtained all the forms required for the use of patwaris and kanungos throughout the United Provinces from Munshi Newal Kishore's press and the Church Mission Press at Lucknow. Resentment against such policy was inevitable.[54]

Even later, when politics became more complicated, the *Aligarh Institute Gazette* remained loyal to the government. For example, it opined that the government had no choice but no enact the Press Act of 1910, as newspapers had been giving sufficient provocation. The editor advised journalists to show, by their loyalty to the Crown, that there was no further necessity for the law.[55] The *Oudh Akhbar,* however, seemed to have changed its stance. It was not disloyal but became more logically critical of the issues involved. For example, it considered the Press Act too drastic. In fact, it seems that after Nawal Kishore's departure the *Oudh Akhbar* seemed to have lost ground with the government.[56]

With the development of extremist journalism and growing Pan-Islamic trends, the government of the UP toyed with the idea of subsidizing loyal newspapers, written in the common language of the provinces, 'in a simple style to arouse and instruct folk under the village pipal tree'. These papers could be distributed to village headmen, patwaris, school masters, etc., either free or at a low rate, to disseminate 'proper' information provided by the government among the people.[57] Some Muslim papers were pampered and even in the midst of the pro-Turkey hysteria these papers generally supported government action. The most prominent of these were the *Al Bashir* of Etawah, *Mashriq* of Gorakhpur and the *Independent* of Allahabad. There is a distinct possibility that at some stage these received government subsidies, perhaps not in the form of money, but hidden subsidies in the form of government advertizing and the purchase of large numbers of copies for distribution to government offices. For example, the Chief Secretary to the UP Government, R. Burn, supported a suggestion that *Al Bashir* be upgraded with government assistance from a weekly to a daily. These newspapers naturally had good circulations and actively countered anti-government activity, whether nationalistic or communal. This was resented by other newspapers—especially the supportive ones—as they felt cheated at having been 'overlooked' when favours were being granted.[58]

Sir Antony MacDonnell, though not a great supporter of the language press, suggested the distribution to all Heads of Districts of the province of the weekly selections from the language newspapers, so that the authorities could be in close touch with the opinions and sentiments of the people and improve thus the administrative machinery.[59]

An effective way of controlling errant newspapers was by using suppressive and repressive methods. Editors were disturbed by the fact that instead of mildly criticizing the press, the government resorted to hostile and virulent disparagement. The language newspapers complained against the police, the magistrates and other government authorities. The police delayed receiving a report of a theft at the press of the *Anis-i-Hind* newspaper at Meerut.[60] At Gorakhpur the police instigated an attack on the editor of the *Riaz-ul-Akhbar* as the latter had exposed police corruption.[61] These complaints were either not brought to the notice of senior government authorities, or the latter were satisfied with the explanations of the concerned officials.[62]

The government did not refrain from abuse of the language newspapers as scurrilous, or seditious, or obscene, and unnecessarily attacking government policy. In the Administrative Report of 1894-5, a complaint of sedition was made which was absurd as no riot or disturbance had occurred which might be attributed to any newspaper.[63] Government officers, as a rule, were hostile to if not nervous of the language press. The newspapers urged the government to issue orders to the effect that no magistrate should try any criminal suit instituted against an editor or proprietor who had frequently made strictures on the proceedings of that magistrate, as such a magistrate was sure to be prejudiced against the accused.[64] An officer suspected of being sympathetic with or of contributing to the language newspapers, was censured by the higher-ups and not promoted. The magistrate of Lucknow, in the days of plague and famine, summoned all the Indian editors to his house and warned them against publishing any inflammatory writings even if they were translations from English papers.[65]

Editors of popular language newspapers suffered harassment and humiliation. The editor of *Riaz-ul-Akhbar*, Gorakhpur, was assaulted and it was feared that the police were behind it.[66] The editor of the *Prayag Samachar* of Allahabad was tried for defamation, and Grey, the magistrate, remarked,

> In this country, the editors of some native newspapers imagine that, as editors, they have full rights and no responsibilities, and have recourse to abusing persons as well as government officials who have no opportunity to reply, and who are not allowed to prosecute the offending newspapers. The sooner they are disabused of these notions the better for them.[67]

The government did not take to criticism from the language newspapers, and even so, in an inverted way, accepted their importance, by taking stern action (imprisonment or fines) against the more vocal ones. The editor of the *Hindu Patriot*, and the editors of the *Rafiq-i-Hind, Naiyar-i-Azam* were punished for publishing libel in 1887. The newspapers felt that the punishment was too severe and would hamper the independence and fearlessness of the editors.[68]

We note that several editors were implicated for libel. In 1894, the *Cawnpore Gazette* was facing a libel charge for voicing anti-government views, and *Anis-i-Hind* was next in the line. The editor of *Qaisar Punch* of Ballia was allegedly imprisoned by the police in a high-handed way with false charges being trumped up against him.[69] The conviction of Abdullah Hasrati, the editor of the *Riaz-ul-Akhbar* of Gorakhpur, for critical remarks on the Collector Hoey, shocked the language press.[70] Munshi Ganga Prasad Verma, the proprietor of the *Hindustani* and the *Advocate* opened a fund for meeting the cost of Hasrati's defence.[71]

As indigenous journalism progressed, government practised further persecution. The *Jam-i-Jamshed* of Moradabad was stopped, consequent on the imprisonment of its editor on a criminal charge in 1897. The plight of the *Jami-ul-Ulum* of Moradabad was the most pitiable. The editor, Amba Prasad, was imprisoned, which led to the closure of the paper. He was released in 1899 and intended to revive the newspaper,[72] but got into trouble again in 1901, and was tried for defaming Mirza Tahawar Ali Beg, late Diwan of the Landaura estate. He was sentenced to two years rigorous imprisonment. Most of the newspapers took this as an attack on the language newspapers, but there were some who blamed the *Jami* for showing disloyalty to the Rani of Landaura.[73]

Another strategy of the government was to accuse the newspapers of publishing obscene advertisements. The editor of the *Ainu-l-Akhbar* of Moradabad was fined Rs.100 for publishing obscene advertisements in 1886.[74] The *Naiyar-i-Azam* of Moradabad, the *Nuru-l-Anwar* of Kanpur, *Nizam-ul-Mulk* and *Sitara-i-Hind* of Moradabad were prosecuted in 1889 for publishing advertisements for the sale of aphrodisiacs. The newspapers were divided in opinion. Some felt that such advertisements were necessary as men would get cured of the diseases mentioned and would then be able to have children. Others accepted that such advertisements were couched in obscene language, but felt they were intended for the public good: 'any language which may be considered indecent on ordinary occasions is perfectly justifiable under special circumstances'. They felt that the newspapers should be specifically told what the government considered obscene, and if anyone had to be blamed, it ought to be the physicians who were the real advertisers, and not the editors.[75]

The government did not let go its determination to prosecute the editors wherever it considered this necessary. Editors argued that the maintenance of the liberty of the press was necessary both in the interests of the government and of the people.

If editors are brought into difficulty by false charges of theft . . . being trumped up against them for exposing the irregular proceedings of officers, government will have no means of obtaining local information from an independent source.[76]

The language newspapers bemoaned the precarious position of editors. Besides other harassments, European magistrates and judges made invidious distinction between European and Indian editors in cases of libel, the former being seldom imprisoned and being let off with fines. The papers felt, and it was true to a large extent, that European judges and magistrates, smarting under the trenchant criticism of the Indian editors, took their venom out on them. 'Indeed they lie in wait for native journalists as alligators and crocodiles do in rivers for their prey.'[77]

Press prosecutions before 1899 could be carried out by the Local Government without obtaining the sanction of the Government of India. But after the passing of the Indian Penal Code Amendment Act of 1898, the government felt that a change was required. The public attention directed to press prosecutions after 1898, necessitated their careful consideration and control. The Secretary of State would naturally hold the Viceroy responsible, so the latter considered the previous sanction of the Government of India necessary in these cases.[78]

With the growth of extremism in politics, the press became more vocal, and even the hitherto moderate ones did not desist from open criticism of government policies. The insidious growth of extremist newspapers that did not mince words in their condemnation of British actions upset the government, who saw how the public mind was influenced. A series of press prosecutions followed and legislation, including the Press Acts of 1908 and 1910, was resorted to so that prosecutions of erring editors was easier. The 'native' editors were repeatedly accused of stimulating sedition, and the period between 1908 and 1914 witnessed an unprecedented number of deportations or jail sentences on editors. Tilak's deportation for six years for his articles in the *Kesari* created a major ruffle. After 1908 many newspapers of the UP met the same fate.

The *Hindi Pradip* of Allahabad was suspected of extremism and in 1908 its publication was halted by the government. It reappeared, and with a vengeance. Its subscription was enhanced from Rs. 3-6-0 per year to Rs. 25 for the government, while the general public was required to pay only Rs. 2-8-0![79] The most notorious and publicized prosecution was that of the *Swarajya*, a newspaper, blatantly extremist, inaugurated in Allahabad in November 1907. Seven of its editors were in the course of three years either transported or imprisoned or penalized in some way for publishing seditious and instigatory articles. The government realized that a 'more ready procedure' was required to penalize a newspaper which was persistently hostile to the government.

> The fact that the newspapers which wrote most violently had the widest circulation showed that a, general interest was taken in the extremist movement. The writings of the more rabid section were more deeply tainted with the views of sedition than had hitherto been the case.[80]

The *Swarajya* was finally assailed for its objectionable articles on 21 August 1909 on Swadeshi and Boycott, on India's progress and regeneration, and on government's distrust of the people. The last editor, Ladha Ram Khatri, was declared guilty and deported for ten years, and the publication of the paper ceased in February 1910.[81] *Swarajya*, though short-lived, became a symbol of defiant and fearless journalism. It had started a novel method of inciting people through poetry:

> But in your power if you hold the heart
> And do as you have done so far
> And have no mind to use withal
> Opinionativeness and pride to serve your country
> Then you will get your heart's desire
> And full reward for what you ask[82]

The *Karmayogi* was a fortnightly review in Hindi which was started on *Janamashtami* in 1909 in Allahabad. Devoutly Hindu, its editor, Sundar Lal, intended to reproduce translations from Aurobindo's *Karmayogin* and Tilak's *Kesari*. He believed in perpetration of nationalistic ideas based on ancient Vedic religion. The government suspected its motives from the beginning, and found its ideas of 'national regeneration' even more objectionable than the *Swarajya*. The *Karmayogi* believed in students taking part in politics. This angered even the moderate press. Its appeal to students, 'The suffering Mother is looking to you alone for the removal of her ailment. All eyes are turned up to you' was considered impractical by the moderate elements, and the British added fuel to the fire by slyly putting forth the idea that managers of moderate newspapers would not object to the 'forcible suppression of prints which compete unfairly by providing matter of an exciting nature debarred from them'.[83] After just one year of publication, the *Karmayogi* closed down in 1910 as Sunder Lal could not pay the security of Rs. 9000 imposed upon the paper by the government.[84] Hasrat Mohani's *Urdu-i-Mualla* from Aligarh was closed down finally in 1913 after a troubled period during which its editor was imprisoned. In 1916, the fiery Hasrat Mohani was interned.[85]

After 1912, when Pan-Islamism grew more fervent, the government sought out the Muslim newspapers suspected of instigating communal fervour against the British. The important 'outside' papers like Muhammad Ali's *Comrade* and *Hamdard,* and Abul Kalam Azad's *Al Hilal* were closed down by 1915 and the *Muslim Gazette* of Lucknow, established in 1912, came under heavy fire as the govern-ment strongly objected to its incendiary articles. Despite the threat of the security of Rs. 500 being forfeited, the *Gazette* continued to publish articles considered instigatory by the government. Its editor was suspected of 'mischievous' intentions and 'animated by a spirit of obstinate fanatical bigotry'.

The *Muslim Gazette* of 19 December 1913 still wrote, 'To use European goods is against the Islamic religion'. It called boycott a 'Quami Tahrir' movement for the race. With the European threat on Turkey, the *Gazette* affirmed the need to save Mecca and Medina. In April 1913 it wrote, 'Now the Muslims of the world will have to bear the burden of this duty on their shoulders.' The proprietor, Nur Jan, was repeatedly warned by the government and eventually blamed the editor, Manbir Wahiduddin Salim, for his obstinacy. He seemed to have been goaded by the British into taking action as he said, '. . . I, in accordance with your suggestion, am dismissing M. Wahid-uddin Salim from the editorship.' Nur Jan, however could not offend his co-religionists by doing a volteface. After this, despite his best attempts at veiling his criticism, the government sabotaged his efforts at publication. In October 1913, the *Muslim Gazette* finally wound up, and even subsequent efforts by other proprietors proved futile. The story of the demise of this paper showed that the government meant business, and would not tolerate even a murmur of sedition.[86]

For an article supporting the boycott of European goods and expressing consternation at the British impassivity when Russia, France and Italy exploited Persia, Morocco and Tripoli, warning was given to the *Rohilkhand Gazette* of Bareilly on 31 March 1913 that unless the paper adopted a more reasonable line, the government would 'consider the propriety of action under the Press Act'.[87] There were several other such instances involving Muslim newspapers.

With the growing suspicions about political and communal motives of the public, there were occasions when even moderate newspapers were not spared. There was, however, a difference in the way the government acted. It had to be more cautious and circumspect in dealing with moderate editors. When the *Abhyudaya* of Allahabad published an article on 'The difference between the black soldiers of the French and those of the British', the Local Government felt this would incite the Indian soldiers in the British army. The government threatened Madan Mohan Malviya, the keeper of the press, with a security of Rs. 2,500 against prosecution. Malviya was undaunted and denied any attempt at instigation of soldiers in this article. The Lt.-Governor, Meston, was in a dilemma as annoying Malviya or taking strong action would sensationalize the issue. Malviya was a popular figure. In the end, Meston withdrew the security demand on a verbal assurance from Malviya, considered 'the bitterest enemy of the British government that we have in Council, and I am not at all sure that he is not one of the anarchist leaders himself'.[88] Similarly, the English daily, *Leader* of Allahabad, had luminaries like Malviya, Moti Lal Nehru, C.Y. Chintamani and S.C. Sinha connected with it. The publication of an article on the current political situation by Bishan Narayan Dar made the District Magistrate send for the editor and warn him against any more such articles which could result in prosecution.[89]

Press prosecutions thus gradually became more frequent, but the psychology of the government remained the same—an unhealthy and obsessive suspicion of the intentions of the 'native' editor, who, to their chagrin, was surviving all attempts to fetter him.

The language newspapers had to encounter major problems, prosecutions and fines that restricted their independence. They felt that unless the authorities developed confidence in the Indian journalists no healthy interaction was possible.

THE RELATIONSHIP BETWEEN THE HINDI AND URDU NEWSPAPERS AND THE ENGLISH LANGUAGE PRESS

A major dissatisfaction of the language newspapers was the attitude of the government towards the English newspapers in India. The discrimination shown to the English language press by the government was a thorn in the flesh of the language newspapers. However, the language press was gradually becoming more conscious of its power and influence, and repression or discrimination did not really curb it. The English language press abandoned all traces of pro-Indian writings, and came to stand solidly behind the government and the bureaucracy.[90] Consequently, whereas the 'native' press was subjected to rigorous enforcement of the Press Laws, the English newspapers enjoyed considerable immunity. Their strategy was to blindly defend government policies and belittle Indians of every school.[91]

The *Pioneer* was the primary English newspaper of the province. It took pleasure in villifying Indians and won the ire of the language press. For the *Pioneer* Indians were not fit to be made jurors or to hold any other influential position. The 'native' newspapers were allegedly seditious.[92] Similarly, the *Englishman* of Calcutta condemned the entire language press as seditious. The language papers protested that their endeavour was only to expose the high-handed and irregular proceedings of British officers and express public opinion to prevent the growth of popular discontent. 'The fact is that English language journalists being blinded by prejudice, are unable to distinguish between sedition and true loyalty.'[93]

The English language press looked down upon the language press, and constantly reminded the government of the unequal status of the two classes of newspapers. The *Pioneer* held that Indian journals were as far removed from the English language ones as the vagrant 'Dom' or a thieving 'Sansaiya' was from the honourable sections of society.[94] The one good result of this superior attitude was the linguistic and emotional identity of the language newspapers with the people. The English papers were more interested in subjects like legislative reform, separation of the executive from the judiciary, the currency question and university education whereas local language newspapers combined the discussions on important national issues with matters which concerned and agitated the common man: racial discrimination, the woeful plight of the people during plague and famine, unemployment, and matters of local interest.[95]

The Urdu and Hindi newspapers were accused of inciting communal disharmony. They did have strong beliefs according to the religion of their editors and proprietors, but the English language press cannot be absolved of the blame of creating communal tension and actually fostering communal consciousness. The birth of the Congress in 1885 troubled the English language press no end. The way to obviate unity among the people was to incite Hindu–Muslim fervour among the respective communities. When the National Muhammadan Association refused to attend the Congress session in 1886, the *Englishman* of 20 December 1886 praised the courage of the Muslims in keeping away. Gradually, Sir Syed and his *Aligarh Institute Gazette* became identified as anti-Congress. The *Pioneer* praised Sir Syed, and the two together dubbed the Congress brand of agitation as a convenient screen which disloyal elements might use to camouflage their activities, and excite racial and fanatical public upheaval to the tune of the 1857 uproar.[96] The English language papers did not desist from rebuking some native princes, but the latter were intimidated by the knowledge that their critics would never be convicted in a British court, and took no action. In the defamation case which Captain Hearsey, an indigent Eurasian, lodged against Mr. George Allen, the proprietor of *Pioneer*, the High Court inflicted a fine of Rs. 3,000 on the latter. The initial reaction of the newspapers was one of satisfaction, as the Captain had pro-Congress leanings, but later they realized that there was a wide gap between assertion and practice, and felt that the court should have been more stringent.[97]

INTER-PERSONAL RELATIONSHIPS

Besides the lack of fellow-feeling with the English language press, the Indian press itself was overridden with dissensions in its ranks. These were either religious or ideological. Besides the government subsidized newspapers, there were some that were prone to acclaim government policies, while others were diehard antagonists. With the growth of communalism a rift grew between them. Divisions became further reinforced by the cow-protection movement to which the Muslim press was generally antagonistic.

Such examples of dissension are many. The editor and proprietor of *Anis-i-Hind* of Meerut was threatened by Muslims as Id approached in 1897. The hostile attitude of *Al Bashir* towards Hindus was resented even by a few Muslim newspapers. They felt that the *Al Bashir* was only displaying its narrow-mindedness and prejudice, and its inflammatory articles would only widen the gulf between the two communities. The fact was that Hindus had progressed better in education and this irritated the Muslim journalists.[98]

The publication of a book by Sohan Prasad of Gorakhpur created a furore in the language press. The Hindu newspapers supported it while the Muslim newspapers objected to some references in the book. They went to the extent of instituting a criminal prosecution against him.[99]

The Muslim papers, themselves, were divided according to Shia or Sunni leanings. There was a quarrel between the Sunni *Agra Akhbar* and the *Mufid-i-Am*. Apparently the latter printed and published a book by Nawab Sadiq Hasan Khan that was opposed to the Sunni sect. The progressive Muslim papers condemned such quarrels and said that it was for such want of good manners on the part of Urdu papers that educated men and civilized society hesitated to patronize them. The 'native' newspapers ought to mend their ways or else government would deprive them of their freedom.[100]

As the years progressed, politics became more communal and resultantly more complicated. This affected the writings of the language newspapers. The Muslim press gradually grew closer to the British, and praised the government for its sagacity in fostering the Muslims; the Hindu press resented this favouritism.

The advent of Pan-Islamic trends after 1911 left the press most confused. The Muslim papers were divided in their support or condemnation of British moves outside India. Religious fervour had overtaken the political, and loyalty to the British was no longer a foregone conclusion. This new consciousness necessitated increasing closeness between the Congress and certain Muslim sections. It gave a great boost to the Pan-Islamic supporters in the Muslim press. The boost that extremism got on the political and national scene, engendered the sprouting of several new newspapers, who were fed up with the equivocations of their moderate brethren appeasing British sensibilities. The newspapers advocating moderation disliked the sensationalism of the radical newspapers. Besides being against their genre of journalism, the increased circulation of these 'seditious newspapers because of their juicy gossip', made the moderate newspapers contemptuous. The prosecution of the editor of *Swarajya* in 1908, for example, received the approval of the *Riaz-ul-Akhbar* (Lucknow), *Advocate* (Lucknow) and *Indian People* (Allahabad). The *Advocate* of 17 December stated, 'The trash which was published in the paper seldom attracted attention.'

Thus the press was divided on several issues. It was pro-government or anti-government, moderate or extremist, pro-Congress or anti-Congress, pro-landlord or anti-landlord, conservative or modern, important or inconsequential. Editors were either well-educated or had received nominal education. The Muslim-Hindu factor was complicated and divisiveness was more evident there. The Muslim press was a multi-faceted corpus. It had both moderate and extremist elements.

ELITE AND THE LANGUAGE PRESS

The nobility of the province was quite vocal in its condemnation of the language press. In 1888 it protested to the Lt.-Governor against the seditious utterances of the language press, which according to them, was doing more harm than good. Sycophancy and conscious efforts to save their skins were most obvious:

> It is not very difficult to imagine the result of such teachings and preachings in the minds of the masses of our countrymen, who have no ideas of their own, and are easily persuaded to believe all the false accusations of mis-government and mal-administration against the Government of India.

They wanted the law of sedition to be made more severe.[101] The Nawab of Rampur reportedly was disrespectful to the editors of the language newspapers.[102] The Maharaja of Banaras (Varanasi) in a memo to Hewett, the Lt.-Governor, in 1909 wrote scathingly of journalists 'Having little means of getting reliable information and caring less to try to get them they are always in quest of sensational news and pander to the baser tastes and depraved notions of the people.' He suggested that 'the native press should be very effectively muzzled'.[103] Thakur Suraj Singh, an honorary magistrate and son of the oldest Awadh taluqdar, felt, '. . . where law and common sense allow, the offending paper should be forcibly discontinued.' In fact, the Upper India Chamber of Commerce was in favour of security deposits liable to forfeiture.[104] To some extent, the accusation of exaggeration seemed plausible and some papers did advise journalistic moderation. They felt that excessive patriotism and unfair attacks on the government on the part of the newspapers created trouble.[105]

THE FINANCIAL POSITION OF THE LANGUAGE PRESS

The publication of a paper was often unprofitable, remuneration to both proprietors and editors was small. There were only a few successful newspapers, who had a large circulation and who made a profit of above a hundred rupees in a month. Generally the editors of language newspapers were men of limited education, on a monthly salary of Rs. 15 to Rs. 50. In most cases, the proprietors were also the editors, and ran their papers at a loss. They had to fund their own newspapers most of the time. Only the favoured newspapers received government support either ostensibly or covertly.

Despite this, no attempt on the government's part to highlight the indigence of Indian editors was appreciated. When Colvin, the Lt.-Governor, said in 1890 that the language newspapers were in the hands of poor and needy men, who levied blackmail on respectable persons, he received the answer that these editors were in no way more needy than editors and proprietors of well-known English language journals. The proprietor of the *Pioneer*, Mr. Allen, had worn a threadbare coat on arrival in India. This apart, it was insisted that some Indian newspapers were owned by respectable men, who spent thousands of rupees on their publications just for the public good.[106]

Financial problems increased with the inability of editors to recover costs from subscriptions. As it is, the papers sold only for 4 to 8 *annas* a piece. Subscribers not paying up created fresh problems, and District authorities were asked to see to the recovery of money on behalf of the editors.[107]

The language press resented the high postage charged by the post-office and wanted it to be brought down to a quarter *anna* irrespective of the weight of the paper. It complained about the refusal by the post-office to receive copies of privileged newspapers for despatch if presented after the fixed dates. Papers paid postage in advance for three months, and felt they were entitled to special indulgence as regards postage.[108]

THE NATURE OF THE LANGUAGE PRESS

Even so, the language press did not stagnate and was much more popular than the English language press. The throbbing pulse of the country was best reflected by papers in local languages, whose editors displayed remarkable courage.[109]

Newspaper reading became a feature of Indian life. Schoolboys began instructing themselves with the columns of such papers. Classroom tables were littered with journals.[110] Newspapers reached villages where one person read them out to several others. The newspaper, besides becoming the political educator, became a means of political participation. The language newspapers were certain that their influence was not because of blackmail or oppression, but because of the newly-educated classes, whose character and aspirations they faithfully reflected. Inconvenient facts were often disregarded by them, and there was often a lack of accuracy and judgement and a tendency to exaggerate. Yet, these impulsive utterings added a charm and richness to language journalism so distinctive of the Oriental mind.

However, some journalists accepted that their colleagues tended to use abusive language. They felt that abuse tended to prejudice the trust between government and the people. Taking up a particular incident, these newspapers felt that the *Hindustani* was unjustified in calling a Lt.-Governor the son of a carpenter, a District Magistrate, the son of a hatter.[111] Both sides were correct in their stand and both had their problems.

CIRCULATION AND PERIODICITY

There was a vast difference between the circulation of the English language newspapers and the language newspapers.[112] The former had a much larger circulation and were more stable enterprises. The number of local language newspapers was greater, but the majority had a very low circulation, with the fear of closing down always in the background. As we have seen, between 1885-1905 there were nine newspapers with circulation below 200, twenty-five with circulation 200 and 400 and twenty, between 400 and 700. Only the *Bharat Jiwan* stood out with a circulation of 1500-1700 copies. There were many more Urdu papers than Hindi, but it seems that the latter were more important and had a larger circulation—in some cases up to 1500 copies. Some other Hindi papers had a circulation of 600-800 copies, while the Urdu papers had much lower circulation, occasionally only 100. The Muslim papers were frustrated by a circulation that was so low. This was probably because Muslims in general were not as educated as the Hindus, nor so persevering. The Muslim press felt that while Hindus were trying to forward the cause of Hindi journalism, Muslims were disinterested.[113] This contention, to an extent, may have been correct, but the fact that several Hindus were bringing out Urdu newspapers itself meant that Hindus could not only be identified with Hindi papers.

Table 1.1 has shown that there were 43 weeklies amongst the 67 papers listed. There were only two daily papers, the *Oudh Akhbar* and the *Aligarh Institute Gazette*. The paucity of daily newspapers made some people doubt the effectiveness and popularity of Hindi and Urdu newspapers. But, as said earlier, circulation and periodicity could not improve easily. These papers they reached out to the common man, who did not always have the money for them. Initially, journalists were faced with the problem of finding a reading public: printing a newspaper did not itself make it popular. Often they had to take their own papers to shops and read them out to the people to attract their attention. Sometimes, they went into people's homes to induce them to buy. This problem of finding buyers was more acutely felt by the Hindi journalists, for Urdu was the language generally understood by the people.[114] For example, the problem of a small clientele was felt by Balkrishna Bhatt when he launched his *Hindi Pradip*. He was indigent and lack of buyers upset him, but he remained undeterred, and launched his paper with missionary zeal.[115]

Small circulation should not be always taken to mean that the language newspapers were ineffective. As a disseminator of ideas, the worth of the newspaper was very great. It reached out to the common man and influenced those who could not afford to buy it. Proprietors may have suffered financially but their influence was much greater than what the figures showed. The village headman, school-master, *lambardar*, or *patwari* read papers aloud to rural folk.[116] The *Pioneer*, in fury, remarked, 'The disloyal language rags now penetrate into remote villages. . . . The village school-master or accountant is generally the disseminator.'[117] Apparently, rural people came a long way to have a newspaper read out to them. A local 'library' would be organized around a single newspaper. Gradually library movements sprang up all over the province.[118] This was the reason why government was wary of the language press and wanted to curb its free expression. Government realized that it afforded 'a valuable index of the state of public feeling'.[119] The journalists fearlessly continued with their mission probably because they gradually realized that they had caught the public interest and also because they understood the defensive psychology behind repressive government measures.

PROPRIETORS AND EDITORS

Proprietors and editors of language newspapers came from many walks of life. Most proprietors were also their own editors. Besides, the low salaries paid to editors failed to attract the cream of the educated classes who found other remunerative professions. There was no journalistic camaraderie and this profession had no associations or clubs. The *Hindustan Review* of August 1906 observed,

> Journalism in India is not a lucrative profession and those, who conduct it live a hand-to-mouth existence. They are not, like their English colleagues, helped by a staff of well-paid assistants, but mainly depend on amateur contribution.[120]

Table 1.2 gives the types of proprietor and their social standing.[121]

I now give life sketches of a few of the proprietors of the province, so that a better insight can be had into their aspirations and life style and most of all, the papers they brought out.

BABU RAM KISHAN DAS was the founder of the well-known Hindi weekly, *Bharat Jiwan*, started in Varanasi in 1884 when he was 25. He was a Khattri and a man of 'low origin'. He was educated at the Banaras College. Though the *Bharat Jiwan* had the largest circulation and lasted throughout the period of study, its effectiveness remained doubtful. Many journalists regarded this paper as effective in propagating drama, books, stories, anecdotes or poems, but a subservient paper nevertheless. It never had the courage to publish clearly and fearlessly. Despite this, government often remarked on the unjust attacks it suffred from this paper, and accused it of instilling distrust of the government in the minds of the people.[122]

SIR SYED AHMAD KHAN was born in 1817 in Delhi. He was the scion of one of the Mughal Empire's great service families. In 1837 he entered British service as a sheristadar. By 1857 he had graduated to becoming a munsif in Bijnor. He helped the government considerably here, and was held in high regard. He was a great writer, initially mainly on subjects concerning Muslims. He was convinced that education was the answer to India's problems. He founded the Aligarh Muslim College, and very soon Aligarh became the centre of Muslim activity. In 1866 his journal *Aligarh Institute Gazette* came out in Urdu and

TABLE 1.2: TYPES OF PROPRIETORS AND THEIR STANDING

Type	*Number*	*Standing*	*Number*
Also Editors	43	Taluqdars & Zamindars	5
Muslims	30	Educated Men of Standing	27
Hindus	25	Low Social Standing or Inconsequential	22

English. He became a member of the Legislative Council, and never swerved from his loyalty to the government. The government bought a substantial number of copies of his paper for the use of the education department. The paper was very loyal and its circulation was more than most other newspapers, but it had no distinct hold on the people, as it was elitist and was considered an organ of the government. Sir Syed died in 1898.[123]

BALKRISHNA BHATT launched the *Hindi Pradip*, a monthly, in Allahabad, at the age of 33 in 1877. He was a Sanskrit teacher at the Kayastha Pathshala on the meagre salary of Rs. 30 per month. This proud Brahmin, steeped in Sanskrit scholasticism and also tutored in English, was willing to promote a change in society as well as maintain its cultural heritage. His income was about Rs. 275 per annum from the sale of his paper, but he wrote fearlessly. Inevitably he made enemies. At 66, he made a stridently critical speech at Tilak's deportation, and courted unemployment as a result. His was a missionary zeal, and though his paper's circulation was below average, his writings had an impact on the public mind. The government was obviously not happy with the virulent criticisms of its policies in the *Pradip*, and it was ultimately closed down on the charge of seditious writing.[124]

RAJA RAMPAL SINGH of Kalakankar in Pratapgarh district, was a taluqdar with a difference. He had received English education, had lived for ten years in England as a youth, and consequently was anglicized in his ways. His marriage to a European had placed him in an isolated position. Initially an ardent Congressman, he was greatly disliked by the government, as the Congress movement received much encouragement from his newspaper *Hindustan*. This paper was a daily started by him in November 1885 at Kalakankar, in English and Hindi. He had many eminent people like Madan Mohan Malviya, Babu Balmukund Gupta, Pandit Amritlal Chakravarthy, etc., on his editorial board, but after Malviya left, he himself became editor . He became a member of the Legislative Council, and gradually drifted away from the Congress. What was particularly commendable about his paper was its constant endeavour to remain unbiased as regards various controversial subjects. It contained commentaries on and critical evaluation of almost all the important subjects of the period. Raja Rampal Singh could be unquestionably considered the doyen of language journalism in UP, one of the most successful journalists of his time. He died in 1909.[125]

MUHAMMAD BASHIR-UD-DIN born in 1857, of the Sunni sect was initially the editor of *Najm-ul-Akhbar*, a weekly in Urdu published in Etawah. It was an intelligent and loyal paper. Though often critical of government policy, it was decidedly anti-Congress. In 1899, after the *Najm* closed down, Bashir-Ud-Din founded the *Al Bashir* at Etawah. This was also an Urdu weekly but its circulation was almost double that of its predecessor. Bashir-Ud-Din was its proprietor, editor and publisher. It generally consisted of translations of matter from other papers, and was loyal to the government so long as Muslim interests were not threatened. For example, *Al Bashir* criticized MacDonnell whom it considered anti-Muslim.[126]

GANGA PRASAD VERMA was a Khattri and a Vaishnava. His father was Munshi Narain Das. He was born around 1860, and became the Municipal Commissioner and Secretary of the Awadh Standing Congress Committee. The government initially regarded him an upstart and a man of no position, but later accepted his ability, good conduct and education. He was the proprietor and editor of the Urdu weekly, *Hindustani* of Lucknow and was accused of abusing the authorities. This appears rather exaggerated as the *Hindustani* was comparatively less biased than the other newspapers and discussed national as well as local affairs.[127]

SHEIKH SAJJAD HUSAIN, the son of Mansur Ali, was born around 1857. He was educated at Canning College, Lucknow. His father was a Deputy Collector in the employ of the Nizam of Hyderabad. He was a supporter of the Congress. Sajjad Husain was the proprietor of the *Oudh Punch* and *Azad*, both Urdu weeklies of Lucknow. The *Oudh Punch* was an illustrated satirical newspaper that freely criticized government measures. It dealt largely with political matters, but the government did not find it objectionable. The *Azad* too did not annoy the government though it was definitely not pro-government. Probably its anti-Congress stance reassured the authorities.[128]

MUNSHI NEWAL KISHORE was a taluqdar of Lucknow and a great supporter of the British government. He was bestowed with the title of C.I.E. by the government, and had a high position in society on account of his wealth and influence. He was the proprietor of the *Oudh Akhbar*, an Urdu daily. The government initially subsidized the *Oudh Akhbar*, and also bought a number of copies. The paper was anti-Congress, moderate and intelligent, and steady in its loyalty to the government in political matters. After his death in 1895, Nawal Kishore's son, Munshi Prayag Narain Bhargava, took over the proprietorship. The editor was Jalpa Prasad, a Kayastha. The unstinted support to the government made the latter encourage Newal Kishore's publication, but angered his colleagues who, however, lauded him as a proprietor who had attained unparalleled success, his newspaper having the highest circulation among Urdu journals in circulation. He had come to Lucknow empty handed and had died a millionaire.[129]

These and other editors laboured to make Indian journalism a potent force. Compared to Bengal, the language press in UP was still in an early stage of development, but it was efficacious enough to create a viable public opinion. It did reach out to the common man and could feel the pulse of the nation. It created turmoil in government circles by occasionally misstating facts either inadvertently or purposely, but its influence could not be denied. The government was eager to get to know the thoughts of the people through the language media, but at the same time wanted to curb their outpourings. In the bargain, repression was practised, while at the same time an eager desire to make language papers available to British officials also developed. The strategy of the government to give limited or no news to the language newspapers, and make it accessible to the English language press, backfired. The language newspapers would publish their own versions, making them more attractive by adding their own flourishes, and the government wondered what effect this would have on the public. It would not be incorrect to conclude that the language newspapers had come to stay. They were proving to be an effective means of disseminating news to the public, and influencing government policies. They formed the fountainhead of information on social, economic, cultural and political developments. This gave a certain unity to all these diverse phenomena which were threatening the foundations of a firmly-entrenched colonial power.

NOTES

1. Lyton had instituted a press commissionership to provide the press with authentic information. The latter proved to be an official 'moniteur' but an unattractive one. Prem Narain, *Press and Politics in India*, 1885, 1905, New Delhi, 1970, p. 265.
2. S. Natarajan, *Rise of Journalism, A History of the Press in India*, Bombay, 1962, p. 128. This resume of the history of the press has been compiled

from (a) Natarajan, (b) Pandit Ambika Prasad Bajpayee, *Samachar Patron Ka Itihas,* Benaras, 1953, (c) Prem Narain, ibid., (d) Vinod Kumar Saxena, *Indian Reaction to British Politics, 1898-1911*, Delhi, 1978.

3. VNR of NWP&O, *Hindustani*, Lucknow, 3 June 1885. This communication was in response to the newspaper editors' resolve at a meeting at Lucknow to show moderation and refrain from false rumours.
4. VNR of NWP&O, *Hindustani*, Lucknow, 18 March 1885; *Najm-ul-Akhbar*, Etawah, 24 March 1885.
5. Natarajan, op.cit., pp. 132-6.
6. Ibid.
7. Ibid., p. 164.
8. GAD UP, 1885, File No. 696.
9. VNR of NWP&O, *Najm-ul-Akhbar*, Etawah, 20 June, 15 July 1885; *Bharat Bandhu*, Aligarh, 26 June 1885; *Hindustani*, Lucknow, 10 July 1885. The latter said that only three English language newspapers, *Pioneer*, *Times of India* and *Englishman* competed with each other in publishing telegrams from their correspondents, *Bharat Jiwan*, Varanasi, 20 July 1885.
10. *Najm-ul-Akhbar*, Etawah, 28 Jan. 1886.
11. S.N. Paul, *Public Opinion and British Rule*, New Delhi, p. 4.
12. Saxena, op.cit., pp. 2-30.
13. The *Englishman* of 19 March 1886, described the writers of the 'native' press, 'The writers seem to be animated by much the same spirit as the Irishman, who, when wrecked on a foreign shore enquired if there was a government in that country, and being answered in the affirmative replied 'Then I am against it'.
14. VNR of NWP&O, *Hindustan*, Kalakankar, 19 Oct. 1889; *Hindustani*, Lucknow, 20 Oct. 1889; *Nasim-i-Agra*, 7 Nov. 1889.
15. Prem Narain, op.cit., pp. 269-70.
16. VNR of NWP&O, *Hindustani*, Lucknow, 25 July 1894.
17. VNR of NWP&O, *Colonel*, Moradabad, 16 Nov. 1894.
18. VNR of NWP&O, *Shahna-i-Hind*, Meerut, 16 July 1897.
19. VNR OF NWP&O, *Azad*, Lucknow, 20 Aug. 1897.
20. MacDonnell papers, M.S. English History, C 355 BPD 6368, 1887. He said: '. . . the press thus set free from all restraints was doing its utmost, without let or hinderance to instil into the people of India hatred and contempt for the rulers'.
21. VNR of NWP&O, *Hindustani*, Lucknow, 12 Jan. 1898; *Sitara-i-Hind*, Moradabad, 12 Feb. 1898; *Anis-i-Hind*, Meerut, 9 Feb. 1898; *Tohfah-i-Hind*, Bijnor, 13 Feb. 1898; *Dabdaba-i-Aqisari*, Bareilly, 26 Feb. and 11 June 1898; *Najmu-l-Hind*, Moradabad, April 1899 said: 'What an irony of fate it is that while Indians had arms they enjoyed the right of freely criticizing Government, but now when they are disarmed, the

freedom of the press has also been wrested from them.' Press Act had been passed under the name of the Sedition Law.

22. VNR of NWP&O, *The Citizen*, Allahabad, 14 Sept. 1903; *Indian People*, Allahabad, 4 Sept. 1903.
23. GOI, Home Public File No 273/1907, Nos. 1269-79; Prog. 16. VNR of UP; *Advocate*, Lucknow, 7 Nov. 1907; *Abhyudaya*, Allahabad, 25 Oct. 1907; GAD File No. 451/1907; VNR of UP.
24. *Advocate*, Lucknow, 20 Jan. 1910; GAD File No. 293/1910.
25. VNR of UP, *Advocate*, Lucknow, 11 June 1908.
26. Moti Lal Bhargava, *Role of Press in the Freedom Movement,* Reliance, Delhi, 1987, p. 24.
27. *Swarajya*, Allahabad, 18 July 1908; *Aligarh Institute Gazette*, 17 June 1908. Extracts from the Confidential Annual Reports on the language press of 1908 in Bengal, Bombay, Punjab and UP Prog. 21. 'It has been placed beyond doubt that the theory of the safety valve cannot be applied to the press of this country without important reservations . . . discontent can be fanned into the white heat of fanaticism by the calculated malevolence of newspaper writers.'
28. GAD, File No. 320/1909—Control over the newspaper press in India, p. 27, 28 Sept. 1909.
29. Ibid., p. 31.
30. VNR of UP, *Leader*, Allahabad, 9 Feb. 1910; *Oudh Akhbar*, Lucknow 11 Feb. 1910; Bhargava, op.cit., pp. 20-4. The Chief Secretary to Govt. of UP's letter to Sir H.A. Stuart, Secretary to Govt. of India, Home Dept. p. 31.
31. Hardinge, *My Indian Years (1910-16)*, p. 20. *Lady Minto: India, Minto and Morley*, pp. 24-7, 412-14.
32. Fortnightly Report (UP) Home (Pol) D., Dec. 1914.
33. GAD, File No. 589/1914.
34. Home Public B, Sept. 1891, Nos. 129-35; Press memo for 1890; Home Public B, July 1897, Nos. 278-81; Press memo for 1896; Home Public B June 1901, No. 6; Press memo for 1900.
35. Table 1.1 has been drawn up from the VNR of NWP&O between 1885 and 1905, and the press memorandum for Upper India between 1885 and 1905. The available memos were for the following years; 1884 1885, 1886, 1887, 1889, 1890, 1891, 1892, 1896, 1900, 1902, 1903, 1905 All subsequent deductions would mostly be based on this table.
36. Ibid.
37. Home Public B, June 1906, Nos. 104-6; Press memo of 1905, pp. 42-51
38. VNR of NWP&O, *Zamanah*, Kanpur, 26 Nov. 1896.
39. VNR of NWP&O, *Jami-ul-Ulum*, Moradabad, 28 Oct. 1902; *Indian People*, Allahabad, 8 March 1906.
40. Home Public B, Sept. 1887, Nos. 221-7; Home Public B, Aug. 1888 No. 209.
41. Home Public B, June 1906, Nos. 102-4; Press memo of 1905.

42. VNR of NWP&O, *Sahifa* , Bijnor, 12 Feb. 1902.
43. VNR of NWP&O, *Azad*, Lucknow, 29 April 1886; *Hindi Pradip*, Allahabad, Feb. 1887; and *Bharat Jiwan*, Varanasi, 21 March 1887. The last two papers were happy because they received the Gazette free.
44. Home Public A, June 1904, No. 283, p. 15.
45. Home Public B, Aug. 1889, Nos. 386-8.
46. Home Public A, Dec. 1891, Nos. 103-8, p. 6.
47. Ibid. The government selected the following newspapers to receive the Gazette of India: *Azad*; *Oudh Akhbar* of Lucknow; *Bharat Jiwan* of Benaras and *Najm-ul-Akhbar* of Etawah. These were regarded as responsible newspapers representative of the different communities.
48. Home Public A, June 1904, No. 283, p. 15; VNR of UP; *Prem*, Brindaban, 9 Dec. 1914; *Asr-i-Jadid*, Meerut, 3 Dec. 1914; *Indian Daily Telegraph*, Lucknow, 9 Dec. 1914; GAD File Nos. 457/1907; 320/1909. Bhargava, op.cit., pp. 45-48.
49. Prem Narain, op.cit., pp. 266-7.
50. Ibid., pp. 43-4.
51. VNR of NWP&O, *Aligarh Institute Gazette*, 2 Oct. 1897.
52. *Hindustan*, Kalakankar, 23 May 1890; *Hindustani*, Lucknow, 6 July 1890.
53. *Oudh Akhbar*, Lucknow, 5 May 1890; *Hindustan*, Lucknow, 4 May 1890. Later in 1895, after a lot of hue and cry was raised did the Lt.-Governor of UP agree to withdraw these subsidies being paid to the papers. *Hindustani*, Lucknow, 12 June 1895.
54. VNR of NWP&O, *Sham-i-Oudh*, Faizabad, 31 January 1885.
55. VNR of UP, *Aligarh Institute Gazette*, 16 Feb. 1910.
56. VNR of UP, *Oudh Akhbar*, Lucknow 11 Feb. 1910.
57. GAD, File No. 320/1909, pp. 27-32.
58. Burn to Meston, 4 June 1914, Meston papers. Francis Robinson, *Separatism Among Indian Muslims: The Politics of the United Provinces Muslims 1860-1923*, Delhi, Bombay, Bangalore, Kanpur, pp. 191-2.
59. (a) MacDonnell papers, p. 9 of the Appendix of the Committee appointed to consider the question of the enlargement of the functions of the Provincial Councils 1888. (b) Home Public A, Sept. 1901, Nos. 88-9. MacDonnell said: '. . . in spite of its imperfections, extravagance and occasional perversity, it reflects, though in an inadequate measure, native opinion in these provinces, and not infrequently offers sound and intelligent criticism on the measures and administrations of Government . . .'.
60. VNR of NWP&O, *Anis-i-Hind*, Meerut, 17 March 1894.
61. VNR of NWP&O, *Mashir-i-Qaisar*, Lucknow, June 1888.
62. VNR of NWP&O, *Prayag Samachar*, Allahabad, 10 June 1885.
63. VNR of NWP&O, *Jami-ul-Ulum*, Moradabad, 28 April 1896; *Azad*, Lucknow, 1 May 1896.
64. VNR of NWP&O, *Nasim-i-Agra*, 23 Feb. 1891.

65. Prem Narain, op.cit., p. 268.
66. VNR of NWP&O, *Tuti-i-Hind*, Meerut, 16 June 1888.
67. VNR of NWP &O. *Najm-ul-Akhbar*, Etawah, 16 Aug. 1887.
68. VNR of NWP&O, *Mashir-i-Qaisar*, Lucknow, August 1887.
69. VNR of NWP&O, *Police News*, Meerut, 24 Aug. 1894; *Riaz-ul-Akhbar*, Gorakhpur, 1 Sept. 1894.
70. VNR of NWP&O, *Jami-ul-Ulum*, Moradabad, 14 Nov. 1896; *Naiyar-i-Azam*, Moradabad, 12 Nov. 1896; *Jam-i-Jamshed*, Moradabad, 22 Nov. 1896; *Bharat Jiwan*, Varanasi, 8 Feb. 1897.
71. VNR of NWP&O, *Naiyar-i-Azam*, Moradabad, 5 Dec. 1896.
72. VNR of NWP&O, *Rohilkhand Gazette*, Bareilly, 4 March 1899.
73. VNR of NWP&O, *Naiyar-i-Azam*, Moradabad, 12 May and 7 June 1901; *Bharat Jiwan*, Varanasi, 3 June 1901.
74. VNR of NWP&O, *Naiyar-i-Azim*, Moradabad, 19 April 1886.
75. VNR of NWP&O, *Naiyar-i-Azam*, Moradabad, 30 Sept. 1889; *Alam-i-Taswir*, Kanpur, 1 Oct. 1889; *Najm-ul-Hind*, Moradabad, 17 Oct. 1889; *Al Hilal*, Moradabad, 21 Oct. 1889; *Nasim-i-Agra*, 23 May 1892; *Dabir-i-Hind*, Agra, Jan 1890.
76. VNR of NWP&O, *Riaz-ul-Akhbar*, Gorakhpur, 28 Aug. 1891; *Tuti-i-Hind*, Meerut, 16 May 1894.
77. VNR of NWP&O, *Faryad-i-Hind*, Allahabad, 1 Aug. 1895; *Agra Punch*, 16 Nov. 1893.
78. Home Public A, Aug. 1899, No. 125, 'Press Prosecutions', Sept. 1899, Nos. 12-13.
79. GAD, File No. 320/1909, p. 31.
80. Confidential Annual Reports on the language press of 1908, Prog. 21; Home Pol. A, Proceedings Nos. 51-3, p. 3, July 1908; Home Pol. A, Proceedings Nos. 124-8, p. 8, Dec. 1908.
81. Bhargava, op.cit., p. 24; Proceedings Nos. 124-8; GAD, op.cit., File No. 320/1909—Letter from J.M. Home, Chief Secretary to Government of UP, to Secretary to GOI, Home Dept., Allahabad, 4 Nov. 1909.

    The prosecuted editors of the *Swarajya* were: 1. Shanti Narayan, 2. Ram Das Saralia, 3. Babu Ram Hari, 4 and 5. Two editors took out one issue each, 6. Nand Gopal.
82. VNR of UP, *Swarajya*, Allahabad, 9 Nov. 1907.
83. GAD, File No. 320/1909, op.cit.; VNR of UP; *Karmayogi*, Allahabad, 4 Feb. 1910.
84. Bhargava, op.cit., p. 24, Arun Chandra Guha, *First Spark of Revolution: The Early Phase of India's Struggle for Independence 1900-1920*, Bombay, Madras, Calcutta, New Delhi, pp. 307-10; VNR of UP, *Abhyudaya*, Allahabad, 28 April, 1910.
85. Bhargava, ibid.; Robinson, op.cit., p. 216; VNR of UP; *Urdu-i-Mualla*, Aligarh, May 1910.

86. GAD, File No. 195/1913-14, *The Muslims Gazette:* Question of taking security under the Indian Press Act of 1910; VNR of UP, 1912 and 1913.
87. GAD, File No. 360/1914, Letter by R. Burn, Chief Secretary of UP to P. Harrison, Magistrate and Collector, Bareilly, 31 March 1913.
88. GAD, File No. 473/1914, Letter of Sir R.H. Cradlock, Secretary to Government of UP to Meston, 19 Sept. 1914; Bhargava, op.cit., pp. 24-6.
89. Bhargava, ibid., p. 45; VNR of UP, 1911.
90. Paul, op.cit., p. 208.
91. Natarajan, op.cit., p. 163. Gokhale commented 'The terms of race arrogance and contempt in which some of these newspapers constantly speak of Indians, and especially of educated Indians, cut into the minds more than the lash can cut into the flesh.' He, however, refuted the contention that all writings of the English language press were 'dipped in government ink'.
92. *Hindustan*, Kalakankar, 29 Sept. 1886 and 12 Oct. 1889.
93. VNR of NWP&O, *Najm-ul-Akhbar*, Etawah, 30 Sept. 1896.
94. Prem Narain, op.cit., pp. 228-86.
95. Ibid., pp. 285-6. The matters discussed by the language newspapers form the main topics of the subsequent chapters.
96. VNR of NWP&O, *Anis-i-Hind*, Meerut of 2 Feb. 1895, Prem Narain, ibid., pp. 15-28.
97. VNR of NWP&O, *Hindustani*, Lucknow, 23 Feb. 1890, *Hindustan*, Kalakankar, 7 Jan. 1890.
98. VNR of NWP&O, *Anis-i-Hind*, 5 May 1897; *Sahifa*, Bijnor, 26 Jan 1904.
99. *Hindustan*, Lucknow, 28 Oct. 1885, VNR of NWP&O, *Dinkar Prakash*, Lucknow, Oct. 1885; *Riaz-ul-Akhbar*, Gorakhpur, 1885.
100. VNR of NWP&O; *Nasir-i-Hind*, Agra, 1 July 1892; *Al Bashir*, Etawah, 25 Sept. 1899; *Jami-Jamshed*, Moradabad, 18 Feb. 1900, accused the *Jami-ul-Ulum* of enemity towards Muslims and ill-will towards the British Government.
101. MacDonnell Papers, p. 58 of the Appendix of the Committee appointed to consider the question of the enlargement of the functions of the Provincial Councils, No. 44.
102. VNR of NWP&O, *Najmu-l-Hind*, Saharanpur, 20 April 1894.
103. GAD, File No. 320/1909, op.cit.
104. Ibid.
105. *Hindustan*, Kalakankar, 4 Nov. 1897.
106. VNR of NWP&O, *Najm-ul-Akhbar*, Etawah, 24 Feb. 1890; *Hindustani*, Lucknow, 23 Feb. 1890.
107. VNR of NWP&O, *Jalwa-i-Ezidi*, Meerut, 13 April 1890, *Agra Punch*, 16 November 1893.
108. VNR of NWP&O, *Akhbar-i-Tammanai*, Lucknow, 8 Nov. 1890; *Najm-*

ul-Akhbar, Etawah, Jan. 1889; *Oudh Akhbar*, Lucknow, 25 Sept. 1885; Home Public B, March 1886, Nos. 125-62. A study of the statement showing periodicals and newspapers published in NWP&O, in 1886 will prove the point that language newspapers suffered on account of subscribers not paying up. Out of 25 English language and British newspapers 9 had pending arrears of subscriptions. About 80 of the 100 language newspapers had to be paid arrears and this was when the circulation of the former was between 300-50 while that of the latter was anywhere between 40 and 1900, with the average somewhere at 200 copies.

109. Natarajan, op.cit., p. 164.
110. Prem Narain, op.cit., p. 279.
111. VNR of NWP&O, *Azad*, Lucknow, 28 Feb. 1890.
112. Home Public B, March 1836, Nos. 125-62, p. 43
113. VNR of NWP&O, *Al Bashir*, Etawah, 22 May 1898.
114. Soochna Vibhag Uttar Pradesh, *Hindi Patrakarita Ank*, 1976.
115. Sudhir Chandra, *Literature and the Colonial Connection (Occasional Papers on History and Society)*, New Delhi, 1983, pp. 32-3.
116. Prem Narain, op.cit., p. 287.
117. Ibid., cited *Pioneer*, 16 Nov. 1893.
118. Natarajan, op.cit., pp. 71-2; Bipan Chandra, *India's Struggle for Independence*, New Delhi, p. 103
119. Home Public A, Sept. 1901, Nos. 88-9.
120. Saxena, op.cit., p. 84; *Advocate*, Lucknow, 26 Jan. 1902.
121. Tables derived from information in the list of newspapers given earlier.
122. Home Public B, March 1886, Nos. 122-4; Press memo of 1885; Home Public B, June 1895, Nos. 74-6; Memos of 1894 and 1905; Bajpayee, op.cit., p. 193.
123. Memo of 1905, op.cit.; Robinson, pp. 86-95.
124. Sudhir Chandra, op.cit., pp. 32-8; Bajpayee, op.cit., pp. 130-60, Press memo of 1905.
125. T.R. Metcalfe, *Land, Landlords and the British Raj: Northern India in the 19th Century*, Delhi, 1979; Press memo of 1905; Bajpayee, ibid., p. 330; Press memo of 1889; *Saptahik Hindustan,* 10 Jan. 1987, p. 53.
126. Robinson, op.cit.
127. Press memos of 1890, 1896 and 1905.
128. Press memos of 1885, 1890, 1896 and 1905. The proprietor in 1890 of the *Azad* was Ahmad Ali and he was definitely anti-Congress. Later Sajjad Husain took over, but somehow the *Azad* could not assume a pro-Congress stance.
129. VNR of NWP&O, 1895: *Hindustani*, Lucknow, 20 Feb; *Akhbar-i-Alam*, Meerut, 26 Feb.; Press memos of 1885, 1890, 1896, 1900 and 1905.

PART II

Society and the Press

2. The Challenge to Orthodox Society

Several factors contribute to the progress or stagnation of a society: religion, economics, traditions, human eccentricities, political consciousness and the policies of rulers are some of these. The task of exercizing colonial control was most difficult in the social sphere, as it entailed interference with some age-old beliefs of the people that were fiercely guarded.

THE SOCIO-RELIGIOUS STRUCTURE

Society in NWP and Awadh was a heterogeneous mass. The divisions within this mass were along the lines of religion, caste, and income. The two great religions were Islam and Hinduism and most of the new socio-religious movements were offshoots of these. In the province there were 8,579 Hindus and 1,380 Muslims to every 10,000 of the population. Out of 47 million, over 40 million were Hindus; only 13 per cent were Muslims. Hence only 178,000 were followers of other creeds, half of which were Jains, 58,000 Christians, 22,000 Modern Theistic Aryas and 11,000 Sikhs. Buddhists were almost negligible, and there were 350 Parsi shopkeepers and 60 Jews.

The customs and observances of Hindus and Muslims differed. The Hindus venerated the cow, and as a rule did not kill animals; while Muslims loathed pigs and dogs, but were not averse to animal sacrifice considered necessary in their religion. The Hindus were not particular about abstention from narcotics and spirits, while Muslims rejected them. The Hindus shaved their heads but kept a scalp-lock intact, but not so the Muslims. The Hindus burned their dead, Muslims buried them. In matters of clothes, colours, cooking utensils and other practices too, the two communities differed. The Muslims, though adhering to caste rules, had no hesitation in drinking and eating from the hands of Hindus, but the latter generally avoided food or water from the hands of the Muslims.[2]

These divisions did not, however, mean that Hindus and Muslims respectively were held together by any bonds of solidarity within their communities. Each was divided into several castes—a division which was observed more stringently than probably communal differences. The great religious communities were so internally divided and their levels of social hierarchy were so different, that to treat them as cohesive entities would be a mistake.

Among the Hindus, the family was of primary importance and caste regulated relations between families. It laid down a ritually prescribed scheme of social status for the four prescribed varnas or orders. Below these were the untouchables. In the lower scale precise ranking was very difficult since under the general designation of Shudra came a host of sub-castes of controversial rank.[3] The worshippers of godlings of disease, of hill and forest, saints, ghosts and demons amounted to no less than 7 million or nearly a sixth of the whole population.[4]

The majority of the people were Vaishnavas. Even among these there were a number of subdivisions distinguished either by some minute differences of ritual, or by their special veneration for the god in one of his myriad forms. They believed in faith leading to the salvation of souls and in a single benevolent Providence. The nineteenth century saw the growth of different sects who were more modern and less ritualistic in their approach. Kabir, Ramanand, Raidas were some of the 'gurus' whom the people venerated in large numbers. The fact that Kabir was a weaver and Raidas a tanner, showed the democratic trend of the times.[5] Nevertheless, this did not mean that the higher castes accepted the existence of the lower castes at an equal level. This was the whole paradox of the situation which resulted in so much divergence among the castes even if their religions were the same. Yet any effort of the government to interfere in their social practices temporarily unified the Hindus.

The Muslims, too, were divided into several castes, and the contempt of the higher castes for the lower castes was as obvious as it was among the Hindus. They, as a monolithic bloc, grew more rapidly[6] than the Hindus. The reasons accorded to this were—the definiteness of Islam as compared to the scepticism of the Hindu religion, democratic acceptance of Hindu converts and conferment of status[7] on them and flexibility in social customs (acceptance of widow remarriage).

Despite all this democratic approach, the Muslims were no less divided socially, and the elite found nothing in common with the lower classes. The Sheikhs and the Syeds could not identify themselves with the Julahas, or the castes like Bhangis or Chamars.[8] The divisions between the two sects Shias and Sunnis were so great that they surpassed Hindu-Muslim differences. The Shias recognized Ali, Mohammed's son-in-law, as his successor. Whereas the Sunnis believed in the supremacy of Prophet Mohammed alone. The Sunnis abhorred the Shia celebration of Muharram. The feast of the Muharram as a season of mourning and humiliation was observed by Shias who carried in procession *tazias*, a ritual which orthodox Sunnis abhorred, though village Muslims, almost without distinction of sect, joined in its observance.[9]

While differences of caste and belief prevailed among these two major communities, as time progressed, divisions on the basis of professions and wealth came to dominate. Social position became more important than caste. In Allahabad itself, there was an enormous gulf separating the 1,071 professional and trading people who paid income tax on incomes exceeding Rs. 1,000 a year in 1886-7, and the overwhelming majority of the population which earned less than Rs. 10 a year.[10] The zamindars, landlords and princes and the higher bureaucracy formed an elite united only partially by religion. As a class they were loyal to foreign rule.[11] Hindus and Muslims of the same class found much more in common among themselves than with co-religionists belonging to lower rungs of society In fact in the nineteenth century, Kashmiris, Kayasthas, Rajputs, Muslims, Banias and Khattris, whose forefathers had served, or were still serving the government of northern India, were the people in power. They could be classified as an urban section which adhered to government bred culture. Their language (Persian and later Urdu), was common, and their lifestyle predominantly Muslim. They showed contempt for people below their status, irrespective of religion. Several examples were known of Hindus venerating the shrines of Muslim saints, and a Hindu pleader still took out a *tazia* float during the Muharram festival of the 1880s.[12]

Peasants, weavers, butchers and others were the impoverished classes. They had problems with their daily sustenance, and could not find common cause with the brethren higher up. The class which was most vocal was the high caste educated middle class, from which lawyers, doctors, teachers and journalists were drawn. They felt deprived of their rightful share of government employment and patronage and received modest salaries, which they believed to be grossly unfair to their talents. The educated unemployed formed an important bloc and were resentful of government attitudes. It was from these middle classes that most of the political activists were drawn. Hence it would not be incorrect to say that there was a marked divergence between the ranking based upon ritual, and the dominance based upon local position.

A society divided on the basis of religion and caste on the one hand, and social position on the other, responded by either supporting, opposing, or criticizing endeavours at social reform. The language newspapers of our period were totally embedded in these forces, and were considered a means of letting the government, or the people, know what a particular group felt about a particular social issue. The concept of a neutral and unbiased Indian press was still to develop. Group affiliations were more important than independent perception or objective assessment.

THE IMPACT OF THE WEST

Contact with the West and growth of education had made a tremendous impact on Indian society. Modern industries, new means of transport, growing urbanization and increasing employment of women in factories, offices, hospitals and schools promoted social change. The new intellectual and political stirrings among the people were conducive to social change.[13] Initially, the rulers encouraged the new movements among the Hindus in the hope that the weakening of Hindu orthodoxy would be in the interests of British rule. Later, however, they realized that the metaphysical ferment was strengthening endeavours to resist the proselytizing influence of Christian missionaries, and teaching ways and means to combat British rule.[14]

Society gradually came to be divided at one level into three broad groups: the conservative and orthodox elements; the imitators of the West; and the religious revivalists. The conservative element resisted the forces of change tooth and nail, and considered their age-old religious practices sacrosanct and not to be interfered with. Orthodox Hinduism also had its reforming sects, devoted to reconstitution of religious endowments and control of the *mahants* of temples. The Sri Vaishnava Mahasabha was a good example. Sanatan Dharma Sabhas were active but to treat them as a coherent whole would be wrong, as the only clear concept they had was the retention of Hindu orthodoxy. However, the movement did manifest itself in groups and associations like the Bharat Dharm Mahamandal in 1900-1. Its meetings were held at Haridwar in 1887, Lahore and Delhi (1890) and Varanasi in 1892.[15] Varanasi, always a centre of religious orthodoxy, became a centre of Hindu religious revivalism under the aegis of Madan Mohan Malviya in the nineteenth century.[16] The assertion of Hindu individuality was manifested in Malviya's attempt to establish a Hindu University at Varanasi in 1909. Though initially he entered into an understanding with Mrs. Besant, around 1913, he stressed the necessity for total Hindu representation in the first governing body of the proposed University. The more neutral elements in society feared that 'A sectarian university will foster a feeling of exclusiveness and of hostility to Western civilisation and to the British race and government as representatives of that civilization.'[17] However, many editors of the language newspapers represented orthodox revivalist trends.

Prominent among orthodox revivalists were Balmukund Gupta, editor of the *Advocate*, Lucknow, and the editor of *Muttra Samachar*.[18] By and large, however, Hindu revivalism was limited to a few rich patrons who sponsored religious functions and financed religious foundations, and was centred around the great bathing fairs at Allahabad, Mathura, Varanasi and Haridwar. Its publicists were Brahmins and its adherents were 'Shankaracharyas' and 'Mahants' UP was the centre of this Hindu revivalism.

The orthodox elements naturally resented the dissemination of Western ideas: Muslims among them refused to accept Sir Syed Ahmad as their leader. He wore European clothes, drank liquor, did not offer his daily prayers, did not fast during Ramzan and preferred a trip abroad to Europe to the Haj. All this modernism was unacceptable to traditionalists.[19] In contrast to these orthodox groups, some middle- and upper-class Indians blindly imitated Western life and culture. They aped European manners and customs; and the superficial appeal of Western culture was more attractive to them than its inherent values and depth.[20] However, some of them were thinking men, prominent in their various professions. By the 1890s a few families of highly Westernized lawyers, led by Motilal Nehru and Sachinanda Sinha participated in social and literary activities very much like the Europeans. These Westernized barristers, pleaders and newspaper editors formed a link between the rulers and the traditional, not necessarily orthodox, sections of society.[21]

British criticism of Indian culture, awareness of the more modern institutions of European life and government, and reaction against the Westernized Indians, created rumblings in Indian society. This resulted in an impulse to look into the past and glorify the old culture and tradition.[22] The British, who had initially supported these religious reformers, withdrew their support when the latter grew vocal in criticism of European systems. The religious reformers formed several organizations like the Prarthana Samaj, Theosophical Society, Brahmo Samaj and Arya Samaj. Their aims were quite similar, but they differed in their notions as to how these could be achieved. All wanted to purge Hinduism of its degenerate forms and virtually propagated new religions. They realized that they would have to come to terms with Christianity. They wished to pursue social reforms, but though they agreed generally about the abolition of *sati, thuggee,* female infanticide and child marriage, they differed on abolition of caste.[23] What was important was that though orthodoxy and revivalism were contradictory elements, they both engendered a new Hindu consciousness and opposition to Western influence.

The revivalist movements, especially the Arya Samaj, appealed to a larger section of the people than did orthodox sects. Although the role of UP in this great nineteteeth-century reassessment of Hindu culture was small—for it was the home of orthodox reaction—it felt the influence of religion especially the Brahmo Samaj and the Arya Ṣamaj The former was brought in by Bengali government servants and the main seat of its revival was Varanasi.[24] The Arya Samaj appealed to the mobile professional elite of the service communities. Its publicity was primarily in Urdu, and it attracted fewer noblemen than clerks. Kashi Prasad, and Ram Das Chakravarti, who was Joint Secretary of the Allahabad Arya Samaj, were prominent among the contributors to local social reform. The Samaj was responsible for the Gaurakshini Sabhas or cow-protection and the movement spread to UP in 1886, until by 1893 it had become so widespread, that the British realized the necessity to contain if not curb it.[25]

The Arya Samaj gradually grew in importance and became the symbol of a democratic social reform movement. The language newspapers supporting it extolled its contribution to revolutionizing Indian society. Swami Dayanand was acclaimed for his propagation of unity in religion by sweeping away all the diversity of languages, of education and of manners and customs in the dissemination of the catholic Vedic religion.[26] Its increazing effectiveness, however, gave rise to much criticism. The inauguration of the Shuddhi Sabha for the conversion of Muslims to the Arya Samaj and the starting of a fund to maintain itinerant preachers, inevitably disturbed those Muslim diehards who saw it as a threat to their social position. The orthodox elements took strong exception to the Arya Samaj policy of interdining with converts to their faith after certain purifying ceremonies, as this was considered contradictory to the teachings of the Vedas. The Arya Samajists were also accused of hypocrisy in practising the Shuddhi movement with regard to Chamaras, Churas and other low castes. The poor Dhunias and Julahas readily accepted this faith to eke out a living, but the Aryas neither dined with them nor did they admit them into their own *gotras*. The Aryas did not even give their daughters to them in marriage, and they remained 'impure' even after being purified![27] Despite the vituperative against it, the Arya Samaj became a binding factor in the heterogeneous society. This perturbed the Muslims as well as the government. While its supporters doggedly tried to prove that it was a purely socio-religious body, its opponents accused it of having political aspirations. This feeling increased as the years progressed, and the government went as far as labelling its followers 'high priests of sedition and anarchy'. Some leading Arya Samajists, like Pandit Daulat Ram of Jhansi, were convicted, which was considered a gross injustice.[28]

Muslim society, part and parcel of Indian society, was also stirred by the influence of new ideas. Literary movements were closely followed by educational movements on traditional as well as modern lines. Maulana Altaf Hussain Hali and Shibli Mohammad Nomani were leaders of the new literary movements in Urdu. They wrote with a social purpose, and roused people to face the new situation. Sir Syed Ahmad's contributions to social awareness and upliftment among the Muslims were phenomenal. The Aligarh school became a force to be reckoned with He wanted education for the Muslims, and desired them to shed their restrictive religious practices. His efforts to bring about social reform among the Muslims by convincing them of its conformity to practices permitted in the Koran, were opposed by a considerable section of Muslims. The Aligarh school was thought of as '. . . upstarts, poor as leaders and reformers of the Musalman community; but the Musalmans do not consider them to be even Musalmans and are far less prepared to recognize them as their leaders and reformers'.[29] The Deoband School of Muslims was also opposed to Sir Syed and had more in common with the Congress initially.[30]

Gradually a rigidity on religion seeped into the ranks of the communities. Implicit faith in the superiority of their own culture acted as a bulwark against the alien cultural thrust, but also brought the threat of vitiated relations between Hindus and Muslims (in view of the different pasts from which they chose to derive inspiration).[31]

TABLE 2.1: NUMBER OF PERSONS EMPLOYED IN THE EXECUTIVE AND JUDICIAL BRANCHES OF THE UNCOVENANTED SERVICE AMONG THE HINDUS (1886-7) IN NWP AND AWADH[32]

Brahmins Prabhus	*Kshatriyas Vaishyas*	*Kayasthas*	*Baniyas*	*Shudras*	*Others*
89	37	107	25	1	3

Despite this serious effect, social reform, as a movement, had come to stay. Various castes, sub-castes and groups formed associations or held conferences for the purpose of initiating reform in society. The Kayasthas, as individuals or in groups, were very conscious of this need. They were as a rule an educated class and held government positions. Allahabad seemed to be their main centre.

Kayastha newspapers constantly reported members' activities. In fact, the idea of caste-backed newspapers had taken a firm grip on Indian society. The second Kayastha Conference was held in Allahabad on the 16 and 17 September 1888. About 750 Kayasthas attended, the majority from NWP and Awadh. They condemned social ills like early marriage, extravagant marriage expenses, and previous settlement of the value of dowries.[33] These Conferences were held every year, and consequently Kayastha associations grew. The fifth conference at Bareilly emphasized non-interference by Kayasthas in political or religious matters. Social reform was their sole aim.[34] The Kayastha Conference at Varanasi in 1895 resolved to establish a Kayastha Family Pension Fund, encourage the study of Hindi and Sanskrit among the Kayasthas, grant aid to the poor Kayastha widows and orphans from the National Fund, and form a marriage provision fund.[35] However, it became clear that these caste conferences, while advocating social reform in society as a whole, were more concerned about the upliftment of their own members. The non-selection of any of the three successful Kayastha candidates at the competitive Deputy Collectorship in 1898 in NWP and Awadh was bemoaned by the Kayastha newspapers.[36]

Individually too Kayasthas tried to bring about social reform. As social reformers, cowprotection lecturers and educationists, many of them attained prominence. Some were connected with the Kayastha Pathshala in Allahabad and were in the vanguard (in terms of social attitudes), of those who brought out the *Hindustan Review* and the *Leader* after 1900. Ramanand Chatterjee, the Principal of the Kayastha

Pathshala, brought out the English *Kayastha Samachar* in 1899.[37]

Similarly, other castes also began to meet periodically to form associations which would work towards social reform in general, and the upliftment of their own community in particular. The Agarwals of Mathura established an association for the encouragement of social reform in 1890.[38] At the anniversary of the recent Agarwal Sabha in 1892, the participants includeed luminaries as Lala Lajpat Rai, Lala Nihal Chand of Muzaffarnagar, Babu Ganga Saran of Agra, and Lala Sanwal Das of Farrukhabad. The principal objects of the Sabha were to initiate social reform, curtail marriage expenses and promote education. Lajpat Rai rebuked Indians for sending their children to Mission schools. The Agarwals should open their own schools, and should promote their own welfare by contributing to a fund meant to help out their needy brethren.[39] The Bhargavas, too, held their social conferences annually. Munshi Nawal Kishore, C.I.E., a well-known newspaper owner and completely loyal to government, could not detach himself from the welfare of his caste fellows and took an active part in these conferences. He wanted his community to break the shackles of conservatism.[40]

Whether it was the Khattris or the Kshatriyas, most caste groups had their own newspapers, which aired their particular grievances, and brought members together on a common platform. Through them the members of the particular caste came to know the maladies prevailing in society, and assimilated remedies suggested by the papers. For instance, the *Kshatriya Hitopdeshak*, regretting the decline of the Kshatriyas, had valuable suggestions to give—Kshatriyas should give a sound education to their children; put a stop to the pernicious custom of early marriage; curtail marriage expenditure; and check other vices. A school had been established for the education of Kshatriya boys at Surayan in the Mainpuri district, and the paper urged well-to-do men to help it by donating generously.[41]

The Brahmins, more orthodox than the rest and more concerned about preserving the sanctity of their caste, were not left behind. They participated in large numbers at the bathing fairs. A meeting of Sarjupari Brahmins was reportedly held at Ayodhya in 1889 where a resolution was passed that every Brahmin on the occasion of a birth or wedding in his family should make a contribution to a fund for the encouragement of education among his caste fellows.[42] Brahmins made fiery journalists too, though many were quite strained financially. Balkrishna Bhatt for example, launched the *Hindi Pradip* from

Allahabad and was fearlessly advocating reform in social practices.[43]

To a lesser degree, but inconspicuous were some Muslim associations perpetuating social reform. There were some with high sounding names like the *Anjuman-i-Himayat-i-Bewagan-i-Islam* or the association to help Muslim widows. Its annual meetings appeared to be highly charged. Its meeting at Barabanki in 1892 recorded an emotional address by its President, Sheikh Wajid Hussain Khan, which touched the hearts of the audience and brought tears to their eyes.[44]

It soon became clear that except for a few totally committed men, the social reformers were mostly drawn from the upper or middle classes. They glorified the past and felt inspired by it. Even so, a compromise with Christianity was desired by most. Many had even converted, but still endeavoured to reconstruct the glorious Indian cultural past. These men, under Western influence, talked of reform but had no emotional commitment to the cause, and somehow were quite happy with their privileged position in society.[45] However, the influence of these reformers and journalists and littérateurs in enunciating the importance of the need for reform cannot be minimized, even if at this time reform was considered efficacious only under the benevolence of the British government. The rejection of Muslim rule and the deliverance which the British had brought from it was the favourite theme of litterateurs and journalists. Bharatendu Harishchandra was a striking example. His plays dwelt on the belief that the ruin of India would have been complete but for British interference. However, later he did not desist from dwelling on the destructive qualities of the British rule and likened it to tuberculosis. Pride in being Indian even while recognizing the existence of evils in contemporary Indian society and trying for their removal, was his idea of a social and national revival.[46] Such ambivalence was common.

Closely connected to this was the difference in views regarding the right of the rulers to interfere in bringing about social reform in India. There was a section who resented government interference in social matters. They were critical of the so-called emancipated Hindu youths who, claiming to be educated, constantly appealed to government regarding religious and social matters. As *Bharat Jiwan* scathingly said, 'Nothing could be more unwise than that natives should endeavour to voluntarily lose the freedom which they still enjoy in religious and social matters and which government itself desires to maintain.'[47] The Indian journalists felt that governmental interference gave a means of oppression to the police.[48] When matters like child-marriage, restitution of conjugal rights and age of consent came up, government interest in them was not favoured by even some professedly modern newspapers like the *Hindustan*.[49]

The Muslims, too, were protective about their customs, however oppressive they might have been. When the question came up of courts in NWP and Awadh being empowered to reduce the amount of jointures settled on Muslim women by their husbands at the time of marriage, the Muslim press generally rose up in arms against such an infringement on privacy.[50] A supposedly minor matter regarding the curtailment of Muharrram holidays in the High Court by the Chief Justice, was resented by a known supporter of government, Justice Mahmud. The matter escalated to such an extent that Justice Mahmud openly protested against the Chief Justice's orders.[51]

Government interference in promoting consciousness for social reform among the people was however welcomed by another section of people. This was evident from the various meetings held for this purpose by government officials. For example, the Magistrate of Jaunpur held a public meeting at the house of Raja Shankar Dutt Dube on 27 March 1893 and recommended the curtailment of marriage expenses, the establishment of agricultural banks and a poor house, and the revival of the panchayat system.[52] The language newspapers, enumerating the evils government interference would lead to in the Indian social scenario, sadly accepted the fact that social ills would not cease 'until . . . expressly forbidden by law'. [53]

THE PREVAILING SOCIAL PROBLEMS IN NWP AND AWADH AND GOVERNMENT STRATEGIES OF CONTROL

The social problems existing during this period were not limited to the province of NWP and Awadh but were country-wide problems and forces working for their solution were widespread. However, what is important in dealing with them is their local impact.

ALCOHOLISM

Drunkenness and drug-addiction were major problems. Liquor shops and drug houses were considered no less than slaughter houses or slave markets, and it was considered the duty of the government to put a stop to this 'slave-trade'.[54]

The most unpopular of the addictions seemed was liquor, and drugs like *chandu* and *charas*. There was a general outcry against them. In a description of a *chandu* house, one of the newspapers voiced its disgust at the scene of the smokers laying their heads on shoes instead of pillows. 'The wise do not smoke it (*chandu*) but those who are the slaves of the devil.'[55] Drinking alcohol was thought to be the worst: it was prohibited by all religions. The papers presented a bizarre picture of the way liquor was sold in these provinces. A particular newspaper wrote:

> The vendors provide attractions for the people to encourage its sale. Number of men are to be found drinking and singing in a body at a shop, and young prostitutes are also generally present on such occasions. Many young men who are not accustomed to the use of liquor are attracted to the shop by the singing of drunkards and the presence of prostitutes and soon begin to drink. The drunkards on their way home from the shops harass and even assault men and women on the streets.[56]

Temperance meets were held all over the provinces to promote conscious boycott of liquor. The *Hindustan* gleefully reported a temperance meeting at Agra under the presidentship of Raja Lachman Singh.[57] The laudable efforts of Mahant Kesho Ram, an energetic member of the Banaras Temperance Association, were acclaimed as being instrumental in decreasing the consumption of liquor which fell from 157,549 gallons in 1885-6 to 85,895 gallons in 1890-1.[58]

Drunkenness was blamed on the defective excise policy of the government. Government was blamed for following an anomalous policy, where, on the one hand, it was trying to persuade people to avoid drinking, and on the other, could not reconcile itself to a loss of revenue. While drinking was on the increase, the Lt.-Governors were feigning ignorance.[59] Any increase in the sale of liquor was explained away by the government as being due to a good *rabi* crop or to the celebration of many weddings but the newspapers attributed the spread of drunkenness to an increase in liquor shops. The *Pioneer* protested that there was only an apparent increase in drunkenness, as distillation was now done openly instead of secretly. The government's excise policy could not be blamed for it. This did not convince the language newspapers who rejected this assertion as reeking of pre-judice.[60] Another plea taken by the government regarding increased drunkenness was the public character: people would resort to illicit distilling if government reduced legal distilling.[61] Its contention that the cost of liquor should be escalated to restrain people from illegal distribution seemed rather unpalatable.[62]

Constant appeals were made to the government to change its excise policy and bring about a reduction of alcohol and opium. As exhibited in the other policies of the government wherein it used the men of influence in a particular area to justify its actions, its dealing with the opium question was no different.

The 1891 resolution of the British Parliament regarding the stoppage of licences for the cultivation of poppy and the sale of opium was heartily welcomed by most of the language newspapers. The government authorities, however, showed their inner feelings when the ministers protested against the resolution on the ground that revenue loss could not be made up by other taxation.[63]

Nevertheless, the Opium Commissioner was appointed in 1893 to debate upon the opium question.[64] Thinking Indians regarded the Opium Commission with some scepticism and doubted its genuineness. Some papers were trenchant in their rejection of the Commission's approach. The *Oudh Punch* minced no words in classifying the witnesses before the Commission as sycophants. The writer even listed the names of the people who had given evidence before the Commission—The Deputy Commissioner, the Civil Surgeon, Raja of Bhinga, the Maharaja of Ayodhya, Munshi Nawal Kishore, C.I.E. and others. They had all spoken in favour of opium.[65] The press regretted the untruthfulness of their evidence. The entire working and progress of the Commission was farcical, as all the witnesses were nominated by the government and resultantly gave evidence in favour of opium.[66]

Sir Charles Crosthwaite's evidence before the Opium Commission completely disillusioned the major section who wanted reform. His assertion that opium was a harmless drug convinced them of the government's underhand desire to retain its use, or to even encourage its increase. Crosthwaite's assumption that restrictions on poppy cultivation would be ruinous to agriculturists was also considered baseless, as surely the agriculturists could take up some other cultivation, like sugarcane, which would be less harmful.[67]

The fact that opium was considered an essential part of the Indian genre was highlighted both by the government and the sycophantic newspaper editors. Opium had medicinal properties too. These qualities were exaggerated to lend credence to the government's excise policy. The *Oudh Akhbar* of Lucknow in keeping with its 'loyal to the government at any cost' policy, wrote on 22 December 1893,

'If its use were stopped thousands of the people would die, and millions suffer great pain. Why, the stoppage of opium will cause much discontent whose consequences need not be anticipated here.'

Such a desperate attempt to highlight the good effects of opium was naturally viewed with suspicion by a large section of the language press. It refused to accept the theory—that Rajputs and Sikhs became more valiant on use of opium. In fact, it argued that opium was enervating and made people cowardly. All Indian religions condemned the use of intoxicants.[68] This was the attitude of a large section of the press, who, nevertheless, did not desist from evaluating any sincere effort made by the British to deal with the growing use of intoxicants. Some newspapers felt that even though government had introduced reforms such as the reduction in the number of liquor shops, the closing of shops preparing opium, the raising of the still-head duty on spirits, and increazing the price of opium, the consumption of intoxicants had increased.[69] The government did try to contain the use of intoxicants by taxing *ganja* and *charas* imported into the Provinces, and controlling drug trafficking, but all these measures did not meet the success they should have. The government expressed its inability to achieve the results it wanted because of the psyche of the drug abusers; meanwhile the reformers condemned the government for not making a sincere effort.

The financial stranglehold of the imperial power at the cost of persisting evil was evident. The consumption of liquor continued to rise and with that the revenue. A sudden spurt in 1902 was considered indicative of 'good harvests and money to spare', and was not 'disquieting'.[70] The Excise Commissioner's hesitation in prescribing a special rate of duty for opium was attributed to his fear, that it would encourage smuggling of opium. Obviously the intelligentsia could not swallow the reasons put forward by the government for their excise policy being what it was. An interesting set of figures was given by Shri Ram Bahadur before the Provincial Legislative Council's meeting in 1904, which clearly showed a rise in the revenue and consumption of *charas* and *ganja*—the latter at the rate of 3.3 per cent and former at 11.3 per cent. He rejected the government's contention that drugs were taxed for the sake of decreasing consumption.

The government made disinterested efforts to combat drunkenness. The United Provinces Excise Bill for the control of liquor shops in 1909 was considered less progressive than the existing provision. The language press and leaders like Madan Mohan Malviya were not impressed by this display of government concern.[72]

TABLE 2.2: CONSUMPTION OF INTOXICANTS (1900-2)[71]

Year	*Total of Revenue*	*Consumption in Seers*		*Total*
		Charas	*Ganja*	
1900	11,82,356	88,430	14,855	103,285
1901	12,69,849	92,660	1,2300	104,960
1902	13,15,990	93,624	13,061	106,685

PROSTITUTION

Another social ill which the government was constantly being asked to suppress was prostitution and the institution of dancing girls. Whether it was Lucknow or Varanasi, this evil seemed to have taken firm root everywhere. The language newspapers reported constant appeals to the government by residents of areas with rampant prostitution for their removal.[73] Some even wanted prostitution to be declared a penal offence as it was 'opposed to every system of religion and morality'.[74]

From all corners, there were regular complaints of an increase of prostitutes, whose houses were frequented by drunks, thieves, robbers and other anti-social elements.[75] Prostitutes at the windows of their homes in the bazars in the evenings incited youth to perform immoral deeds, it was said.

The evil of prostitution grew from extreme poverty. When rendered destitute, especially during famines, people sold their daughters to the highest bidder. Ostensibly, a marriage ceremony was performed, but it was entirely farcical and meaningless as small girls of seven or eight years were married off to men over forty-five. This system was practised among several Hindu tribes. Brahmins and Khattris also followed this practice and it seemed especially rampant in the territory between Faizabad and Bhojpur. When the old husbands died, the girls had to undergo the miseries of widowhood for life. Such young widows often became women of loose character as they had nothing to look forward to and were defenceless in a male-dominated society. This pernicious custom was nowhere mentioned as being acceptable in any religion. The government was thus repeatedly asked to put a stop to the selling of girls in the garb of marriage.[76]

Worse than the above initiation to prostitution was the practice of decoying little girls of respectable families by clandestine prostitutes and procuresses to their homes, after which they were handed over to 'reckless, lustful young men'. The tragedy was that often the offenders received protection from the influential men of the vicinity.[77] So many times girls from the lower classes were kidnapped and sold off to men of higher classes. They were treated like slaves and heavy work was extracted from them, or they were sold to other men. The government did endeavour to criminally prosecute the offenders, but more stringent methods were required to put a stop to this disgusting practice.[78]

The most debasing practice was the system of procuring women for European soldiers. The language press was convinced that government officials were involved in such traffic. Magistrates were expected to provide young and handsome women procured from among the wives and daughters of peasants. It was an age-old custom to settle prostitutes in cantonments, to be periodically examined by doctors for venereal disease. A thought provoking case was cited, wherein a certain Commander-in-Chief reportedly issued orders that good-looking, respectable women were to be provided for European regiments.[79] The Chakrata rape case, in which a European soldier was charged with having outraged an Indian girl of seventeen created a furore, especially because the British judge, presiding over a jury of five Europeans and four Indians, made the insulting observation that Indian girls often gave their consent for money, and raised an outcry only when caught red-handed by their relatives. Such insolence was indicative of how lightly the authorities took the appeals of Indians.[80]

In 1898 the Municipal Boards of leading towns in UP introduced a Bill forbidding prostitutes to loiter in the streets. The Municipal Board was empowered to expel a prostitute from her house on receipt of a complaint from three respectable residents in the street to the effect that her residence there was a source of annoyance to the neighbours. A draft Bill was prepared to prevent poor girls from falling into the hands of prostitutes. The press appreciated this need for legislation but wanted adequate punishment to be meted out to the male relatives of the prostitutes who procured the minor girls by deceit and exchange of money.[81]

Marriage Rules

Some marriage rules prevalent among Hindus and Muslims were outrageous, to say the least. Two underlying phenomena of vital importance were money and the inferior social position of women in that period. The necessity for parents to give large dowries for their daughters was replete with unsavoury connotations. Among Kshatriyas, Brahmins and Vaishyas dowries often caused impoverishment for life.[82] The refusal of the parents to give dowries meant girls would remain unmarried until the age of twenty or twenty-five, or even die unmarried.[83] The Rajputs were especially guilty of demanding dowry, as the honour of a girl's family depended on her alliance with a youth of a higher social standing. This entailed heavy marriage expenditure and dowry which crippled 'the resources of a man whose quiver is full of daughters'.[84] Despite government claims that female infanticide had lessened, there were constant reports in the Hindi and Urdu papers about people incurring heavy marriage expenditures; or worse still, of fathers killing their daughters because they were too poor to arrange for them to marry.[85]

Mild efforts were made at the local level, both by social reformers and government officials, to influence people to give up this practice. C. Whish, the Joint Magistrate of Hamirpur, was praised for his efforts to influence Kanyakubja Brahmins to abolish this evil custom.[86] The Raja of Bansi was praised for not demanding a dowry at his son's marriage, and setting an example for his countrymen. But these were rare instances.

The newspapers were sharply divided over the enforcement of decrees for the restitution of conjugal rights. The government desired to modify Section 260 of the Civil Procedure Code, with a view to abolishing imprisonment in the execution of a decree for the restitution of conjugal rights Surprisingly, this endeavour of the government to improve the position of married women met with some support, but more opposition. The supporters argued that if it was not obligatory on the husband to live with the wife he disliked, a woman should not be forced to live with a husband she disliked. The man could practice polygamy after paying a mere subsistence allowance to his wife, so where was the justice in imprisoning a wife if she wished to leave? However, one fact was clear—even the supporters objected to government interference in social matters in general. '. . .The *Hindustan* is in favour of exemption of women from liability to imprisonment in execution of decrees for the restitution of conjugal rights, though . . . it is opposed to government interference in social matters.'[87]

The opposition to this proposal was very strong. The fear of imprisonment often induced women to live with their husbands, and if imprisonment were abolished, they would leave their husbands whenever they pleased, like European women. The Hindu Samaj of

Allahabad opposed it and one is astonished by the depth of feeling evidenced in the outbursts of professedly modern sections of society. They felt that this reform would affect both Hindus and Muslims, whose women would take recourse to law at the slightest pretext. The *Oudh Akhbar* was vociferous in its condemnation of this proposal. To make his point, the editor published an imaginary dialogue between a Hindu woman, her husband, and his mother in which she was represented as declining to attend to domestic matters, and to live in the same house as her mother-in-law. She was threatening to depart from the house and apply to the Court for a divorce despite the entreaties of her husband and mother-in-law.[88] The attempt of the Arya Samaj to modernize relationships between the two sexes was naturally disapproved by most of the newspapers. This was the introduction of the practice of *Niyog* according to which a chaste woman could have sexual intercourse with a man and contract a temporary marriage if her husband was sterile, cruel, quarrelsome or away for three years or more. Even in cases of the husband being sick, the woman could contract a temporary marriage with another man. Besides this, a widow was allowed to marry eleven times. This created a furore in Indian society and Swami Dayanand's reforms were considered immoral.[89] Somehow one feels that it was not only the interference of the government in social and religious customs and usages that were resented. These men were alarmed by the prospect of the emancipation of their wives, which would put a stop to their domination.

The prospect of governmental interference in altering the obsolete rules framed twelve hundred years ago for marriages among Muslims, created an uproar in Muslim society. Despite the fact that the Muslims were even more eager to keep their women under control, the male prerogative of divorcing their wives or even abandoning them whenever desired, made them realize the need for the women to be comfortably off in the face of such an eventuality. The talk of empowering courts in the NWP to reduce the amount of jointures settled on Muslim women by their husbands in cases they deemed it necessary was regarded as an unnecessary interference on the part of the government in the personal matters of Muslims. These women when abandoned were in any case in a sorry plight, having lived in *parda* without any education, and with no hope of remarriage. Their only anchor was their jointure. This system had been established by the Prophet to protect women, and to extend to the entire province what the courts were already practising in Awadh would be sacrilegious and an unnecessary infringement on the Muslim law. 'If courts were empowered to reduce jointures it would simply be paying no consideration to the miserable life which women lead, and encouraging men to commit still greater excesses on them.'[90]

Probably no matter received so much attention as the prevalence of child marriage, and the prejudice against widow-remarriage among most Indians. To an extent, the two seemingly distinct phenomena were interdependent though people were constantly emphasizing the basic separateness of the two problems.

Child marriage was widely prevalent among Hindus. Not marrying one's daughter by the age of ten was considered against social norms. Many people had, however, begun thinking on different lines and realized that infant marriages were undesirable. The travails of early widowhood would also be avoided. The differences of opinion were only on two scores—the minimum age fixed as the marriage age for girls; and whether the latter should be established by the government or by the people themselves. The newspapers generally favoured ten or twelve years as the minimum age, though one wanted it to be fifteen years.[91]

The much publicized case of Rukmabai gave impetus to the efforts at reform. Rukmabai was married to Dadaji Bhikaji in childhood. She was educated and he ignorant, hence she had no sympathy with him and did not want to live with him. The Bombay High Court ordered her to live with her husband, or in case of default to undergo six months' imprisonment. Much of the language press was furious as the people were gradually realizing the cruelty of forcing a woman to stay with a husband she hated. The evil custom of child marriage that had caused this to occur in so many households, must be modified.[92] The *Hindustan* revealed something interesting. Quoting verses from Manu, the editor showed that he had not been in favour of child-marriage. Hindu law-givers and Hindu physicians were both against child marriage. In the well-known Sanskrit medical work, the *Sushruta*, the marriageable age was sixteen for women and twenty-five for men, according to the editor. The government responded by trying to modify the existing rules which had nurtured this pernicious evil. In 1891, Sir Andrew Scoble introduced The Age of Consent Bill in the Legislative Council of the Viceroy. According to this, any man who had sexual intercourse with a wife under twelve years of age would be liable to imprisonment for seven years, though offences under this Bill would not be cognizable. There was an uproar. Many religious and caste instincts had been ruffled. The government had entered a private precinct, and this was it intolerable. There were several arguments and counter arguments put forth. The papers were afraid that getting correct information about the girls offended against would be well-nigh impossible for the magistrate who would have to depend on the anonymous petitions or information given by unscrupulous informers. The magistrates and the police would be invested with undue powers which they may misuse in harassing the girls' parents. Besides, what irritated most newspapers was the clause about girls being medically examined to ascertain whether cohabitation had taken place or not, before action was taken against offenders. The *Bharat Jiwan* ranted, 'If those ladies, whom the measure is intended to protect from ill-usage, are subjected to medical examinations, many of them are sure to commit suicide to escape such dishonour.'

The opponents took refuge in religion, and stressed the fact that the Hindu marriage was a sacrament and not a contract. According to Hindu scriptures, marriage of a girl after menstruation was unholy. This generally commenced at the age of ten or eleven, so Hindus must marry their daughters early. Consummation of the marriage at the time of puberty was prevalent among both Hindus and Muslims, and the Bill consequently was an 'unjust interference with their religious customs'. Muslims too were up in arms, though early marriages were not common among them. What they objected to was the ban on early consummation of the marriage, which was considered against the law of nature among married couples. Invoking religious heritage, they argued, 'When the Prophet was married to Aisha, the age of the latter did not exceed nine years. A Musalman who disapproves of anything done by the Prophet is guilty of sin.'[93] The period of imprisonment also required curtailment as a wife would not be able to subsist alone without her husband's protection for such a long time.[94] However, a number of persons welcomed this measure, and gave it a fair measure of support. In NWP and Awadh, girls were seldom married before ten and even after that had to live with their parents for three years, so in general this Act would not affect these provinces as much as it would affect Bengal where girls attained puberty very early when the consummation of marriage had to be effected. However, the evil custom of child marriage which prevailed among some classes of Brahmins, Vaishyas and Khattris, would be discouraged by this proposal. About the danger of police interference they felt it was a useless apprehension as offence under this Act would not be a cognizable one. Besides, no action would be taken by the Magistrate until a complaint was made by a doctor or an application was filed by a girl or her parents.[95] The advantage to the girls' parents would be that they would be able to ascertain the character and the prospects of the boys before marrying their daughters to them. This would put a stop to the misery of an unsavoury marriage and would curtail the evil of early widowhood. It would also protect unmarried girls under twelve from prostitution. 'No religion allows cohabitation with a wife until she has attained puberty. Even if the Bill involved an interference with religion, government would be justified in passing it in the interests of humanity.'[96]

The newspapers which advocated passage of the Bill realized that the hope of people voluntarily abandoning this custom was dim as neither public associations nor newspapers exercized much influence on them. The Bill finally became an Act with some modifications. The District Magistrate would only consider the information of reliable persons; and local inquiries would be made by an experienced 'native' magistrate and not by the police. The Local Government would submit a report annually to show the working of the Act. The supporters took it as reflective of 'great credit on the sagacity, shrewdness, and sympathy of Lord Landsdowne'.[97]

The encouragement of widow remarriage met with even greater opposition than did the child marriage issue. This too was considered a direct infringement upon religious practices. The sorry plight of widows had long been under discussion, and the proposals of B.M. Malabari of Bombay regarding infant marriages in India and enforced widowhood, escalated the issue. He wanted government to make rules that minor Hindu girls should not be condemned to permanent widowhood if they lost their husbands; that it must be ascertained whether a widow had adopted her seclusion voluntarily or it was a case of 'enforced widowhood'; that all widows should be allowed to make appeals against social harassment to the authorities by making procedures easier and cheaper for them; that priests had no right to excommunicate the relations and connections of the parties contracting second marriages, besides excommunicating the principals.[98]

Sir Alfred Lyall of NWP and Awadh found the idea of governmental interference in the question of 'enforced widowhood' unacceptable.

Besides the basic resistance which people had for any sort of government manoeuvre, he felt that in this province, the caste customs of Hindus imposing enforced widowhood did not apply. Quoting statistics, he showed that little more than a fourth of the Hindu castes followed any such customs, and that the proportion of widows was scarcely greater among the Hindus than among the Muslims. Spinsters were fewer in number than widows, but this was because of physical and social causes not specific to Hindus, and probably inseparable from the ethnological and climatic conditions of the country. The incidence of this evil was confined to the wealthier and more educated classes, who could themselves effect reform without appealing for governmental help. However, he accepted the fact that the machinery provided under Act III of 1872 (an Act to provide a form of marriage in certain cases) was not sufficient if this desire of a certain number of people to renounce Hindu law or marriage custom gained momentum and became a mass movement.[99]

The government was hesitant to interfere with this age-old practice, and stressed that only an infinitesimal number were suffering from the malady of enforced widowhood.[100] The authorities stressed on the caste divisions among the Hindus, which incapacitated them for united action in doing away with social evils. Dividing Hindu society into four classes, they tried to show the weight of prejudice against doing away with enforced widowhood. Only an extremely advanced class of educated men sympathized with it but were apprehensive about the additional burden of so many more girls to marry. More vociferous and in greater majority were the moderately educated who did not want to unnecessarily go against the 'Shastric' prohibitions. Below these were the mass of uneducated men who had a vague knowledge of the Shastras and depended wholly on the propagation of religious practices by the learned Brahmins whom they revered. Widow remarriage was a badge of social degradation linked with the Doms, Boonas, Bagelis and other low castes. It was the low castes at the bottom of the social hierarchy, who practised widow remarriage and adult marriage, and these also sometimes endeavoured to identify with the higher castes by shaking off these lowly customs. The Hinduizing movement had received impetus because of improvements in communication, which made it easier for feeling against social reform to be aroused. If the incidence of widowhood among the Muslims were taken as a yardstick, only one per cent more widows existed among Hindus, where, unlike the Muslims, widow remarriage was unacceptable to a large number of people. The government argued that consequently only about a million and a half Hindu widows in the whole of India would represent the utmost effect of the Brahmanical doctrine. For this small number, it was not worth simultating a tornado of emotion in reaction to government's interference. The government felt that education had hampered the progress of social reform instead of furthering it, as it had made Indians conscious of their lost heritage which had to be revived. These men, were 'even now defending infant marriage and enforced widowhood, because they conceive those practices to be home-growths as opposed to alien importations'.[101]The authorities felt that nothing could be achieved unless numerical strength of the remarriage party was won over carefully. The higher classes, if convinced of the efficacy of this social reform, would draw the lower classes also towards it.

The apprehensions of the government were not unfounded. They had already experienced the exacerbated emotions of the Indians at the time of the abolition of *sati*, and the legislation of 1873, which had legalized widow remarriage. The Hindu Mahasabha claimed celibacy to be meritorious in all castes. Birth and death were effects of '*Karma*' and adult-marriage was the execution of that law. 'Hindu religion and law recognize and regulate the evil but cannot condemn, or honour it as a merit.'[102] There were instances of *sati* being praised, the poor victims being lauded as being noble and faithful women.[103] The *Indian Standard* of Allahabad of 3 September 1906 idolised women who had committed *sati*. 'If the Hindu society has survived the ravages of time and has outlived so many attacks upon it, it is because of the exemplary character and unparalleled devotion of Hindu women to their husbands.'

In the face of all this orthodoxy, the task of social reform was difficult and the government had to tread carefully. Yet it was not an impossible task as there was a large section of the intelligentsia which condemned these evil practices. Pandit Ishwar Chandar, Diwan Raghunath Rao and others published pamphlets promoting the cause of widow remarriage.[104] Cases of widow remarriage were highlighted and applauded: widows led a miserable life; the police harassed them and extorted money from them; there were many instances of widows killing their new-born children out of despair.[105] Citing the example of the sale of a widow in the Samthar State in Bundelkhand, the *Agra Punch* of May 1893 pleaded the cause of widow remarriage. These women were so young that loneliness often drove them to way-wardness and frustration. Some language papers endorsed the view that 'It is really far better that young widows should be remarried than that they should secretly misbehave themselves and bring themselves and their relatives into disrepute.'[106]

The reformists could not perceive the discrimination made between men and women. A man could marry as many times as he wished while women had no support.[107] The progressive elements stressed the fact that the Hindu religious books expressly permitted the remarriage of those widows whose marriage with their deceased husbands had not been consummated. They tried to arouse the superstitions of their fellowmen by bringing in concepts of divine will.

> Owing to the prohibitions against widow remarriage no Hindu household is happy but rather resembles hell and there exists a great deal of avoidable crime in the shape of abortions, elopements etc. No wonder if famine, plague and other visitations are due to Divine vengeance for the suffering of widows.[108]

There were trend setters, too, who were courageous enough to defy social ostracism. Striking among these was the case of a Saksena Kayastha, Roshan Lal, who on his return from England practised law in Allahabad. He married Hardevi, a Bhatnagar Kayastha widow, daughter of Rai Kanhay Lal of Lahore. This created a furore among the Hindus and even advocates of widow remarriage felt such sudden and radical actions would tend to injure rather than promote the cause of widow remarriage, even though the lady was educated and working for female upliftment. It would give a rude shock to the cause of female education as people would associate it with having a bad influence on women.[109] However, the way had been shown, and Roshan Lal became a leading social reformer and educationist.

Women's Problems

It is now clear that women enjoyed a dubious social position. There were several complaints about the neglect of the basic amenities which women should enjoy. The holy cities of Allahabad,Varanasi and Mathura had *ghats* where women bathed and were exposed to the lecherous eyes of mendicants, as there were generally no provisions for privacy or safety.[110]

Raping of Indian women was rampant and the thinking Indians naturally resented it. From Brahmins to railway personnel, to the police and the soldiers—all took advantage of women on their own. There was no separate accommodation for women in the trains and several instances of rape involved railway personnel. The case of Price, a railway guard, who raped a 'native girl', was indicative of the sensitive position of Indian women. What was shocking, and revealed the prejudice behind a benevolent facade, was the acquittal of Price by a European majority jury in the Allahabad High Court. The suggestion made by the language press was that women should be appointed in the railways to take care of women passengers.[111]

Police atrocities committed on women were widely condemned. There were cases of policemen forcibly lifting women from the streets and exposing them to the indignity of a medical examination to prove that they had procured abortions. *Pardanashin* women had to suffer trauma in police lockups. An interesting and revealing case was cited by the *Prayag Samachar* of 7 July 1890: in the Barah tahsil of the Allahabad district, a woman was raped and robbed by some Brahmins. Neither her husband nor she reported it to the police for fear of blackmail and extortion.

The social reform movements were anxious to promote the cause of women and improve their position in society and newspapers were their main spokesmen. Reporting the case of the three girls at Barah in Allahabad district whose property was denied them by their uncle on their father's death, the newspapers declared that according to the Hindu law, daughters inherited the father's property in the absence of a son. It was the government who should give wide publicity to this law. These reformers wanted to espouse the cause of women's education and required government assistance. There were a few Homes for destitute women established in the Provinces by missionaries. The newspapers appealed to well-to-do Indian citizens to support such useful associations, instead of patronising Brahmins and priests. Some leading Indians did form Stri Samajs to help destitute women. The papers reported the anniversaries of the Meerut Stri Samaj and Kanya Pathshala at the house of Babu Ram Chandra, a medical practitioner. His wife and other prominent women attended these meetings and gave meaningful speeches.[112]

However, with the National Movement picking up, there were instances of women actively participating in it. There was the remarkable example of one Kshiroda Sundari of Mymensingh joining the extremists in Bengal. Starting with giving protection to political absconders, she moved from place to place and finally reached Varanasi. Here she stayed for some time before returning to her husband's village.[113] A married woman taking such a courageous step was in itself striking and made one feel that a change was in the air, however imperceptible to begin with.

The Problem of Racism

The problem of racism was created by an inextricable complex of social, psychological and economic factors. The feeling of ethnic superiority was predominant among the Englishmen, while educated Indians found this concept unpalatable. The arrogance of the British was further exacerbated in the late nineteenth century as a wave of racist doctrines preaching the inherent superiority of white people over the others spread over Europe.[114] Even more painful was the emulation of Europeans by subordinate Indian officials, who mistreated their less fortunate countrymen.[115]

Cases of negligence while shooting, whereby peasants working in the fields or walking along roads were indiscriminately shot, occurred with frequency. The Indian press protested that if the European officers were so careless, they should not be allowed to carry arms. To add insult to injury the authorities often blamed Indians for coming in the way of the Europeans. There was indignation that 'the natives who have given ample proofs of their loyalty, should be shot like dead beasts of prey by Europeans, and that the offenders should be allowed to escape scot free by European judges'.[116]

The lowest in the rung of European officialdom—the private corporal or the sergeant in the army, the railway guard and the station master—were conspicuous offenders. The poorest and the weakest sections of the Indian population (peasants, labourers and women) were the greatest sufferers. The *pankha coolies*, cooks and other menials were kicked or beaten to death. The cruelty of British officers was proved in the famous 'rupture of spleen' cases cited by many Indian newspapers wherein the officers beat *pankha coolies* mercilessly, for indolence, and ruptured their spleen by kicking them in the stomach. The doctors generally hushed up the cases by confirming that the accused was either mad or drunk at the time or attributed the deaths to a diseased spleen. The language newspapers pointed out that an enlarged spleen among Indians only caused death when touched by a European! Assaulters, hitherto perfectly sane suddenly developed signs of insanity. Consequently, what happened was that very few such cases were put before the courts. Even here the bias was naturally in favour of Europeans. The young 'Boy Magistrates' were inadequately acquainted with the customs of the people, and pleading a lack of knowledge of the Indian language, believed in the misstatements in the English press that Indians were offensive by nature and there was no alternative except to be stern with them.[117]

The railways offered ample opportunity to the Europeans to emphasize their racial superiority. There were frequent occurrences of Indians being forcibly ejected from first—and sometimes second—class compartments. There were instances of Indians not being permitted to sit in the same compartment as the Europeans, even if the place was limited and there was overcrowding in the other compartments.[118] The guards on these trains were cruel and uncomprising. They insulted both passengers and coolies. They refused to pay the latter wages and when they protested, beating was all they got.[119]

The papers protested that there was a 'White Law' and a 'Black Law', and never would the twain meet.[120] The pressures of bureaucratic change had pushed some poor Europeans into temporary alliance with dissident Indians yet all levels of European society were not accessible to even the Indians higher in the hierarchy. There were some Indians on the Bar Association, but there was generally little social mixing between the two races. 'Indians were also expected to put up with European exclusivism in regard to clubs, hotels, public roads, and even barbers' shops.'[121] There were instances of high officials like the Judicial Commissioner of Awadh, Burkett, using foul language when dealing with 'native' lawyers in his court.[122]

This assumed superiority, irritating in itself, generally generated a feeling of inferiority among the majority of Indians. Indians clamoured to be accepted in European circles, but even this with a tinge of subjection. In the words of Premghan, 'Just as a child gets no milk without crying, a beggar no alms without begging, and the thirsty no water without asking for it, the ruled do not obtain justice from the ruler without petitioning and wailing.'[123] The feeling of superiority which some better placed Indians developed towards other Indians, and their callous attitudes were all indicative of their desperate attempts to be on par with the Europeans.[124] Attitudes of submissiveness and awe extended even to officials like magistrates. These 'native' officials were hesitant in dealing boldly with criminal cases.[125]

In the administrative sphere and the judicial departments, there was great discrimination between the appointments of Europeans and Indians. The language press highlighted this and said that while the number of posts had risen at the turn of the century, the number of Indians in high posts was still inadequate. The Governor-General answered by instituting an enquiry comparing the years 1877, 1887, 1897, 1903. The government happily concluded that almost in all the grades the number of 'natives' had risen while that of the Europeans had fallen. The aggregate cost of the civil establishment of government had nearly doubled, while the average cost had appreciably declined, proving thereby that more Indians at lower salaries had been employed.[126] The assertion seemed self-contradictory. On the one hand the number of posts had risen over the years and on the other very few highly paid posts had been created. Where did this leave room for the Indians who, it was claimed, manned more high posts?

Great differences existed in criminal laws for the trial and punishment of Indians and the British. A magistrate who could punish an Indian with three years imprisonment could not give even three months notice to a British-born subject. A Sessions Judge could sentence a 'native' to transportation for life or even to death but he could not imprison a British-born subject for more than a year.[127]

The case of Pandit Hriday Narain stood out in the minds of the editors of the language press as one in which justice had not been done to the Pandit. He had been assaulted in Kanpur and had sustained injuries. The Commissioner supported District Magistrate Wright, though the latter had refused to take action when the Pandit had reported to him. The injustice of this stumped the newspapers who realized that '. . . when it is difficult for a native to obtain justice against an ordinary European it is more so against a heaven-born civilian, particularly when political and imperial considerations are at stake.'[128]

Even senior judicial posts were not manned by Indians. The highest posts they could hold were those of subordinate judges and munsifs. As time progressed some Indians of the judicial branch were raised to District Judgeships, for example, Saiyad Akbar Husain, Babu Pyare Lal and Babu Baijnath. The local language papers were unhappy that the government ignored the claims of the subordinate judges or judges of the small-cause courts to officiate as District Judges.[129] Indians manning high posts was such a rarity that the appointment of Mr. Mahmud as a permanent judge of the Allahabad High Court caused a stir in the local press.

The salaries Indians received were lower than what Europeans on the same posts were paid This was true of all departments including the army wherein it was more economical to recruit Indians. The colonialists regarded it as a matter of right and as a sound way of keeping Indians in tether, as is evident in a letter written by the Secretary of State for India to the Governor-General commenting on Maulvi Sami-ul-lah's appeal for a higher salary as District Judge.

> I concur with your Excellency in Council in thinking that there is no reason for excepting these judgeships from the operation of the general rule under which natives of India receive two thirds of the pay drawn by Europeans discharging similar duties.[130]

Compulsory Labour

The practice of forcibly employing Indians for work, or impressing their carts, vehicles, etc., for the use of Europeans, was prevalent and widely so. Apparently European officials had no qualms about pressing into service even 'native' women. Sometimes these women were 'outraged' and the relatives had to be satisfied with a paltry amount of compensation.[131] Abduction of small boys by a certain class of men to sell them into slavery, was common. The main target, however, were the labouring and artisan classes who were freely seized by tehsil peons and policemen to do work for which they were given no payment.[132] Although, in a particular case the impressment of labour was declared illegal by a judicial court, the Lt.-Governor, LaTouche, was not convinced of the existence of this crime. The language press was vehement in its claim of the evil present in 'every district in these provinces, and that it is a synonym for slavery'. The prevalence of *begar* or forced labour had a demoralizing effect on workers who felt justified to shirk even when paid a full day's wages. Consequently, they became dishonest and slothful.[133]

Employment of underage children in factories was a grave problem and the government of India sent a complaint to the Chief Secretary, United Provinces, that the Indian Factories Act of 1881 was not being duly enforced as regards the employment of children below nine years. The main evil was the impersonation of children regarding age. In some labour centres the practice of employing the same children in two shifts, under a double set of names, was resorted to, and in such cases it was extremely difficult for inspectors to ascertain the exact number of hours a particular child worked. The Chief

Secretary responded by issuing an order to all Civil Surgeons in the UP that to prevent this they should take a thumb impression on the certificate of the person to whom it related.[134]

BEGGARY, *BEGAR*, AND CONVERSION

The existence of beggars was an evil connected with the contemporary economic crisis. There were professional beggars all over the provinces, persistent and making a nuisance of themselves. The sight of children sent by poor parents to beg upset the people. The newspapers appealed to people to form associations to provide food, clothing and technical instructions to these deprived children.[135]

Rai Nihal Chand Bahadur, a member of the Legislative Council, proposed certain measures to combat this menace. He attributed the prevalence of beggary among able-bodied men and those of higher castes to the so-called religious spirit of the Indian which forbade him to refuse alms to anyone, needy or otherwise, old or young, sick or healthy. There were many orthodox Hindus who regarded beggary among Brahmins as dictated by religious considerations. Improving the material condition of the people and education of public opinion were ways in which this ill could be combated, but these were slow processes and until the state interfered nothing concrete would come out of it.

The establishment of orphanages in the province, with or without government help, helped in meeting the problem of destitute children, to an extent. For instance it was reported that the Lt.-Governor granted Rs. 2-8-0 an orphan per month to the Bareilly orphanage established by the Arya Samaj.[136]

There were instances, too, of individuals establishing orphanages without distinction of caste or creed. Pandit Jaishankar established an orphanage at Varanasi for both Hindu and Muslim children. They were given literary and technical education and appropriate religious instruction. The only problem was paucity of funds. Such institutions were often supported by the public, but religion was a matter on which the more conservative elements backed out. Christian missionaries had established these institutions and were doing laudable work, but were looked on with suspicion by most Indians.[137]

The conversion of a Kayastha boy of thirteen to Christianity at Agra was enough to raise an uproar in the language press. Quarrels ensued at such conversions, between the Hindus or the Muslims, and the missionaries, who were accused of all sorts of deviousness. Few persons were allegedly converted by being convinced of the superior merits of the Christian religion. Some were lured by the promise of a valuable gift, some by offers of employment, and some by fraud.[138] Missionary schools, however good the education they might offer, were generally condemned as anti-Hinduism and there were instances of Hindu schools desperately competing with the Christian institutions for Hindu enrolment.

Hindi and Urdu papers were vehement in condemning the zeal of the missionary ladies of the zenana mission to influence Hindu and Muslim ladies. Under the pretext of spreading education among women, they unhesitatingly entered their homes, and tampered with their faith. They were accused of encouraging young girls to flee from their homes and convert to Christianity.[139] The only way to put a stop to this was banning female missionaries from Indian homes; and a boycott of the ladies, who allowed themselves to get influenced, by their relatives.

This was an over-reaction, but not entirely unjustified. At religious fairs, the Christian missionaries unhesitatingly abused the Hindu and Muslim religions, and distributed pamphlets villifying them. Indians often rioted in response. The government was openly accused of surreptitiously furthering the cause of these missionaries by bestowing special benefits on them. The sanctioning of the seat of a bishop at Lucknow by the government; on a salary from the government treasury—stocked with revenues derived from Hindus and Muslims—was resented, as the government had always claimed to be neutral.[140] The building of a church between two temples at Mathura, despite the fact that there were two churches already there, aroused the worst suspicions and Colvin's intervention was sought.[141]

Low-caste men were generally attracted to the Christian fold, and hence the fear of Christianity taking a firm grip on Indian society. The discrimination made by the genuine Christians against converts was pointed out. The Europeans kept as much aloof from 'native' Christians and even Eurasians as from Hindus and Muslims, so conversion would not improve matters as far as social intercourse with the ruler was concerned.[142] The government accepted the feeling of superiority felt by the Christians brought up at mission centres and the converts at the villages. The civilized Christians were contemptuous about the roots of their less fortunate village brethren, generally Bhangis and Chamars. Hence conversion did not dissipate long-standing caste prejudices.[143]

A reaction to the proselytizing influence of the Christian missionaries was the religious revival among the Hindus and Muslims. There were consequently constant tiffs between the orthodox Hindus and these revivalists who believed that to get back a Christian convert into the fold of the Hindu community was one battle won. They disagreed with the orthodox that such a dissenter should be ostracized.[144] The language press claimed that the preachings and writings of revivalists like Swami Dayananda Saraswati, Babu Kesava Chandra Sen and Munshi Kanhaya Lal, had stemmed the tide of Christianity.

Casteism and Sectarianism

It is obvious that caste and caste groups and untouchability prevailed. For the upper castes the touch of a shoemaker or sweeper meant pollution. Constant complaints were lodged by the higher castes against seating the lower classes in the same railway compartments as they. There was a cry for separate accommodation for the lower castes.[145] This was ironical because the same Indians felt slighted when Europeans practised racial discrimination against them!

Caste differences became sharp and men tended to further the cause of their particular castes. Caste conferences were held periodically. The educated man was a part of the political scene which was based on common kinship and religious persuasion, and at the same time was a leading member of his own caste group Thus, he had to play a dual role.[146]

There was condemnation of the government policy of educating low classes—weavers, washermen and shoe-makers—as this engendered a feeling of equality in them, which produced contempt for the high castes. All this boycott of the lower castes, and social ostracization by the higher castes, was responsible to a large extent for conversions to Christianity. Urdu and Hindi newspapers were divided on the caste issue. While some felt that the caste system should be abolished, as it would make 'the tie of humanity stronger', the others felt that the social, moral, economic and political degeneration was chiefly due to the fact that the caste system had been discarded, and foreign culture was being imitated. In 1910, the question of the inclusion of the depressed classes as Hindus in the final census list arose. Most reformist newspapers favoured it, but the Muslims newspapers vehemently opposed the idea. This could have been because of their fear of the number of Hindus in the political reckoning swelling up, enabling them to get more political representation and importance.[147]

Sectarianism was pronounced among the Muslims. Shias and Sunnis were irreconcilable over their interpretation of the Muslim religion. The Shias were the educated class and Sunnis the weavers, butchers etc. Their many appeals to the government to resolve their disputes, left it in a dilemma as to how best they could be reconciled.[148] The language press was generally not in favour of escalating issues on a religious basis. 'The existence of religious animosity is very regrettable, and the conduct of the men who foolishly endeavour to increase it is highly reprehensible.'[149]

Public Health

Outbreaks of epidemics in the province affected the attitudes of people towards government, and towards each other. Epidemics had religious, social, and economic connotations in the public mind. At the time of such occurrences, the government tried to use them as an excuse to practice social control. Since 1857, the government had resorted to the practice of controlling social evils through the so-called 'natural leaders of the people'. This was witnessed very clearly during the outbreak of epidemics. Misbehaviour by the police and the medical officers was also overlooked, if not actively condoned, by the authorities.

Efforts to revive lost religious practices to prove 'selfhood' gave tremendous importance to the bathing fairs in some holy places. The Magh Mela and the once in-twelve-years Kumbh Mela were events when the Hindus were able to wash away their sins by taking a dip in the holy Ganga. It was to these places that thousands flocked. Consequently, it is not surprizing that incidence of disease rose. Epidemics broke out with terrifying frequency, during which constant mutual recrimination between the people and the government regarding sanitation, habits, religious beliefs, rules, arrangements, etc., was not an uncommon occurrence. Cholera broke out at the Magh Mela at Allahabad in 1890. The government ascribed it to the 'dirty habits of the Hindu pilgrims', while the press was generally vehement in its condemnation of the Municipal Commissioners-in-charge of the fair. They said that latrines had been constructed too near the fair and the filth was buried close by. This really poisoned the air. Besides, sweetmeat sellers who had to pay Rs.1000 per month as ground rent, to sustain themselves, were inclined to sell polluted stuff. Their living places were inadequate and overcrowded and exposed them to severe inclemencies of winter. These fairs were purely religious gatherings and so government was not justified in making them a source of revenue, at the risk of hurting religious sentiments and causing epidemics.[150]

The hasty dispersal by Sir Auckland Colvin of the pilgrims at the highly sanctified Mahabarni fair at Haridwar, on the suspicion that cholera might break out, was enough to raise a furore. Some newspapers doubted the veracity of government's claim of suspected cholera cases, but others were more circumspect. They resented the high-handedness of the police, and the inadequate arrangements on trains for pilgrims to be hastily transported back to their respective places. Colvin himself, after an enquiry, declared that the police were not guilty of tyranny or high-handedness, which completely stumped the Hindu press. The government's efforts to combat the outbreak of the dreaded disease met with even more apprehension in the columns of the press.[151]

The Leprosy Bill introduced in 1889 was viewed with suspicion by the general public, as it introduced segregation of the inflicted. As a rule, a man who was infected with a contagious disease was attended by his friends and relatives, who did not remain aloof. Yet thinking persons, of whom journalists were good representatives, generally approved of this bill.[152] Government efforts at social control were most obvious in meeting the outbreak of the plague. Plague control became a political issue. Anthony MacDonnell, the Lt.-Governor of UP stressed the importance of keeping the social issue in mind, which should not lead to disturbances beyond control. An Epidemic Diseases Act was passed in 1897, wherein government laid down rules for the treatment of a suspected plague case—segregation and burning of his possessions. These were anathema to the people. The inspection of houses on the merest suspicion of plague was considered obnoxious. Almost the entire press rose up in arms against these unsavoury rules. They were generally premature, and clashed with the sentiments, prejudices and circumstances of the people.[153] The issue of sanitation was again raised, and this appeared to be the main cause of the spread of plague. In fact, the furore about plague rules resulted in the gradual dissipation of Hindu-Muslim acrimony. MacDonnell prophesied, 'The plague is sure to depart sooner or later, while the union which it bids fair to effect, will continue to benefit the country for hundreds of years.'[154] Plague broke out at Kanpur in 1900 and government endeavours to enforce the relevant rules resulted in the outbreak of serious riots. There were instances of Hindus of the lower castes at Ballia converting to Islam in the false hope of gaining immunity from the plague rules.[155] MacDonnell suspected that the Congress and other outside elements were instigating these riots. He realized that he had to somehow arrive at a balance between controlling the disease and controlling the people. The latter assumed greater importance and MacDonnell consulted the community leaders such as the landed aristocracy or leaders of particular areas, to learn their views. He ascerbically affirmed that the Kanpur riots could not be controlled as there were no 'natural leaders' there!

Yet there did exist some individuals who realized that disinfection, inoculation and segregation were necessary to fighting the plague that had spread to Allahabad, Agra and Varanasi.[156] The only way in which the people could be convinced of the sincerity of the government in imposing the rules was by government publicizing their real aims to the people and explaining to them the efficacy of each. The Chief Secretary subscribed to this view, and felt the secret Plague Regulations of 1898 should be widely published.[157] The failure of the government in meeting the plague epidemic effectively was widely criticized, and by 1904, 6000 deaths had already occurred in the province. Ghazipur, Lucknow, Ballia and Jaunpur were the worst affected areas.

What was again ironical was the ambivalent public attitude. On the one hand, government measures were causing riots, and on the other, government withdrawal from active interference in plague matters was construed as negligence and apathy. Government was accused of not wanting to spend on combating plague. This paradoxical approach could only be explained on the basis of the inherent fear of governmental interference in social and religious practices. Besides, the Hindu Pandits proclaimed that natural calamities had been caused by the sins of the people. A bath in the Ganga would cure disease. The use of piped water, so essential to maintain good health, was considered by the old fashioned Hindus to involve a loss of religion.[158] The presence of quacks, and the medicines they prescribed, was also a deterrent to acceptance of English medication. Besides, the attitude of the authorities executing the plague rules was allegedly high-handed. Police was blamed for forcibly picking up suspected plague victims without ascertaining whether they were genuine cases or not.

Vaccination was one genuine attempt by the rulers, which generated a mixed reaction. It was regarded as a salutary measure by a section of people, and government was praised for establishing the Vaccination Department. The supportive newspapers emphasized upon their fellow men the need to accept vaccination as a preventive against smallpox, which led to the death of ten to twelve children of the province everyday, and to give up dependence upon charms and amulets for cure.[159] However, the outcry against vaccination outrode the support. The negligence of vaccinators in ascertaining the health and age of the children before vaccinating them, the use of bad lymph, the lack of after-care of vaccinated children, allegedly led to a deterioration in the health of those vaccinated, and sometimes severe reactions were also visible, thus doing more harm than good to the general public. In fact it would not be incorrect to assume that people preferred smallpox to vaccination. Needless to say, religious considerations played a major role in fanning prejudices. Basic suspicions regarding the attempts of the British in ameliorating sickness and disease were never so evident as in public opposition to vaccination.[160] The vaccinators were incompetent and low-paid, and due care was certainly not taken to ascertain the quality of the lymph used. This was probably more an indication of the casual attitude the rulers had towards their subjects, rather than of a devious design of purposely harming them.[161]

The adherence of most Indians to their age-old prejudices and religious practices seemed to them the surest way of preventing the inroad of British culture into their own. This clinging on to an established set of rules was often to their detriment and retarded progress. Going abroad for education was regarded by a majority of the Hindus as amounting to a loss of religion. They boycotted such persons; and those among them, who were professedly modern, also could not accept a 'foreign returned' fellow back into the caste unless he underwent the prescribed penance.[162] Human sacrifice, for the propitiation of the goddess, or for procuring a better yield, or for even a minor achievement like water-works, was not uncommon. Protection of cows was considered more important than protection of human life, which could be sacrificed for the former.[163] Most religious endowments, whether it was the Hussainabad Trust at Lucknow, or the mosques at Agra, were managed by their own priests. There were constant complaints that the latter either mismanaged funds, or were old or incompetent. On their part they were loth to relinquish their hold on this important religious position, which enhanced their social position considerably. The newspapers were happy at the government endeavours to take on the management of these endowments as it would save them from bankruptcy but did not favour total governmental control.[164] In fact, the religious endowments question became a battle between conservative and practical men.

Crime

In the NWP and Awadh crime covered a broad spectrum including theft, dacoity, highway robbery, etc. Thefts were reported at Moradabad, Etah, Etawah, Barabanki, Allahabad, Lucknow and most places of the provinces. The presence of bad characters was often lamented by the language press, a sure sign of the possibility of theft in the particular district.[165]

The names of dacoits like Tantia Bhil and Jhanda were a source of terror. People found it increasingly difficult to protect themselves from their attacks. Everywhere the inability of the police to deal with these marauders was lamented. Either the police were allegedly hand-in-glove with the criminals, or too few to tackle these crimes effectively. The subordinate police officers often persecuted innocent and harmless persons, so that perforce they became thieves and criminals. To give the policemen their due, they were hampered by the orders of their superiors, badly paid, and justifiably only interested in making a living by whatever means.

Poverty was reason enough for growing crime. Shortage of grain was a potent problem, which was responsible for all sorts of unsavoury acts. Bhils and other groups were present in large numbers, and their attacks were so sudden and unpredictable that controlling them needed grit, determination and planning on the part of the authorities. Besides the suggestions to improve the economic situation, reinforce the police force, most newspapers were in favour of the repeal of the Arms Act, which had left the common man defenceless against marauders and thieves. Providing this sort of security to the people would ensure the loyalty of the public towards the government.

CONCLUSION

Social norms and beliefs could not be changed in a hurry or within a short span. Society took a long time to evolve, and was the creation of various economic, administrative, political, psychological and traditional influences. The presence of social ills was something which was an established fact, and their removal could be effected only gradually. The psychological and traditional factors were of paramount importance, and reform had to come from within. The government, of course, could help in bringing about reform, but its unwillingness to interfere in these sensitive matters was understandable. It was difficult for social reformers to impose social reform upon the people so the imponderables faced by a foreign regime would obviously prove quite insurmountable.

However, it was clear that the colonial rulers were more interested in keeping the people in tether. As in other areas, the social phenomena too had to be controlled and not allowed to either endanger the imperialist stranglehold or to result in losses on the economic front. The methods adopted were familiar but the goal was the same—complete control, whether social, economic or political. The opinions of the public voiced in the press were considered only in a limited way and only as long as they did not contribute to the erosion of colonial power.

NOTES

1. W. Crooke, *The North West Provinces of India—their History, Ethnology and Administration,* Delhi, 1897, p. 234. These figures differ in some books but approximately are the same. 'It is difficult to define a Hindu as this term can be attributed to everyone from a Brahman to a low Caste', p. 240.
2. Ibid., pp. 238-9.
3. Anil Seal, *Emergence of Indian Nationalism: Competition and Collaboration in the later 19th century,* London, 1968, pp. 27-8.
4. Crooke, op.cit., pp. 241-53.
5. Ibid., pp. 253-6.
6. Raghuraj Gupta, *Hindu Muslim Relations,* Lucknow, 1976, p. 20.
7. Crooke, op.cit., pp. 260-1.
8. Robinson, op.cit., pp. 24-5.
9. Crooke, op.cit., p. 263.
10. C.A. Bayly, *The Local Roots of Indian Politics: Allahabad, 1880-1920,* London, 1975, p. 39.

11. Bipan Chandra, Amalesh Tripathi and Barun De, *Freedom Struggle*, New Delhi, 1972, p. 37.
12. Robinson, op.cit., pp. 30-1, Bayly, op.cit., pp. 40-4.
13. Bipan Chandra, op.cit., pp. 27-8.
14. Ganeshilal Verma, *Party Politics in UP (1901-1920)*, Delhi, 1978, p. 15.
15. Bayly, op.cit., pp. 108-15.
16. Paul R. Brass, *Factional Politics in an Indian State: The Congress Party in UP*, Bombay, 1966.
17. VNR of UP, *Leader*, Allahabad, 12 Nov. 1911.
18. Bayly, op.cit., p. 114.
19. VNR of NWP&O, *Nasim-i-Agra,* 7 June 1888.
20. Bipan Chandra, op.cit., pp. 28-9.
21. Bayly, op.cit., pp. 56-63.
22. Bipan Chandra, op.cit., p. 29.
23. Robinson, op.cit., Brahmo Samajists eschewed caste altogether. The Prarthana Samajists decided they could best reform Hinduism from within. The Arya Samajists, however, were bitterly divided over caste. Dayananda had envisioned a casteless society but the failure of the Arya Samajists to implement this was responsible for the lack of cohesion in their ranks, p. 67
24. Robinson, op.cit., p. 69.
25. Bayly, op.cit., pp. 116-17; Robinson, ibid., p. 78
26. VNR of UP, *Saddharm Pracharak*; Bijnor, 24 June 1908.
27. VNR of UP, *Shahna-i-Hind*, Meerut, 16 July 1910; *Brahman Sarvaswa*, Etawah, Dec. 1910; *Musafir*, Agra, 23 Aug. 1908.
28. VNR of UP, *Musafir*, Agra, 8 Dec. 1908 and 15 Feb. 1909; *Saddharm Pracharak,* Bijnor, 24 June 1908; *Bharat Sudhsha Pravartak*, Farrukhabad, Oct. 1907.
29. VNR of UP, *Shahna-i-Hind*, Meerut, 16 April 1898.
30. Padmasha, *Indian National Congress and the Muslims,* Rajesh Publications, New Delhi, 1980.
31. Sudhir Chandra, *Dependence and Disillusionment: Emergence of National Consciousness in later 19th Century India,* New Delhi, 1975. 'Everytime Hindus evoked their ancient glory, they could not but lament its eclipse following the Muslim conquest. Muslims, on the contrary, could scarcely feel attracted to an Indian past prior to their arrival and revelled in the memories of their ascendancy,' p. 58.
32. Public Service Commission's report, pp. 34-41. Cited in Seal, op.cit., p. 118.
33. VNR of UP, *Kayastha Akhbar*, Lucknow, 24 Sept. 1888.
34. VNR of UP, *Dabdaba-i-Qaisari,* Bareilly, 9 Jan. 1892.
35. VNR of NWP&O, *Kayastha Conference Gazette*, Kanpur, 4 Jan. 1895.
36. Ibid., 30 Oct. 1898.

37. Bayly, op.cit., p. 116.
38. VNR of NWP&O, *Hindustani*, Lucknow, Jan. 1890.
39. VNR of UP, *Arya-Darpan*, Shahjahanpur, Jan. 1892.
40. VNR of UP, *Oudh Akhbar*, Lucknow, 2, 9 and 14 Jan. 1891.
41. VNR of UP, *Kshatriya Hitopdeshak*, Agra, Sept. 1891.
42. VNR of NWP&O, *Prayag Samachar*, Allahabad, Nov. 1889.
43. Sudhir Chandra, op.cit., *Literature and the Colonial Connection*, pp. 32-3.
44. VNR of NWP&O, *Nur-ul-Anwar*, Kanpur, 2 Jan. 1892.
45. Sudhir Chandra, op.cit., *Dependence and Disillusionment*, pp. 51-2.
46. Sudhir Chandra, op.cit., *Literature and the Colonial Connection*.
47. *Bharat Jiwan*, Varanasi, Jan. 1888.
48. VNR of UP, *Nairang*, Agra, 8 Sept. 1890.
49. *Hindustan*, Kalakankar, 10 Feb. 1888.
50. VNR of UP, 1899: *Riaz-ul-Akhbar*, Gorakhpur, 24 Aug.; *Mihr-i-Nimroz*, Bijnor, 28 Aug.; *Nizam-ul-Mulk*, Moradabad, 30 Aug.
51. VNR of UP, *Azad*, Lucknow, 19 Aug. 1892.
52. VNR of NWP&O, *Nagri Nirad*, Mirzapur, 6 April 1893.
53. *Hindi Pradip*, Allahabad, June 1890.
54. VNR of NWP&O, *Hindustani*, Lucknow, 16 Jan. 1885.
55. VNR of UP, *Hamid-ul-Akhbar*, Moradabad, 12 Dec. 1893.
56. VNR of UP, *Alwaqt*, Gorakhpur, 24 May 1893.
57. *Hindustan*, Kalakankar, 28 Jan. 1891.
58. *Bharat Jiwan*, Varanasi, 1 May 1893.
59. VNR of UP, *Shahna-i-Hind*, Meerut, 8 Jan. 1899.
60. VNR of UP, *Azad*, Lucknow, 9 Jan. 1891.
61. VNR of UP, *Naiyar-i-Azam*, Moradabad, 5 Feb. 1898.
62. Administrative Report of NWP&O, 1889-90, p. xv.
63. VNR of UP, *Hindustani*, Lucknow, 15 April 1891
64. Home Public B, June 1894, Nos. 232-4, Memorandum on the Vernacular Press of Upper India during 1893, pp. 7-8
65. *Oudh Punch*, Lucknow, 18 Jan. 1894.
66. VNR of UP, *Hindustani*, Lucknow, 17 Jan. 1894.
67. VNR of UP, *Azad*, Lucknow, 26 Jan. 1894; *Nizam-ul-Mulk*, Moradabad, 31 Jan. 1894; Administrative Report of NWP&O, 1889-90, p. xv.
68. VNR of UP, *Dabdaba-i-Qaisari*, Bareilly, 9 Dec. 1893.
69. Ibid., 1894-5, p. xi.
70. Ibid., 1902-3; 1903-4.
71. UP of Agra and Awadh, Legislative Proceedings, 1903-4, p. 41.
72. VNR of UP, *Leader*, Allahabad, 3 Nov. 1909.
73. VNR of NWP&O, 1885; *Waqaya-i-alam*, Ghazipur, 5 Jan.; *Hindustani*, Lucknow, 11 Sept.; *Rafiu-l-Akhbar*, Varanasi, 19 Oct.; *Prayag Samachar*, Allahabad, April 1887.
74. VNR of UP, *Waqaya-i-Alam*, Ghazipur, 5 Jan. 1885.

75. VNR of UP, *Amiru-l-Akhbar*, Meerut, 16 Dec. 1890.
76. VNR of UP, *Azad*, Lucknow, 13 Jan. 1887; *Amiru-l-Akhbar*, ibid., 16 Feb. 1886; *Hindustan*, Kalakankar, May 1889.
77. VNR of UP, *Rohilkhand Gazette*, Bareilly, 24 Jan. 1897.
78. VNR of UP, *Azad*, Lucknow, 16 Feb. 1886.
79. VNR of UP, *Bharat Bandhu*, Aligarh, 15 June 1888; *Prayag Samachar*, Allahabad, 18 June 1888.
80. VNR of UP, 1896: *Al Rashid*, Allahabad, 22 Aug.; *Jami-ul-Ulum*, Moradabad, 28 Aug.; *Azad*, Lucknow, 28 Aug.; *Prayag Samachar*, Allahabad, 24 Sept., says the unlucky girl did not get justice from Justice Blennerbassett.
81. VNR of UP, *Al Bashir*, Etawah, 27 Oct. 1903; *Indian People*, Allahabad, 29 Jan. 1905.
82. VNR of UP, *Rajput*, Agra, 15 Sept. 1901.
83. VNR of UP, *Nasim-i-Agra*, 23 April 1898. This was especially among Kayasthas and may be growth of education and consciousness had something to do with it.
84. Crooke, op.cit., pp. 136-7.
85. VNR of UP, *Arya Darpan*, Shahjahanpur, Feb. 1896. A Brahmin girl is killed by her father in Etawah.
86. VNR of UP, *Kanyakubj Prakash*, Lucknow, April 1887.
87. *Hindustan*, Kalakankar, 10 Feb 1888; *Azad*, Lucknow, 5 Aug. 1887.
88. VNR of UP, *Oudh Akhbar*, Lucknow, 24 Aug. 1894.
89. VNR of UP, *Zamana*, Kanpur, June 1913; *Al Bashir*, Etawah 29 Nov. 1910.
90. VNR of NWP&O, *Riaz-ul-Akhbar*, Gorakhpur, 24 Aug. 1899; *Mihr-i-Nimroz*, Bijnor, 28 Aug. 1899.
91. VNR of UP, *Oudh Akhbar*, Lucknow, 16 Oct. 1885 wanted the minimum age to be fixed at 15; *Sajjan Vinod*, Agra, 24 March 1886 preferred 12 years; *Prayag Samachar*, Allahabad, March 1886 advocated government interference; *Bharat Jiwan*, Varanasi, 30 Dec. 1890 wanted the social reformers to effect this reform; *Hindustan*, Lucknow, July 1887, wanted the age to be 13 for girls and 18 for boys.
92. VNR of UP, *Prayag Mitra*, Allahabad, 29 April 1887.
93. VNR of NWP&O, *Najmu-l-Akhbar*, Etawah, 1 and 8 Feb. 1887.
94. I have drawn up this resume from various newspaper extracts; *Almora Akhbar*, Jan. 1891; *Bharat Jiwan*, Varanasi, 19 Jan. 1891; *Hindustani*, Lucknow, 21 Jan. 1891; *Nasim-i-Agra*, 23 Jan. 1891; *Tohfa-i-Hind*, Bijnor, 13 and 20 Jan. 1891; *Khichri Samachar*, Mirzapur, 17 Jan. 1891; *Nairang*, Agra, 2 Feb. 1891; *Anjuman-i-Hind*, Lucknow, 7 Feb. 1891; *Tuti-i-Hind*, Meerut, 31 Dec. 1891.
95. VNR of UP, *Hindustani*, Lucknow, 14 Jan. 1891; *Prayag Samachar*, Allahabad, 19 Jan. 1891.
96. *Oudh Akhbar*, Lucknow, 6 March 1891.

97. VNR of UP. *Najmu-l-Akhbar*, Etawah, 24 March 1891.
98. Public Proceedings, Sept. 1884, Nos. 81, 82 and 83.
99. Home Public A, Nos. 131-III-408-3, 5 Feb. 1885 and Nov. 1886.
100. Home Public A, Nos. 131-8 E, Nov. 1886, p. 31.
101. Ibid.
102. *Hindu Mahasabha Series*, 7 Dec. 1885; Home Public A, Nov. 1886, Nos. 131-8 E.
103. VNR of NWP&O, *Bharat Jiwan*, Varanasi, 3 Aug. 1896, *Anis-i-Hind*, Meerut, 7 April 1897.
104. *Hindustan*, July 1887.
105. VNR of UP, *Anis-i-Hind,* Meerut, 7 April 1897; *Khichri Samachar*, June 1890, *Alwaqt*, Gorakhpur, 12 Oct. 1892. However, there were the opponents who took child killing to be indicative of the desire of widows to get married and felt that the non-prevalence of this custom was 'a great safeguard of the honour of their families' (*Almora Akhbar* and *Advocate,* Lucknow, 1898).
106. VNR of UP, *Almora Akhbar*, 25 April 1896; *Arya Darpan,* Shahjahanpur, Feb. 1895.
107. GO 1902, File No. 226—reported 'marriage with a deceased wife's sister in the case of an East Indian'. VNR of UP, *Arya Darpan*, Shahjahanpur, Sept. 1903, said a Hindu woman had deserted her illegitimate child at Allahabad and blamed her guardian who did not perform her remarriage.
108. VNR of UP, *Arya Darpan*, Shahjahanpur, May 1902.
109. *Hindustan*, Lucknow, 21 Sept. 1890; VNR of UP, *Soldier*, Moradabad, 7 Oct. 1892; Bayly, op cit., p. 116.
110. *Bharat Jiwan*, Varanasi, 31 May 1886; VNR of UP, *Kanauj Punch*, 1 Aug. 1892; *Prayag Samachar*, Allahabad, Nov. 1887.
111. VNR of UP, *Nasim-i-Agra*, 15 Feb. 1888; *Prayag Samachar*, Allahabad, 7 July 1890; *Akhbar-i-Alam*, Meerut, Aug. 1888; *Hindustani,* Lucknow, 31 May 1893; *Halat-i-Hind*, Allahabad, 31 May 1893; *Riaz-ul-Akhbar*, Gorakhpur, 1 June 1893; *Prayag Samachar*, Allahabad, 1 June 1890; *Najmu-l-Akhbar*, Etawah, 1 June 1890.
112. VNR of UP, *Arya Darpan,* Shahjahanpur, Jan. 1892; *Hindustan*, Kalakankar, 7 Feb. 1893.
113. Guha, op.cit., pp. 310-11.
114. Bipan Chandra, op.cit., p. 39.
115. VNR of UP, *Prayag Samachar*, Allahabad, 29 Dec. 1885, reported that a tahsildar at Chibramau forced a lady and child to vacate a carriage and pressed it into government service.
116. VNR of UP, *Nasim-i-Agra*, 7 May 1887; *Naiyar-i-Azam,* Moradabad, July 1886; Prem Narain, op.cit., p. 170.
117. Prem Narain, op.cit., pp. 170-1,

118. Sudhir Chandra, op.cit., *Dependence and Disillusionment; Oudh Akhbar*, Lucknow, 26 March 1888.
119. GAD, UP, File No. 587C, 1900, Report regarding the death of a coolie from injuries inflicted by one, Hemisphere, a guard employed on the BNW railway.
120. VNR of UP, *Cawnpore Gazette*, 1 July 1895.
121. Bayly, op.cit., pp. 54-7; S. Chandra, op.cit., p. 67.
122. VNR of UP, *Hindustani*, Lucknow, 18 May 1892.
123. Sudhir Chandra, op.cit., *Literature and the Colonial Connection*, cited from *Bharat Saubhagya*, p. 86.
124. VNR of UP, *Cawnpore Gazette*, 1 Sept. 1892, reported the death of the woman struck by the carriage of Babu Baldeo Prasad, Deputy Collector, Kanpur.
125. Home Police A, May 1892, Nos. 115-240
126. GAD, File No. 247, Home Dept., Nos. 419-35, 1904.
127. VNR of NWP&O, *Jami-ul-Ulum*, Moradabad, 14 May 1896.
128. VNR of NWP&O, *Hindustani*, Lucknow, 27 July 1890.
129. *Advocate*, Lucknow, 13 Sept. 1903.
130. Home Judicial A. March 1888, pp. 276-9.
131. VNR of UP, *Halat-i-Hind*, Allahabad, April 1892.
132. *Hindustan*, Kalakankar, 21 Nov. 1900; VNR of UP, *Riaz-ul-Akhbar*, Gorakhpur, 12 Dec. 1905.
133. VNR of UP, *Indian People*, Allahabad, 17 Dec. 1905.
134. GAD, UP, Lucknow, 1906, File No. 56, Nos. 4-7.
135. VNR of UP, *Oudh Akhbar*, Lucknow, 17 March 1886; *Azad*, Aug. 1887, *Chirag-i-Aiman*, Agra, June 1888.
136. VNR of UP, *Arya Patra*, Bareilly, Sept. 1886; *Dabdaba-i-Qaisari*, Bareilly, 4 Aug. 1888.
137. VNR of UP, *Azad*, Lucknow, Jan. 1888; *Bharat Jiwan*, Varanasi, 25 March 1895.
138. VNR of UP, *Muttra Akhbar*, 24 Oct. 1885; *Nasim-i-Agra*, 15 Aug. 1885; *Najmu-l-Akhbar*, Etawah, 20 Aug. 1885; *Almora Akhbar*, 28 Sept. 1891.
139. VNR of UP, *Muttra Akhbar*, 24 Oct. 1885; *Jam-i-Jamshed*, Moradabad, 3 April 1892.
140. VNR of UP, *Hindustani*, Lucknow, 9 Feb. 1890.
141. *Brij Basi*, Mathura, July 1891.
142. VNR of NWP&O, *Alwaqt*, Gorakhpur, 21 June 1893.
143. GAD, UP, 1899, File No. 357C, Progress of Christianity in the Rohilkhand Division.
144. VNR of UP, *Dhela Akhbar*, Moradabad, 11 Sept. 1895.
145. VNR of UP, *Surub-i-Qaisari*, Rampur, 31 Dec. 1886; *Bharat Jiwan*, Varanasi, Jan. 1889; *Police News*, Meerut, 24 April 1894.
146. Seal, op.cit., pp. 12-16.

147. VNR of UP, *Sahifa,* Bijnor, 19 Nov. 1910; *Zul Qarnain*, Badaun, 21 Nov. 1910; *Rahbar*, Moradabad, 21 Nov. 1910; *Tafrih*, Lucknow, 21 Nov. 1910; *Hindustani,* Lucknow, 21 Nov. 1910; *Leader*, Allahabad, 24 Nov. 1910; *Al Bashir*, Etawah, 29 Nov. 1910; *Hindi Pradip,* Allahabad, 1910.
148. GAD, UP, 1896, File No. 1060/64. Dispute between Shias and Sunnis of Amroha, Moradabad district.
149. *Hindustani*, Lucknow, 7 Dec. 1890.
150. *Hindustan*, Kalakankar, 8 Feb. 1890; VNR of UP, *Halat-i-Hind,* Allahabad, Jan. 1890; *Prayag Samachar*, Allahabad, 17 Feb. 1890.
151. VNR of UP, *Rahbar*, Moradabad, 6 Dec. 1892; *Hindustani*, Lucknow, 7 Dec. 1892.
152. *Bharat Jiwan*,Varanasi,1 July 1889; *Azad*, Lucknow, 5 July 1889; *Karnamah*, Lucknow, July 1897.
153. VNR of NWP&O, 1897; *Jami-ul-Ulum*, Moradabad, 14 March; *Ainah*, Lucknow, 16 March; *Anjuman-i-Hind,* Lucknow, 13 March; *Naiyar-i-Azam*, Moradabad, 19 March; *Anil-i-Hind,* Meerut, *Bharat Jiwan*, Varanasi, 22 March.
154. VNR of NWP&O, *Jami-ul-Ulum*, Moradabad, 21 March 1897.
155. VNR of UP, 1900: *Prayag Samachar*, Allahabad 29 March; *Jami-ul-Ulum,* Moradabad 14 April; *Oudh Akhbar*,Lucknow, 9 April; *Al Bashir*, Etawah, *Hindustani*, Lucknow, 18 April; *Oudh Punch*, Lucknow, 19 April; *Indian Daily Mail*, Lucknow, 24 Sept. 1901.
156. *Bharat Jiwan,* Varanasi, 11 March 1901; *Aligarh Institute Gazette*, May 1901; *Kalidas*, Varanasi, 2 June 1900.
157. GAD, File No. 486-C, 1900, Plague riot at Cawnpore.
158. *Bharat Jiwan*, Varanasi, 1889; *Hindi Pradip*, Allahabad, 1899.
159. *Hindustan*, Kalakankar, Jan. 1889; VNR of UP, *Mirutu-l-Hind,* Lucknow, Feb. 1885; *Tohfa-i-Hind,* Bijnor, 27 Nov. 1890.
160. VNR of UP, *Nasim-i-Agra*, 15 Dec. 1892; *Alam-i-Taswur*, Kanpur, Feb. 1888; *Azad*, Lucknow, 2 Jan. 1891; *Nasim-i-Agra,* 15 April 1892.
161. VNR of UP, *Anjuman-i-Hind*, Lucknow, 31 Dec. 1893.
162. *Oudh Akhbar*, Lucknow, March 1889, gave the example of Pandit Bishan Narain, Barrister at law
163. *Bharat Jiwan*, Varanasi, 14 Aug. 1893 gave a gory description of a boy of the Kundri caste found beheaded at the temple of the 'Devi' in a village in Varanasi district, his body marked with vermilion and wearing a garland of flowers. VNR of UP, *Godharm Prakash*, Farrukhabad, Sept. 1891; *Hindustani*, Lucknow, 5 April 1893; *Hindustan*, Kalakankar, 7 Sept. 1894.
164. VNR of UP, *Oudh Punch*, Lucknow, 27 Nov. 1891; *Azad,* Lucknow, 18 May 1888; *Almora Akhbar*, 16 Feb. 1885.
165. VNR of UP, *Prayag Samachar*, April 1888; *Najmu-l-Akhbar*, Etawah, Feb. 1888; *Sahifa-i-Qudsi,* Delhi, 1888; *Mihr-i-Ninroz,* Bijnor, May 1888.

PART III

The Relationship between Communities in the Eyes of the Press

3. The Indian Reaction to British Educational and Administrative Policies

Muslims were the rulers in the NWP and Awadh before the advent of the British, so even after the establishment of the British rule they retained their position as the dominant favoured class. So also the great landlords and the higher officials. They were on good terms with the British, and enjoyed the top positions and maximum emoluments permissible to Indians. Despite Macaulay's stress on English education, until the middle of the nineteenth century British educational policies had a very limited effect on the province. Most people preferred the indigenous schools for classical and religious education. They were taught Arabic and Persian which was sufficient to make them eligible for government jobs.[1]

The rebellion of 1857 changed this relationship between the rulers and the ruled. Muslims were henceforth regarded the culprits who had conspired against the British, and were looked upon with suspicion for long afterwards. They had never been traders or men of commerce, and depended for their survival on 'the army, the administrative services and sycophancy at court'.[2] According to government policy, the number of government primary and secondary schools gradually increased and private schools closed down. There was a rapid growth in enrolment in government schools in comparison with private schools. From 83,000 boys in government schools and 65,000 boys in private schools in 1860-1, the numbers went up to 350,000 and 80,000 boys respectively in 1900.[3] Higher education, less popular, also too expanded. All the same, stress was laid on English education and Western learning in higher education, for the British felt that in 1857 Indians with an English education had proved more loyal.[4] Besides, the authorities suspected many of the professors of oriental learning to have taken an active part in the rebellion. Consequently, oriental learning in Persian, Arabic and Sanskrit was almost wiped out of the system.

At the lower levels, indigenous languages were stressed as it was felt that 'the vernacular will be the best medium, if . . . we wish to produce any perceptible impression on the general mind of the people in this part of the country'.[5] The British encouraged the translation of English works into Hindi and Urdu as Indian language textbooks had to be written. 'To encourage the growth of vernacular literature nearly half of the circulation of the native newspapers published in the province was bought by the Education Department and distributed to its schools.'[6] It was only later, when the press became more vocal, that the government withdrew its patronage.

With the growth in education, to get jobs became more and more difficult for the uneducated. Muslims were slow to go to government schools, while Hindus took to Hindi and Urdu as they had earlier taken to Persian and Arabic. According to Sir Syed Ahmad, the social and political traditions of the Muslims made them contemptuous of attending schools along with Hindus whom they had always regarded as being inferior. They would not accept any study before the study of the Koran, which took a long time. They firmly believed that the study of English was incompatible with Islam. 'Their antipathy was carried so far indeed, that they began to look upon the study of English by a Musalman as little less than the embracing of Christianity. . . .'[7]

Until now official careers were monopolized by particular families rather than being open to talent. The Muslims were content as they got the major share. But 1857 changed it all. Bureaucratic reform was implemented by the introduction of caste and communal proportions in recruitment, and by the introduction of educational qualifications. To give a few examples, the communal principle was applied in the 1860s to the police establishment, and in 1873 to the subordinate revenue and judicial service. From the 1860s, police officers had to pass a literacy test. In 1874 examinations were made compulsory for tehsildars. From 1877 the Middle Class vernacular examination was a condition for appointment to any office of ten rupees or above.[8] From 1882 every munsif had to pass the lower standard examination and would get promoted only if he passed the higher standard.

There was consequently turmoil in the minds of the already disturbed Muslims. As Noman has aptly asserted,

> the educational policy of the British was responsible for the increase of unemployment and the closing of other avenues for the Muslims. . . . In the Army their recruitment was limited; in arts and crafts they were crippled and rendered helpless.[9]

The repression of the Muslims was both ruthless and callous. They were 'reduced to the position of illiterate masses with their spirit broken and their pride humbled to the dust'.[10]

THE POSITION OF THE COMMUNITIES IN NWP AND AWADH UP TO 1885

In the NWP and Awadh the effect of British repression of the Muslims was initially not as acute as it was in Bengal. Francis Robinson has given statistics to support this, showing that in 1882 Muslims in the province held nearly 35 per cent of all government posts. Ram Gopal held that 'Muslim boys freely entered the government managed schools and in proportion to their population did not lag behind Hindus and sometimes were more than the Hindus.'[11] He said it was a misconception on the part of the leading Muslims in northern India that Muslims were generally not taking part in English education, the reason being that Muslim landlords and aristocrats considered it derogatory to their position to allow their children to associate with commoners at educational institutions. He said that according to Reverend B.H. Badley (Report of the then Education Commission, NWP and Awadh), while the Muslims formed about 10 per cent of the population of the Province, Muslim students at schools and colleges numbered about a quarter of the total.

Despite this, the assumption persisted among the leading Muslims in northern India that Muslims were generally not taking advantage of English education. Sir Syed Ahmad had long felt uneasy at the inability of Muslims and the ability of Hindus to adapt to English education.[12] In 1875, he opened a high school in Aligarh for Muslims. In 1878, this was raised to the level of a second grade college, the Muhammadan Anglo-Oriental College. However, at its inception and for some years after that, there were many Hindus studying there (expectedly the elite).[13] He successfully impressed upon the British that the leading and intelligent Muslims were all for imparting a genuine and sound education to their co-religionists, so that they would make loyal and better subjects.[14] The Aligarh College became the basis of the Anglo-Muslim camraderie. Its chief teachers were Englishmen of ability; leading among them were Theodore Morrison, Thomas Arnold and Walter Raleigh.

REACTION AFTER 1885

To assume that the Aligarh College, with Sir Syed at the helm of affairs, was separatist from the beginning would be wrong. Sir Syed never wanted it to become a political institution. How it was gradually transformed into an institution which enhanced Muslim separatist consciousness is another story.

Muslims

Gradually a difference arose in the approach of the Muslim and the predominantly Hindu papers. The latter, and even those without communal bias, considered education very important. A perfect example is in the divergence of views between the *Hindustani* and the *Najm-ul-Akhbar* over the government order that tahsildars would be recruited from among those who had passed the Anglo-vernacular middle class examination. The *Hindustani* felt that 'When University men could be obtained without difficulty for the office, there was no necessity for fixing such a low standard.' The *Najm-ul-Akhbar*, on the other hand, said

> A Tahsildar should be a man of active habits but it is well known that graduates and students have not generally a good physique. Even some shoemakers' sons have received high education, but surely no right thinking man could be prepared to recommend the elevation of such low classes of people for Tahsildarships.

The Hindu papers were glad that Dufferin had not acceded to the request of the Muslims that they should not be required to meet the educational qualifications fixed for eligibility for government service.

Yet Muslims were convinced that they were not getting their due share in public service. In 1885 in the NWP and Awadh there were 170 Deputy Collectors, of whom 96 were Hindus, 59 Muslims and 15 Christian; and the total amount of money paid every month on account of their salaries was Rs. 59,150. Of this Rs. 34,000 went to the Hindus, Rs. 19,400 to the Muslims, and Rs. 5,750 to the Christians. This was not considered adequate because the Hindus received twice the Muslim share. The number of tahsildarships awarded to Muslims was satisfactory, but the government was trying to curb the number.[15] The Postal department too was imbalanced as of 43 post-masters, 15 were European, 27 Hindu and only 1 Muslim. What was especially acrimonious was Muslim exclusion from the Postal department was not due to any lack of proficiency in English: most incumbents there knew only a smattering of English.[16] As late as 1894, the Muslim newspapers were bemoaning the fate of the Muslims who they claimed were poor and educationally backward.

At the turn of the century, Muslim protestations had become more vehement, probably because of other political and socio-religious developments taking place. Their contention was that the number of Hindus exceeded that of Muslims in the Legislative Councils and the Municipal, District and Local Boards. 'The Hindus are prejudiced against the Musalmans, their object being to gain ascendancy over the latter by way of revenge for the late Muhammadan supremacy.[17] Constant complaints were being levelled against the Universities. The Allahabad University reportedly had 105 Fellows out of whom 70 were Englishmen, 23 Hindus and only 12 Muslims.[18]

Gradually, the feeling grew in them that Hindus were denying them their due, and were it not for the British, the Muslims would be completely eliminated from important positions. They still denied any sort of prejudice against the Hindus but felt the latter were not blameless. For example, the editor of *Al Bashir* asserted that in the Islamia High School at Etawah, of which he was manager, Hindu children were treated on equal terms with Muslim boys. This was not the case in the Kayastha Pathshala at Allahabad and the Hindu College at Varanasi, where, he alleged, the Muslims were discriminated against.

Considering such heightened emotional beliefs of the Muslims, we may subscribe to the theory of W.W. Hunter, reiterated by the Muslim press in general, that blamed the government for not establishing its own schools at the outset but leaving education to missionaries. Muslims, highly religious, would naturally not send their children to such schools. When government schools were established, Hindus were appointed teachers and ill-treated Muslim students there so that they were compelled to leave school.[19]

However, one cannot subscribe to this theory *in toto*. There were several papers which were pro-Muslim and yet blamed their co-religionists for their backwardness. They took the Muslims to task for making frequent appeals to government for aid in education, and argued that other communities also needed aid. The Muslims should help themselves by educating themselves as government would eventually discontinue to provide for higher education at public expense. They did not blame the British for the condition of the Muslims.[20] An example may suffice. The *Azad* of Lucknow of May 1889 did not approve of the appointment of Mirza Mohammad Abbas as officiating District Judge in Awadh on the ground that he was unfit for the post. It went on to say that Awadh was the only province which had been retrograding as far as the intellectual qualifications of its officials was concerned.

Hindus

Hindus never looked upon themselves as a favoured race and repeatedly voiced grievances against the partiality shown to Muslims. In 1887 Hindus contended that the Hindu population being six times the Muslim population, and the Hindus also being ahead of the Muslims in education, the number of Hindus in public service should be at least six times that of Muslims. Yet actual figures of the Civil list showed an extreme predominance of Muslims in both the Executive and the Judicial Services. 'Sir Alfred Lyall has added insult to injury by appointing two Musalmans and only one Hindu to the Statutory Civil Service, this year.'[21] The *Hindustan* of Kalakankar, one of the most popular Hindu papers, said on 25 June 1887 that the complaint of the Muslims about low representation in the provincial public service was unfounded, as Muslims were predominant in these provinces.

The annoyance of Hindus over the neglect of their language and community interests was evidenced in a book by Munshi Sohan Prasad, a teacher, on the question of Hindi *versus* Urdu. The pamphlet was in the form of a dialogue between a good and virtuous woman and a shrew, the former representing Hindi and the latter Urdu. The tyranny and oppression to which Hindus were exposed at the hands of their late Muslim rulers were mentioned. This annoyed the Muslim papers like the *Riaz-ul-Akhbar* of Gorakhpur, and some Muslims were even ready to initiate criminal proceedings against the author.[22] The furore abated only when the author agreed to delete the objectionable passages. What was important was that a linguistic matter had attained religious overtones.

Madan Mohan Malviya, the founder of the Banaras Hindu University and a leader of the Hindu Mahasabha, was a great protagonist of Hindu culture. The Hindu Mahasabha gave the organizational form to the politics of Hindu communalism.[23] The Allahabad Kayasth Pathshala was potentially a formidable weapon for both the authorities and Indian leaders. It had almost no European staff unlike the Aligarh College. Yet the need to be recognized officially as an institution fit to teach up to University Entrance standard, and hope of eventual college status, limited the trustees' freedom of action and made possible a degree of official control. The Kayasthas accounted for a high percentage of the English educated class in the province.[24] In fact the Kayasthas showed their distress when the government announced its plans to limit the recruitment of Kayasthas as kanungos.[25]

THE ESSENCE OF SEPARATISM

The growing cleavage between the Muslims and the Hindus emerged from several factors, but educational disparity and job denial were useful slogans. Most writers agreed that in NWP and Awadh the Muslims were a minority of some 13 per cent but more influential, more prosperous and better educated than Muslims in any other part of India. The reason for this was probably because Muslims were predominant in towns. While 9.7 per cent of the total population was urban, the Muslims were 26.6 per cent of the urban population. 25 per cent of the Muslims lived in towns while only 7 per cent Hindus lived in urban areas.[26] There was far less English education in the NWP and Awadh than in the coastal Presidencies. Western schooling here was estimated as being almost a quarter of a century behind Bengal, and almost in its infancy. Yet Muslims were more than holding their own among the indigenous communities as far as state education was concerned. They were more eager to avail of English education than Hindus.[27] In fact, English schools flourished more in the Muslim towns of Kakori, Bilgain and Jais than in conservative Hindu towns, like Ayodhya. 'In Awadh itself, the political danger, if there is one, lies in there being too many educated Mahommedans to find employment in the public service.'[28]

Tables 3.1 and 3.2 reinforce our arguement that Muslims were not the educationally deprived people that they were presented to be.

The attendance at the Anglo-vernacular and vernacular middle class examination had enormously increased.

1884—2,734 candidates
1888—4,440 candidates

In the matter of government appointments, the Muslims definitely did not lag behind as Table 3.3 shows.

TABLE 3.1: COMPARATIVE SUCCESS OF HINDU AND MUSLIM CANDIDATES[29]

	Anglo-Vernacular		*Vernacular*	
	Actual Number	*Proportion to Successful Candidates*	*Actual Number*	*Proportion to Successful Candidates*
Brahmins	300	25	440	19.5
Banias	142	12.6	194	8.6
Kayasthas	333	28	595	26
Muslims	212	18	685	30

TABLE 3.2. THE NUMBER OF GIRLS ATTENDING SCHOOL BETWEEN 1885-9

	Europeans & Native Christians		*Hindus*		*Muslims*	
	Primary	*Secondary*	*Primary*	*Secondary*	*Primary*	*Secondary*
1885	1,270	1,317	4,914	34	2,969	None
1889	916	1,744	5,590	13	3,088	15

TABLE 3.3: THE NUMBER OF APPOINTMENTS IN THE UNITED PROVINCES[30]

	1867					*1877*					*1887*					*1897*					*1903*				
Pay (Rs.)	*Total*	*European*	*Eurasian*	*Hindu*	*Muslim*	*Total*	*European*	*Eurasian*	*Hindu*	*Muslim*	*Total*	*European*	*Eurasian*	*Hindu*	*Muslim*	*Total*	*European*	*Eurasian*	*Hindu*	*Muslim*	*Total*	*European*	*Eurasian*	*Hindu*	*Muslim*
75-500	1678	601	78	681	318	1821	468	97	919	337	1661	328	67	894	372	1920	394	75	1012	439	2020	382	87	1113	438
500-1000	269	243	0	11	15	335	301	0	17	17	318	253	6	39	20	301	218	3	54	26	238	205	3	50	25
1000-2000	68	68	0	0	0	98	98	0	0	0	100	100	0	0	0	109	105	2	1	1	117	106	3	4	4
2000-4000	69	69	0	0	0	67	67	0	0	0	52	51	0	0	1	60	58	0	2	0	50	49	0	1	0
4000 & Over	4	4	0	0	0	2	2	0	0	0	2	2	0	0	0	2	2	0	0	0	7	6	0	1	0
Total	2088	985	78	692	333	2323	936	97	936	354	2133	734	73	933	393	2392	777	80	1069	466	2477	748	93	1169	467

In Table 3.4 below it is evident that Muslims occupied almost 40 per cent of the posts to those occupied by the Hindus.

Why then was the factor of educational backwardness and denial of government posts taken up time and again as one of the causes of Muslim separatism? The reason could well be the Muslim fear, after 1857, of the Hindus riding roughshod over their confirmed territory —government appointments. This could become a reality as elsewhere in India things were not as rosy for Muslims as they were in the NWP and Awadh. They were afraid that the majority would sweep over the rights of the minority, as the Congress movement was threatening to do. Between 1867 and 1887, Hindus had increased their share of government patronage. In particular, the determination of the Kayasthas to improve their conditions was beginning to threaten

TABLE 3.4: THE PROPORTION OF APPOINTMENTS[31]

Pay	*1867*	*1877*	*1887*	*1897*	*1903*
Total Rs.	00000□□□++	0000□□□□++	000△□□□□++	000□□□□□++	000□□□□□++
75-100	0△□□□□□++	0□□□□□□□++	0□□□□□□□++	0□□□□□□□++	0□□□□□□□++
100-200	000□□□□□++	00△□□□□□++	00□□□□□□++	00□□□□□□++	00□□□□□□++
200-300	0000△□□□++	000△□□□□++	00△□□□□++	00□□□□□+++	0△□□□□□+++
300-400	0000000△□+	0000000□□+	00000□□□++	0000△□□□□+	0000△□□□□+
400-500	0000000□□+	000000□□++	00000□□□++	0000△□□□++	0000△□□□++
500-600	000000000+	000000000+	000000△□□+	000000□□++	000000□□++
600-700	00000000□+	0000000□++	00000000□+	0000000□□+	0000000□□+
700-800	0000000000	0000000000	000000000□	000000000□	000000000□
800-900	000000000+	000000000□	000000000+	0000000□□+	0000000□□+
900-1000	0000000000	0000000000	0000000000	00000000△□	000000000+
1000-2000	0000000000	0000000000	0000000000	0000000000	0000000000
2000 and over	0000000000	0000000000	0000000000	0000000000	0000000000

Note: In the diagram the symbol 0 represents Europeans, △ Eurasians, □ Hindus and + Muslims.

Each symbol represents 10 per cent of the total number of appointments. Ordinarily proportions under 5 per cent have been ignored and those between 5 and 10 taken as 10.

the Muslim preserve. Munshi Kali Prasad of Lucknow preached to fellow Kayasthas that their salvation lay in applying themselves to the study of Western arts and sciences and availing themselves of the means of education placed within their reach by the government.[32]

Besides this, the unevenness of development in India had produced disparities among the Muslims of different provinces and also among the Muslims of the UP. Common interests between the Muslims of differing status were almost non-existent.[33] It would not be a misstatement to affirm that initially social divisions ran according to standing in the social order rather than religion. In fact, upper caste Muslims preferred to associate with Hindus of matching social status and profession, rather than with low caste Muslims. Even Sir Syed, who claimed to represent Muslims (among whom equality among men is a fundamental tenet) and who had also been to England, in his famous Lucknow speech expressed his abhorrence at the idea of Chamars and others having political power.[34] Similarly, popular language papers expressed their disgust at high caste and low caste students sitting together in schools.[35]

Muslims of the higher castes were experiencing a feeling of insecurity in the changing of the caste and communal composition of the services, which had hitherto been their preserve. It would be correct to say that 'by and large reforms in the bureaucracy were putting pressure on the traditional government service groups'.[36]

THE ALIGARH MOVEMENT AND EDUCATION

The Aligarh College was representative of a movement that propagated complete loyalty and allegiance to the British, and a way of showing this was to prove that Western learning was compatible with Muslim faith. 'On the assumption that the Koran was the only reliable guide to Islam, Syed set himself to formulate traditional Koranic teachings anew, so as to extirpate all that was irrational in Islam.'[37] He dismissed the Muslim schools of the old sort at Deoband, Kanpur, Delhi, Jaunpur, and Aligarh as useless, and felt that their books and syllabi were irrelevant, a misrepresentation of actualities, vague and biased.

> If the Muslims do not take to the system of education introduced by the British, they will not only remain a backward community, but will sink lower and lower until there will be no hope of recovery left to them. . . . The adoption of the new system of education does not mean the renunciation of Islam. It

means its protection. . . . How can we remain true Muslims, or serve Islam, if we sink into ignorance?[38]

For such revolutionary views, he was indicted by the conservative Muslims. Dislike of his overbearing attitude was evident in 1889 when the question of his successor at the Aligarh College came up. He wanted his son, Justice Mahmud, to be appointed as life secretary, or else he would severe his connections with the College. *Najm-ul-Akhbar* (Etawah) commented that

there is every reason to hope that the severence of his connection with the College would be as conducive to the prosperity of the College as has been the withdrawal of the management of the Lucknow Paper Mill from the hands of Munshi Newal Kishore, to that of the Mill.[39]

To counter Muslim orthodoxy and encourage people to become educated, Sir Syed established the Muhammadan Anglo-Oriental Conference in 1886. In education, his views matched those of the Congress which wanted the encouragement of English education among Muslims, as then they might become discriminating enough to ally themselves with the Congress, even as he opposed it politically. He considered India unready for elections, popular government and representation as it was overridden with differences of race and creed. He actually feared that the larger community would devour the minorities, who would then blame the benevolent government for its measures.[40] He did not want the Civil Service examination to be held in India as this would throw the Covenanted Services open to all and sundry. He did not consider Muslims sufficiently educated to be successful in competition with others in India.[41]

Sir Syed tried to collect funds for the betterment of Aligarh College. For this he won the ire of the orthodox Hindus who felt that he had already collected enough from so many sources and should not apply to the public for aid. That poor students could not get admission was irksome.[42] Sir Syed's suggestion of special scholarships for the Muslims of the province on the plea of the latter being poor and backward roused opposition.[43] In any case Sir Syed was not popular with all sections of Muslims. Even after his death in August 1898, the Muslim paper *Anis-i-Hind* of Meerut vituperated against him. And all writers did not regard the Aligarh College as the most important base of Muslim consciousness.[44] However, Sir Syed Ahmad's contribution to Muslim upliftment via education was considerable. That the Aligarh Movement prospered on account of the patronage of the British was undeniable. That it gradually became the communal base from which educated Muslims waged war was also a reality.

As the years passed, a growing sectarianism and communalism in education became evident. It seemed as if the two major institutions of UP were geared for a battle of wits, each representing its own communal ideology. To counter the influence of the Aligarh College, the Hindu College at Varanasi became a seedbed of Hindu consciousness. The language newspapers had their own ideas regarding the establishment of the proposed university at Varanasi. The Education Report of the UP for 1908-9 said that Muslims had made greater progress than Hindus, and the endeavour to establish the Hindu University henceforth became more serious. Malviya's insistence on the governing body being totally Hindu put off Annie Besant, who dissociated herself from the scheme. She accused Malviya of conspiring against her, but the supportive newspapers denied this allegation. Some even went to the extent of expressing relief at her withdrawal as a propagation of her esoteric theosophy could have an injurious effect on students.[45]

Despite the prominence of Aligarh and the imminent establishment of a Muslim University there, a section of Muslims felt threatened by the Hindu University scheme. They egged on their co-religionists to take more interest in education. For example, the *Nasim-i-Agra* of 31 July 1910, referring to the keen interest Hindus were taking in educating their women (some had passed their B.A. at Allahabad University), urged Muslims to give at least primary education to their women. While some newspapers felt the need for a non-denominational and non-communal university, some gave a political complexion to the developments. They said that the Hindus were realizing their separate existence and also the futility of the Congress propagation of communal unity.

Colonial Attitudes

Until the turn of the century most Viceroys and Lt.-Governors of NWP and Awadh supported the Aligarh College. They were constantly encouraging fund raising for it. It is commonly held that the British purposely assumed that Muslims were educationally backward in order to divide the two communities.[46] The belief that the absence of religious teaching was responsible for Muslim aversion to government schools was thoughtfully engineered by the British, 'had its effect in combining religion with education and thus effectively dividing the Hindu and Muslim students'.[47] It was this combination which was the special feature of the Aligarh College.

Among the principals of the Aligarh College the name that was most associated with furthering Muslim race consciousness was that of Theodore Beck, who became the Principal in 1885. The fostering of the Aligarh movement by the government was resented by most language newspapers. The case of Munshi Awadh Behari Lal was often quoted. His candidature for Deputy Collectorship had been rejected by Auckland Colvin, though he was a graduate of the Allahabad University and had been recommended by many Englishmen. It was generally felt that 'Sir Auckland Colvin's government has exhibited undue favour to the followers of Sir Sayyid Ahmad Khan in the matter of patronage, in utter disregard of the claims of educated Hindus.'[48] Colvin and Crosthwaite were throughout portrayed by Hindu papers as being pro-Muslim and the greatest proof of this was the disproportionate predominance of Muslims in public services.

This policy received a check in Sir Anthony MacDonnell's time. With him is associated the famous Nagri Resolution. MacDonnell was appalled at Muslim predominance in every rung of the bureaucracy and imposed reforms to reduce it. The Muslim service class was horrified when a list of candidates was rejected because it had too many Muslims. In addition to other things, orders were issued that no more than three Muslims should be appointed for every five Hindus in any branch of the government.[49] The *Pioneer* contended that out of 56 approved candidates for the next competitive examination for the executive branch of the Provincial Civil Service only 6 were Muslims as against 50 Hindus.

James Digges LaTouche was a Lt.-Governor in the traditional mould and Muslims came back into favour. They found it easier to get jobs, and, as Hindus bitterly pointed out, Muslim numbers in the bureaucracy rose.[50] The newspapers complained against this and blamed Muslim pre-eminence on the partiality of the government.

Hewett found it difficult to maintain a balance between Hindus and Muslims. It was during the Lt.-Governership of James Meston that the unpleasant decision of the government to disallow affiliation of outside colleges to the Banaras Hindu University was made. Already the newspapers had been accusing government of favouritism towards the Aligarh scheme, 'For it there is perpetual and balmy breeze, while for the Hindu college there are only sleet and frost, snow and hail, and the weather never shows any sign of a break.'[51] When the government decided to limit the scope of the institution and put it under greater official control the press was resentful. Loud protests were raised and warnings issued that

> the unwillingness on the part of government to entrust the people with the affairs of the proposed university will give rise to deep dissatisfaction' and this at a time 'when both the Congress and the Muslim League have set before themselves the goal of self-government.[52]

CONCLUSION

The growth of the educated class and the resultant scarcity of government jobs were important issues and added to the furtherance of Muslim separatism. But, as said earlier, these grievances emanated from basic psychological insecurities which had been simmering for a number of years before they were actually recognized. That the British instigated division between the two communities is accepted by most. What is debatable is whether they initiated the alienation, or whether it was already there and required only to be nurtured. It was, nevertheless, the British who earned the dubious distinction of having made Muslims conscious of being a distinct race. The divisions between the so-called Hindu and Muslim language press became obvious, and in their inimitable style the colonialists exploited it. It was a display of socio-religious engineering in education and government jobs. It succeeded in escalating social divisions, thus keeping colonial control over the people intact.

NOTES

1. Franics Robinson, *Separatism among Indian Muslims: The Politics of the United Provinces Muslims 1860-1923*, Delhi, Bombay, Bangalore, Kanpur, pp. 34-5.
2. Ishwari Prasad and S.K. Subedar, *Hindu-Muslim Relations,* Allahabad, 1974, p. 4.
3. Robinson, op.cit., p. 35.
4. T.R. Metcalfe, *The Aftermath of the Revolt in India: 1857-1870*, Princeton, 1965, pp. 124-6.
5. Education Commission, NWP and Oudh, p. 8.
6. Robinson, op.cit., p. 36.

7. Evidence of Syed Ahmad Khan before the Education Commission of NWP & Oudh, p. 77.
8. NWP Police Administration Report, 1869-70, p. 53 B, quoted in Bayly, *Political Organisation in the Allahabad Locality,* p. 57; E. White, Officiating Director of Public Instruction, NWP and Oudh, to Chief Secretary, Govt. of NWP and Oudh, 9 Jan. 1885.
9. M. Noman, *Muslim—India Rise and Growth of the All-India Muslim League,* Allahabad, 1942, pp. 23, 26, 27.
10. Saxena, op.cit., quoted from *The Communal Triangle in India,* Ashok Mehta and Achyut Patwardhan, p. 21, Allahabad, 1942, p. 147.
11. Ram Gopal, *Indian Muslims: A Political History (1858-1947)*; Bombay, Calcutta, New Delhi, Madras, Lucknow, London, New York, 1959, p. 31.
12. Briton-Martin, Jr., *New India 1885, British Official Policy and the Emergence of the Indian National Congress,* Bombay, 1970, pp. 328-30.
13. Prasad, op.cit., p. 11.
14. Circular from the Muhammadan Anglo-Oriental College Fund Committee signed by Syed Ahmad Khan, Life Honorary Secretary, Muhammadan Anglo-Oriental College Fund Committee, Undated but probably published in 1872.
15. VNR of NWP&O, *Najm-ul-Akhbar,* Etawah, 4 Oct. 1887.
16. Ibid.
17. VNR of NWP&O, *Naiyar-I-Azam,* Moradabad, Feb. 1900.
18. VNR of NWP&O, *Al Bashir,* Etawah, 19 Feb. 1900.
19. VNR of NWP&O, *Najm-ul-Akhbar,* Etawah, 28 Aug. 1885.
20. VNR of NWP&O, *Azad,* Lucknow, June 1889.
21. *Hindi Pradip,* Allahabad, January 1887.
22. VNR of NWP&O, *Prayag Samachar,* Allahabad, 24 June 1885.
23. Brass, op.cit., pp. 20-2.
24. Bayly, op.cit.
25. VNR of NWP&O, *Kayasth Reformer,* Bareilly, 2 Aug. 1890.
26. 1881 Census NWP & Oudh, pp. 57, 60, 98. Evidence by A.C. Bannerjee, Additional Subordinate Judge, Agra Education Commission, NWP & Oudh, pp. 158, 162.
27. RDPI, Oudh, 1875, pp. 7-9 (Report of the Director of Public Instruction).
28. Ibid., p. 10.
29. Administration Report of NWP & Oudh, 1888-9, pp. 161-4.
30. I have drawn up this Table from the figures given in the following file: GAD UP, 1904, File No. 247.
31. Ibid., p. 20.
32. A short account of the aims, objectives achievements, and proceedings of the Kayastha Conference and letters of sympathy from eminent rulers

and high government officers, Allahabad, 1893, pp. ii and iv.

33. Seal, op.cit., p. 359.
34. *Pioneer*, 11 Jan. 1885, reproduced the Lucknow speech of Sir Syed, GAD UP, 1904, File No. 247.
35. Prem Narain, op.cit., p. 87.
36. Robinson, op.cit., p. 46.
37. Seal, op.cit., p. 317.
38. Syed Ahmad Khan to Maulvi Tassaduq Husain, quoted in W.T. de Bary (ed.) *Sources of Indian Traditions*, New York, 1958, pp. 744-5.
39. VNR of NWP&O, *Najm-ul-Akhbar*, Etawah, 8 Oct. 1889.
40. Proceedings of the Council of the Governor-General 1883, quoted in Seal, p. 320. Also in Robinson, p. 118. Almost the same excerpts are quoted in C.H. Phillips, *The Evolution of India and Pakistan 1858-1947, Select Documents*, London, 1962, p. 185.
41. Speech at Lucknow, 28 Dec. 1887. Syed Ahmad Khan, *On the present state of Indian Politics*, Allahabad, 1888, pp.10-15.
42. VNR of NWP&O, *Agra Punch*, 4 Aug. 1890.
43. *Hindi Pradip*, Allahabad, Aug. 1887.
44. Ram Gopal, op.cit., p. 58.
45. VNR of UP, *Advocate*, Lucknow, 26 Sept. 1909, *Musafir*, Agra, 6 Jan. 1911; *Tafrih*, Lucknow, 14 April 1911; *Leader*, Allahabad, 16 May, 1913.
46. Ishwari Prasad and S.K. Subedar, op.cit., p. 10.
47. Ibid., p. 10.
48. VNR of NWP&O, *Hindustani*, Lucknow, 20 July 1892.
49. Robinson, op.cit., p. 134.
50. VNR of NWP&O, *Indian People*, Allahabad, 5 July 1906.
51. VNR of UP, *Leader*, Allahabad, 18 May 1910.
52. VNR of UP, *Advocate*, Lucknow, 30 July 1914; *Oudh Akhbar*, Lucknow, 28 July 1914.

4. The Controversy over the Language of Administration

Nothing alienated Hindus and Muslims more than the language controversy. The British had inherited a predominantly Muslim culture which found its greatest manifestation in the literary field. Until 1837, the court language was Persian, which was later substituted by Hindustani, which was essentially a form of Urdu.[1] Many Muslims and Hindus did not approve of this but gradually it gained acceptance. To say that this form of Urdu was spoken only by Muslims would be wrong. There are several examples of prominent Hindus speaking and writing Persian, and later Urdu. The leading Persian poet of nineteenth-century Lucknow was Dwarka Prasad, a Kayastha. What is important to note is that there was no linguistic division between Hindus and Muslims, and the former had completely adopted the culture and literature of the latter. It would be better to call this group the Urdu-speaking elite.[2]

Gradually, as the British imposed English in schools, there followed a linguistic renaissance, and people started having pride in their own languages.[3] UP's part in this great nineteenth-century reassessment of Hindu culture was not as major as that of Bengal or Punjab, but the influence of the Arya Samaj and Brahmo Samaj were felt on the cities of western and eastern UP respectively. Varanasi established itself as the centre of the Hindus. Besides, Urdu was a provincial tongue and not a classical language that Persian had once been. The cultured elite did not find the same satisfaction in Urdu as the medium of their literary expositions and started looking to socio-cultural movements and theosophy for satisfaction. Thus UP was 'a great area with little or no cultural or indeed any other kind of creativity to its credit. The flesh had dried up. The kernel had gone. Only the husk remained.'[4]

One of the important manifestations of the Hindu revival was the demand for the introduction of the Nagri script in government offices and courts in place of Persian. This was initially not an exclusively Hindu movement, and did not receive the support of all Hindus. There were Hindu members of the Urdu-speaking elite who opposed this.

For example, in 1880 Pandit Ajodhianath vigorously opposed the government proposal to suspend the Urdu law classes at Muir Central College, Allahabad.[5] As awareness grew, linguistic differences gained prominence. The Hindus identified Persian with Muslim supremacy while the Nagri script was what Brahmins used and in which Sanskrit was written. The Muslims considered Hindi dirty and degrading.[6] Besides, Urdu had grown rapidly and in 1863, out of 23 newspapers published in the province, 17 were in Urdu and only 4 in Hindi.[7] Moreover, at primary school level, education was being imparted in the regional languages, and the Hindi learning section, mainly in villages, found it useless in court dealings where the language was Urdu with Persian characters. Matters were, brought to a head by Sir Syed Ahmad's demand for a Vernacular University in Upper India with Urdu as its language. This set many Hindus thinking and the question of whether Hindi was their real language provoked them no end. Some Hindus with strong affiliations with the Muslims of the Urdu-speaking elite, changed loyalties.[8] In 1874 printed petitions were presented to Sir William Muir, the Lt.-Governor by the residents of Bijnor and Najibabad praying for the introduction of the Hindi or Nagri characters in all the courts and offices. The movement became less concerned with the introduction of Nagri than with the advancement of Hindi and Hindu interests. The great Hindi litterateur Bharatendu Harishchandra (1850-85) of Varanasi reflected an antipathy in his poems to Muslims, who, he felt, had trampled India for centuries. His newspaper, *Kavi Vachan Sudha* publicized his mood.

> If Urdu ceases to be the court language, the Musalmans will not easily secure the numerous offices of government such as peshkarships, sarishtadarships, muharirships, etc., of which at present they have a sort of monopoly.[9]

This argument gradually gained ground. The language and script questions contributed to a large extent to the growth of communal politics. Two orders of the Local Government in 1878 had sharpened the edge for the agitation for Hindi. The possession of the Middle Class Certificate was made a prerequisite for appointments, and it was essential to have Urdu as the second language. The Muslims of Aligarh, Roorkee, Meerut, Bulandshahr cojointly represented that people were familiar with Urdu as the native tongue of UP for two-and-a-half centuries. The Hindus countered by saying that they had been helpless during Muslim rule.

The government in its inimitable style focused on the communal aspect of this issue. In a Memorandum on the language Press of Upper India during 1884 the colonial view was spelt out.

> Perhaps there are no better arguments, and there is a general impression, which the names of these papers appear to support, that this agitation is almost entirely a Brahamanical one, and that its basis is partly the sacredness attached to the Nagri character and the Sanskrit language and partly a desire to oust Musalmans from government employ. At present nothing is said for Urdu, probably because its advocates do not consider it in danger.[10]

THE LANGUAGE CONTROVERSY AFTER 1885

The government had finally to give serious thought to the language issue. The multiplicity of languages (Urdu and Hindi) and characters (Nagri, Persian and Kaithi) was creating problems for village schools.[11] The language newspapers did cite examples of British government officers being sympathetic to the introduction of Hindi in the Courts of Justice. In 1885, W.E. Ward, Commissioner of Jhansi, recommended this to the Local Government.[12] There were several arguments put forth by the newspapers. The *Hindustani* of June 1885 published the results of the Middle-Class language Examination where 396 had passed in Hindi and 536 in Urdu. It said that Hindi was popular as many candidates who passed in Hindi were Muslims. The ambiguity of the Persian character was repeatedly stressed by these newspapers and all through the period examples were given as to how mistakes were made in courts because of this factor.[13] On one occasion the word *kishti* (a boat) was mistaken for *kasti* (a prostitute), on another occasion Banno Bhatiari in a summons was mistaken for Pannu Pansari.[14] Hindi in contrast was unambiguous. The newspapers felt that pleaders, munsifs and subordinate judges of the Allahabad High Court should also be examined in Hindi as many of them did not know it and when documents were filed in that language in civil suits, they were at a loose end.

The Hindi newspapers were bitter about the fact that in every province except the NWP and Awadh, the language of the people was the court language. Bengali was the court language in Bengal, Gujarati in Gujarat, Oriya in Orissa.[15] Even in neighbouring Bihar Hindi had recently been introduced because of a benevolent Lt.-Governor, Sir Ashley Eden.

The newspapers were perturbed because boys who had passed

the Anglo-Vernacular Middle Class examination taking Hindi as their second language, were not eligible for the public services since the 1878 government order had made Urdu compulsory. The newspapers reported the presence of essentially Hindu organizations who were wanting the introduction of Hindi in law courts, in the Allahabad University curriculum, in the Acts of government, etc. Prominent among these were the Hindu Samaj, Arya Samaj, Dharm Sabha, Nagri Pracharini Sabha, etc.[16]

A proposal was mooted by Raja Rampal Singh to Sir Auckland Colvin in 1892, regarding the introduction of Roman characters to supersede the conflicting claims of Urdu and Nagri.[17] The newspapers both Hindu and Muslim generally opposed it, and the proposal was finally dropped in 1896.[18]

One of the leading protagonists of the Hindi agitation which began in 1883 was Madan Mohan Malviya.[19] Sir Syed Ahmad was an avid supporter of Urdu which he considered essential for gaining Muslim's ascendancy. The Lt.-Governors who ruled over the NWP and Awadh had either Muslim leanings (Colvin) or were middle level un-authoritative men like Sir Alfred Lyall. It was only when Sir Anthony MacDonnell came to power that things moved as far as the Hindi supporters were concerned. His pro-Hindu leanings were because of a variety of reasons. He found the province in many respects 'behind Bengal. The Judicial and Revenue (Native) official I have seen are distinctly inferior in education and class, while the Police are, I fear, even more corrupt.'[20] These were the departments manned mostly by Muslims. He attempted to reduce their strong position in government service.

With a sympathetic Lt.-Governor at the helm of affairs, the Hindi agitation gained momentum and in 1898, a memorial was presented to the government praying for the substitution of the Nagri script for Persian. The Hindi newspapers put forward their arguments for the Nagri character with reinforced vigour. They felt that since Hindi was the mother tongue of the Hindus, its absence from the courts impeded the spread of education. Rajas, maharajas, landlords, Brahmins, Vaishyas and peasants, who had no desire to secure the admission of their sons into the public service, hesitated in sending them to schools and colleges for instruction, and the present backwardness of female education was also because of this.[21] The *Bharat Jiwan* of Varanasi praised the Nagri Pracharini Sabha of Varanasi for its efforts to secure the introduction of Hindi letters in courts and government offices and was glad to notice that the Maharaja of Rewah had already substituted Hindi in place of Urdu in his State.

The Muslim papers now seemed to rise from their stupor and strong protests were made against the memorial. They insisted that the Persian script in which Urdu was written had nothing to do with religion. Persian had made the Hindus civilized and they ought to be proud of it. There were many Persian and Arabic words introduced into the Urdu language and they would cease to be correctly pronounced if this language was written in the Hindi character. Hindi was the language of 'ploughmen' and an Indian could only acquire culture by the study of Persian.

The Hindi character would not only mar the excellence of Urdu but would also take more time and place to write it.[22] The *Aligarh Institute Gazette*, Sir Syed Ahmad's mouthpiece, displayed its modernism by assuming that gradually English would replace Urdu in the courts but until then the latter should continue as it was more popular in these provinces. The paper compared the numbers of Hindi and Urdu newspapers and books published, and letters despatched through the post office, every year in the province.[23] The Urdu newspapers insisted that Hindi had been derived from Persian and the only difference between Urdu and Hindi was that the former maintained more Arabic and Persian words than Hindi. To say that people found themselves at a loss to decipher plaints, etc., written in the Persian was not correct as only educated persons read these. The script was immaterial. Hindi character was difficult enough to even deciphered by Hindi-Sanskrit scholars, while a little practice familiarised a person with the Urdu *Shikasta* (broken hand). To say primary education had suffered was wrong, as Urdu was much more widely spoken than Hindi. Quoting the results of the last language Middle Examination in the province, the papers said that 1,353 and 529 candidates respectively has passed in Urdu and Hindi; and out of them 1,050 were Hindus.[24]

THE HINDI RESOLUTION

Each party was vociferous in condemning the proposals of the other, and amidst this confusion, MacDonnell's Hindi Resolution was issued in 1900. Under this, petitions and complaints would henceforth be filed or written in the Persian or Nagri character, and summons, proclamations, etc., issued from courts would be written in both Nagri and Persian. The Hindu papers were eternally grateful to MacDonnell, the Kashi Nagri Pracharini Sabha and Madan Mohan Malviya for their interest. The Muslim papers were violently opposed to it. The amlas were already overworked and the use of both Devanagri and Persian would certainly make their work still heavier. The papers feared that Urdu would ultimately be given up. Besides, only 1 per cent of the Muslims knew Hindi, while 50 per cent Hindus knew both Urdu and Hindi, so the former would suffer. Since both languages would have to be taught as second languages, educational expenditure would increase phenomenally.[25] The antagonists of the Resolution feared that, Urdu would decay, 'and with its decline, the improvement, liberty and religion of the Musalmans will all disappear, by and by'.[26] There were certain newspapers who accepted the government's decision gracefully. If a just ruler like Anthony MacDonnell considered it right, why should both scripts not be used? Even if only one per cent of Muslims knew Hindi, there was no reason why lakhs of people should be made to suffer from the ambiguity of the Persian alphabet. They felt that it was absurd to allege that government had issued the Hindi Resolution with the object of destroying the concord and goodwill that had lately sprung up between the Hindus and Muslims in connection with the plague rules.[27]

Curzon, though supportive of this Resolution, suggested certain alterations, and the final resolution as it appeared said,

> No one shall be appointed except in a purely English Office, to any ministerial appointment after one year from the date of the Resolution unless he knows both Hindi and Urdu . . . one appointed in the interval who knows one of these languages but not the other shall be required to qualify in the language which he does not know within one year of this appointment.[28]

The Nagri Resolution exacerbated Muslim sentiment, and the previous accusation, that the supporters of the Nagri cause could be identified with the supporters of the Congress, was belied when several Muslim Congressmen joined the general outcry against the Nagri Resolution. Agra landlords, Awadh taluqdars, ulema, Civil Service hopefuls, lawyers galore joined the fray.[29] The government divided the agitators into the 'men of property and influence' and the 'young gentlemen of progressive tendencies'.[30] This distinction was derived on the basis of the capacity of the two types of Muslims to bear government displeasure. Apparently, the latter were more bold and defiant. Mohsin-ul-Mulk, the Secretary of the Aligarh College, would not be cowed. It was only when this young progressive was threatened by

MacDonnell with the possibility of the discontinuance of the government grant to the college that he quietened down.[31] It would not be wrong to say that by 1901 MacDonnell had managed to ostensibly curb the protest movement. Emotions were still raw, and antagonism was simmering more strongly than before. The Muslims took the Nagri Resolution and government's repression to mean that Sir Syed Ahmad's policy of dependence on governmental goodwill was hollow and meaningless. The Muslim sentiment seemed justified. Although the number of publications in UP in Urdu increased substantially in the first half of the twentieth century, those in Hindi increased much faster. By 1921, Hindi publications for the first time began to outnumber Urdu publications. The Muslim position was made more articulate by Ghulam-us-Saqlain, one of the ablest Aligarh graduates.

> The order of Sir Anthony MacDonnell teaches a very serious lesson to the communities of this country. It shows that even a small minority, if it be aggressive and energetic enough, can by sheer persistence succeed in getting such important, indeed revolutionary administrative mandates issued by the government . . . . This is a ready reward to political agitation, a call upon the people to rise and do the same.[32]

He felt the need for the establishment of a Muslim political association as he felt that the Hindi-Urdu controversy and the Resolution was an instance among the many instances of the trampling of the interests of the Muslim community.

The attempts to form a Muslim political association proved abortive. In December 1901 the need became less urgent as LaTouche became Lt. Governor Although he declared his support to the Hindi Resolution, his goodwill for Muslims and Urdu was evident in his statement to Curzon, 'Sir Anthony MacDonnell went too far in acknowledging Hindi as a language.'[33] The Hindu papers were convinced LaTouche was on the side of Hindi while the Muslim papers became bolder and hoped he would support them. The Director of Public Instruction ordered that Hindi be made compulsory for Urdu students in the school classes. This was not received as strongly by Muslim papers as one would have expected. Even a rigid paper like *Al Bashir* said

> the compulsory instruction . . . of Muhammadan children in both the Hindi and Persian characters is calculated to promote goodwill and mutual sympathy between them. Indeed a better means for the purpose could not be thought of.

However, very soon matters settled down and the newspapers began reporting that promotions and appointments were being made in the old way. By the middle of 1903, no bi-lingual examinations had been held for clerical officials and government orders in Hindi and Urdu were rarely issued.[34] Papers complained that despite these orders ministerial officials were not implementing them. A typical example can be found in the complaint of the Honorary Secretary of the Nagri Pracharini Sabha, Shyam Sunder Das. He alleged that the District Judge of Mirzapur refused to accept a plaint written in the Nagri alphabet and pleaded that since he did not understand it, it should be translated into English. The Secretary said this was against the Nagri Resolution, which also said that all 'amlas' should learn Nagri within a year, and only three months were left for the year to be over. The High Court, in its reply agreed that the judge could not return the plaint just because it was in Nagri, but nevertheless said that the Hindi resolution applied to new appointees, who were required to learn Nagri in a year, and not to the existing incumbents.[35] The effect of the Resolution seemed to have waned, and Muslims again found themselves at an advantage in getting jobs. Yet between 1903 and 1906, Muslims were constantly reminded that their position was exposed despite governmental favour. Urdu was constantly under attack from the Hindus. As communal tension increased, the boycott of lawyers of the rival community became a favourite tactic. The Nagri Resolution had cut down the number of briefs going to Muslims.[36] Consequently, by 1909 the number of Muslim lawyers was at its peak, while the number of Hindu lawyers continued to increase at a rapid rate.

Very soon the supporters of Hindi started mooting the proposal that Hindi, being the mother tongue, should be a separate language in schools and courts in UP. Perturbed, the Muslim League passed a resolution that if Hindus wanted cooperation from the Muslims, they should recognize Urdu as the national language. The Hindi Literary Conference was held at Lucknow in 1914, and under the aegis of M.M. Malviya, efforts were made to influence Hindus to discard the Urdu script.[37] The Urdu papers protested. The intention of the conference to extirpate the Urdu language was condemned. Arguments put forth were both political and otherwise. The transitory character of the Hindi press was stressed upon, '. . . numerous papers started in the Hindi language had very brief careers, and . . . if Hindi were not a dead language these papers would have thrived.'[38] *Raises*, rajas, merchants and lawyers promised to conduct their private and official correspondence in Hindi. The conference disagreed with Meston's declaration that the language of the provinces was Hindustani irrespective of it being written in the Urdu or Nagri character.

The Urdu-Hindi controversy was sparked off because of certain basic causes which were the fundamental reasons for misunderstanding between Hindus and Muslims, and could not be treated in isolation. But it definitely contributed towards divisive movements. The government had politicized a purely academic matter. The concerned officials had time and again made suggestive statements which contributed to making this dormant language issue into a major politicial and communal controversy. It helped in breaking up the hitherto socio-economic homogeneous groups which had always symbolized cohesiveness in society.

NOTES

1. GAD, UP, 1906, File Nos. 24, 343C and 461.
2. Robinson, op.cit., p. 32. The Centres of this Urdu-speaking elite were the cities, notably Agra, Allahabad, Meerut, Moradabad, Bareilly and Lucknow.
3. Seal, op.cit.
4. D.A. Low, *Soundings in modern South Asian History*, Berkeley, 1968, p. 9.
5. NWP&O, GAD, Aug. 1880.
6. Evidence of Babu Siva Prasad before the Educational Commission, E.C. NWP&O, p. 314.
7. NWP Administrative Report, 1862-3, p. 91.
8. Robinson, op.cit., p. 74. The example of Raja Jai Kishen Das, one of the closest friends of Sir Syed was given. He urged the cause of Hindi and the Nagri script and wanted a Sanskrit University. He left the Aligarh Scientific Society.
9. Sudhir Chandra, op.cit., *Literature and the Colonial Connection*, Robinson, op.cit., p. 76.
10. Home Dept. Files, March 1885, Public Nos. 3 B-4.
11. GAD, UP, 1906, p. 16.
12. VNR of NWP&O, *Kavi Vachan Sudha*, Varanasi, 1 June 1885.
13. VNR of NWP&O, *Prayag Samachar*, Allahabad, 9 Sept. 1885; *Hindustan*, 21 July 1886.
14. *Hindi Pradip*, Allahabad, March 1890.
15. *Hindustan*, Kalakankar, 13, 14, 15 Sept. 1888; *Hindi Pradip*, Allahabad, March 1890; VNR of NWP&O; *Bundelkhand Punch*, Jhansi, 1 Sept. 1895.
16. *Hindustan*, Kalakankar, 20 March and 9 May 1890.

17. GAD, UP, 1906, File Nos. 24, 343C and 461, p. 14. Provincial Report of 'Question of the Introduction of Hindi as the language and Nagri as the character in the courts of the NWP and Awadh.' VNR of NWP&O, *Deva Nagri Gazette*, Meerut, 1 Aug. 1895; *Bundelkhand Punch*, Jhansi, 1 Sept. 1895; *Azad*, 1886; *Liberal*, Azamgarh, 24 Aug. 1895.
18. GAD, UP, 1906: Serial No. 4, File No. 623, Serial No. 85, File No. 117C.
19. Brass, op.cit., pp. 20-67.
20. MacDonnell to Elgin, 2 Jan. 1896, Elgin Papers (68) 101.
21. *Bharat Jiwan*, Varanasi, 21 Feb. 1898.
22. VNR of NWP&O, *Oudh Punch*, Lucknow, 10 March 1898; *Riaz-Ul-Akhbar*, Gorakhpur, 14 March 1898.
23. VNR of NWP&O, *Marrif*, Aligarh, 1 April 1899.
24. VNR of NWP&O, *Al Bashir*, Etawah, 5 March 1900.
25. VNR of NWP&O, *Al Bashir*, Etawah, 30 April 1900.
26. VNR of NWP&O, *Jam-i-Jamshed*, Moradabad, 13 May 1900.
27. VNR of NWP&O, *Hidiyat-ul-Akhbar*, Moradabad, 24 May 1900; *Shahna-i-Hind*, Meerut, 9 June 1900.
28. GAD, UP, 1906, File Nos. 24, 343C and 461.
29. Robinson, op.cit., p. 136. The Muslim Congressmen were Hafiz Abdur Rahim of Aligarh, Sajjad Hussain, the editor of *Oudh Punch* and Hamid Ali Khan of Lucknow.
30. Miller to Hewett, 21 Sept. 1900; Home Judicial B, Oct. 1900, 200-2 NAI.
31. VNR of NWP&O, *Riaz-ul-Akhbar*, Gorakhpur, 20 Feb. 1901; *Al Bashir*, Etawah, 1 April 1901.
32. An 'Open Letter' to Lord Curzon from Ghulam-us-Saqlain, published in the *Punjab Observer*, Lahore, 16 May 1900 and quoted in Hamid Ali Khan, *The Language Controversy*, p. 45
33. LaTouche to Curzon, 15 May 1902, Curzon Papers (205) 106; *Advocate*, Lucknow, 12 Jan. 1902.
34. VNR of NWP&O, *Prayag Samachar*, Allahabad, 4 July 1903.
35. GAD, UP, 1901, No. 82, U.P.S.A.
36. Letter from E.H. Radice, Commissioner of Lucknow, 24 May 1909; Home Pol. A, Oct. 1913, pp. 100-13.
37. VNR of UP, *Abhyudaya*, Allahabad, 12 Jan. 1911; *Arya Mitra*, Agra, 8 Jan. 1911.
38. VNR of UP, *Zul Qarnain*, Badaun, 14 Dec. 1914.

5. The Religious Factor

In any relationship between two communities, religion plays the role of either dividing or unifying them. Before going into the religious upheavals in UP in the late nineteenth century, the basics of the existing religions have to be enumerated. Semitic religions like Judaism, Christianity and Islam have two distinctive characteristics. They have a very clearly articulated body of religious belief embodied in a sacred work which the members of a religion regard as authoritative (the Bible and the Koran). Semitic religions also have the concept of a community or brotherhood of all who subscribe to them (for example, the Umma or community of Islam).

In contrast a religion like Hinduism has neither the concept of an overreaching community, nor the notion of a single sacred work which authoritatively expounds the tenets of that religion. Thus, it would be appropriate to define Hinduism as a religion resting upon a corpus of philosophical beliefs and organized in a loose and amorphous structure of sects, denominations, *jatis* and tribes, not necessarily arrayed in any clear hierarchical pattern.

Thus it is obvious that there were inherent differences of principle that separated most Hindus from most Muslims. Hindus believed in many gods and worshipped many images, while Muslims were monotheistic and rejected idols. Hindus were ranked in the hierarchy of castes, Muslims—though no less divided—professed equality of all true believers. Hinduism was specific to India, Indian Islam was but one sector of a universal faith.[1]

Despite differences in belief and practice, the importance during the period after 1857 was of social position rather than religious affiliation. Muslims were divided into two major ethnic groups: those who claimed to be descendants of Muslim immigrants, known as *ashraf*, and those of indigenous origin whose ancestors had been converted to Islam. The latter were divided into converts from Hindu high castes such as Muslim Rajputs, converts from clean occupational castes such as Julahas and Qassabs, and converts from unclean occupational castes such as Bhangis and Chamars. The Muslims were sorely divided on issues of their interest in government service and land, with religion playing a secondary role. Landlords did not support the ulema, who taught Islamic sciences and interpreted the holy law. The ulema were orthodox and their main influence was on the masses to whom they could make emotional appeals. The service class could not identify with them as they wanted to gain power in the new secular state created by the British, while the ulema wanted the rule of the priests, and preached a regression to the Middle Ages.[2] Even in religious beliefs they were sharply divided into Shias and Sunnis. It would be appropriate to say that 'The Muslims were more a multiplicity of interests than a community.'[3]

Hindus, had strict caste consciousness and were most uncompromising with each other where the question of caste arose. The most important castes in the UP were the Rajputs, the warrior and landed elite; the Brahmins, the priests and teachers; the Kayasthas, the traditional clerks of northern India, and the Khattris and Banias, the traders and money-lenders. These were further subdivided into sub-castes. At the bottom were the Shudras, menials, who also had several sub-divisions. However, caste organization was a reflection of the social and political ambitions of a few men, not of a caste as such. During those years in the second half of the ninteenth century, the great religious communities were so internally divided, and their levels in the social hierarchy so uneven in the country as a whole, that religious rivalry cannot be seen as a necessary or sufficient factor in generating political activity in India.[4]

Historians have time and again stressed the social proximity of upper class Hindus and Muslims on the basis of profession, interests and relationship with the government. These sections of both communities identified with each other culturally, economically and professionally. Religion was a personal matter. Ram Garib, the Kayastha banker of Gorakhpur, employed a Muslim to manage his bank. The great Kashmiri Brahmin lawyer, Pandit Ajodhianath, appeared in cases with Nawab Abdul Majid and Syed Abdur Rauf.[5] The Kashmiri Brahmin Tej Bahadur Sapru was admired for his fine Persian; while Ghalib's chief disciple was Munshi Hargopal, a Kayastha of Sikandrabad.[6] It was evident that these landlords and government servants from among the Muslims had far stronger connections with their Hindu counterparts than with Muslim weavers or butchers. But as explained above, these affiliations broke because of the educational, professional and linguistic aspirations which were forced into religious categories by the government. Gradually all grievances became religious grievances. Muslim separatism gradually grew and the basic unity among the Muslims became evident.[7] The following observation is self-explanatory:

> When Muslims came to pray in the mosque, they stood in a line, not one inch in front of the other. Potentially the equality of all believers united Muslim society more than the inequalities of descent divided it.[8]

CAUSES OF MUSLIM SEPARATISM AND THE COURSE IT TOOK

Several reasons have been given for the growth of the separatist syndrome. Muslims and Hindus were both responsible. The language press in fact exhibited maximum rigidity on the religious issues.

Religious Revivalism

The earlier cohesion and solidarity of the Hindus and Muslims was considerably affected by new movements that sprang up in the nineteenth century. All these movements were a revolt against the existing order and practice. They sought the press as a platform to air their views and much acrimony ensued between Hindus and Muslims.

The Arya Samaj, the Brahmo Samaj, the Prarthna Samaj, and the Theosophical Society were voices of opposition to Western influences and alien rule. They wanted to revive Indian culture and endeavoured to prevent conversions to Christianity. They were a thorn in the flesh of the Muslims who wanted to clip their wings. These socio-religious movements were enthused with purging Hinduism of all its evils and conservative beliefs.

The Cow was in Danger

The most impressive form of revivalism, and the one which reached the widest segment of the population, was the agitation against the slaughter of cattle, moving towards its first climax in the years between 1882 and 1896. The glorious past of both the communities became their source of inspiration, and in that past they found that Hindus and Muslims had often had ideological differences. The Hindu gradually became the infidel who must be brought back to the ways of God and the Muslim often became the detestable *Mlechha* whose touch was to be avoided.[9]

Hindus had always objected to Muslims sacrificing cows on their annual festival of the Bakr-Id.[10] In the 1880s on the initiative of Arya Samajists, these objections began to take positive form. In 1882, Swami Dayananda formed the Gaurakshini Sabha or cow protection association, and published *Gokaruna Nidhi*, a book which aimed to rouse Hindus against the beef-eating Christians and Muslims and to encourage them to petition government to stop cow killing.[11] This movement, however, became forceful in the NWP and Awadh only in 1886, when a ruling of the High Court stated that a cow was not an object within the meaning of section 245 of the Indian Penal Code, and that the Muslims who slaughtered it could not be held to have violated the legal provisions against incitement to religious violence.[12]

The Muslim Bakr-Id feast slaughters of 1886 became a major issue. The language press reported these riots with full vigour, the Muslim for the Muslim, and the Hindu for the Hindu. The *Prayag Samachar* of Allahabad of December 1886, gave examples of cow slaughter in Allahabad. Allegedly the head of a cow was thrown into the house of a Hindu by a Muslim; the main grievance of the papers was the acquittal by the authorities of the accused.[13] The *Hindi Pradip* of Allahabad warned the government against encouraging an enmity between the two groups that could lead to 'a serious outbreak sooner or later'. The *Tutiya-i-Hind* of Meerut of 16 October 1885 was sore with the Hindus' interference with the religious practices of the Muslims. Muslims could not kill kine at Id and even if they carried beef duly covered through the streets, the Hindus protested. The paper wondered why Hindus did not protest against the practice of the British killing cows.

The ruling of the Allahabad High Court in the Shahjahanpur cow killing case that it was no offence to kill a cow in a public street or thoroughfare, naturally made the Hindu papers doubt the 'justice, impartiality, and sagacity of the judges of that high tribunal'.[14] Such passionate appeals as the following could naturally not leave the Hindus unmoved, especially the Ahirs or the Gwalas among them.[15] The *Brahman* of Kanpur for July 1888, published a short Hindi poem in which cows were represented as appealing for protection to Shri Krishna, who tended cattle in childhood and one of whose appellations was Gopal, or the cherisher of cows.

Hindus became disillusioned with the British as the latter made no concrete move towards cow protection. There was a practical reason also. Cows were useful animals who provided milk, butter, dung, etc. The government was anxious to improve agriculture, but animals that were essential for cultivation were paradoxically not being protected.[16] The Hindu newspapers were convinced about the hostility of some officials towards cow protection. The case of Mr. Wright, the District Magistrate of Kanpur, was cited. He allegedly prohibited Pandit Jagat Narain, Balkrishna and others to deliver lectures on cow slaughter in public streets and thoroughfares.[17] This could have been motivated by a desire to prevent unnecessary disturbance, but some Hindus, led by the language press, took it as interference in religious matters. Their contention was that if Christians and Muslims could be allowed to preach publicly, so should Hindus.[18] The public sale of cooked beef was offensive to Hindus. The *Dabdaba-i-Qaisari*, Bareilly, of 5 July 1890, protested against its sale at the railway station, as this was offensive to Hindu passengers who outnumbered the Muslims.

The cow protection movement had advanced rapidly from its initial aim of building *gaushalas* or homes for sick and aged cattle. Its leaders were pressing for the impounding of stray cattle, and the collection of fees for cattle so impounded at rates to be fixed by zamindars and utilized for the promotion of *gaurakshini* purposes.[19] Some Hindu newspapers, though very few, agreed that mischief was being caused by the anti-cow killing agitation of the Arya Samaj, whose preachers in their zeal embittered relations between the two communities. The *Prayag Samachar*, a Hindu paper of Allahabad, advised Hindus to give up their rigid religiosity as they were under foreign rule. Some Hindu papers even accepted the fact that though these societies had unquestionably good objects in view, which had won them the sympathy of sensible Muslims, they had become hotbeds of sedition and strife. They should have explained the advantages of cattle protection to the lower classes of Muslims, and, using friendly pressure, persuaded them to abandon it.[20]

Hindus meanwhile were forcing their own brethren to subscribe to the cow protection societies. This system of intimidation was exemplified in an incident that occurred in the village of Panda Kunda in Azamgarh in 1893. A well-to-do farmer, Lachman Paure, was boycotted for selling a bullock to a Muslim. He was beaten, his belongings broken and his family and he ostracized. There is evidence that Muslim villagers, weavers and landowners were threatened with boycott, social and economic, and plunder if they did not contribute to the Sabha.[21]

The cow protection movement culminated in the Bakr-Id riots of 25 June 1893. Azamgarh was the main centre of these riots. The Azamgarh riots did not have only local participants,

> of 35 cases of unlawful assembly and rioting (in Azamgarh) nearly all were the work of large bodies of excited Hindus, who had collected from distant villages and from the Ballia and Ghazipur districts to join in an attempt to prevent the Muslims exercizing their lawful custom of sacrifice. . . .[22]

The main points of rioting were the Mau and Chandpur districts.[23] Most Muslim papers blamed the riots on the cow protection societies, but Hindu newspapers felt differently. The *Hindustani* of Lucknow of 20 September complained that the Gaurakshini Sabhas were being unjustly harassed on the bare suspicion of having had a hand in the Bakr-Id riots. Another Hindu newspaper protested that cow protection societies were receiving the sympathies of a number of Muslims. Disputes only occurred during Bakr-Id, when cows were slaughtered in public. Hence Bakr-Id riots were a result of cow slaughter and not cow protection.[24]

The Muslims were at a loss to understand as to why the Hindus were protesting against cow killing when this practice had been prevalent for such a long time. They had a nagging doubt that these protests were only against the Muslims, and not really for cow protection. Or else why were the English allowed to carry on killing cows? A very suggestive observation was made regarding an incident where Hindus plundered a Muslim's house because he had made two cow sacrifices. 'Their object was plainly to punish the Muslims for the performance of cow-sacrifice. They appear to have made no enquiries regarding cattle owned by the local Muslims, let alone attempting to rescue any.'[25]

The *Zamanah* of Kanpur of 4 September 1893 and *Nizam-ul-Mulk* of Moradabad of 16 September 1893, attributed these dissensions to the spread of English education, which had created a strong love of freedom in the minds of Hindus. The educated unemployed Hindus had taken recourse to joining cow protection societies as preachers.

The Hindus also felt that cow sacrifice was not inherent in the religion of the Muslims. Sacrifice was required at the festival of Bakr-Id but it could be sheep or goats and not necessarily cows. The Sultan of Turkey had ordered the prohibition of cattle slaughter as the use of beef encouraged the spread of cholera and leprosy. As the Sultan was the head of the Islamic world, the Indian Muslims should listen to him. The cow was definitely not particularized for sacrifice in such a way as to offend Hindu sentiments.

The riots of 1893 in Bareilly and Azamgarh saw the most brutal outrages. The call for revenge against Muslims who had performed *qurbani* at the Bakr-Id was widespread in 1893 in the Bhojpuri districts. However, some people were keen on amicable relations being established between the two. They felt this collision between the two communities had pushed back progress considerably, and the press and influential men of both communities should endeavour to bring them together again.[26]

The social and economic aspect of the cow protection movement and its violent consequences, are undeniable. Teachers, lawyers, clerks and officials were active in the establishment of the Gaurakshini Sabhas. Goading them on were the new socially respected *swamis, samnyasis* and *fakirs*. However, the main supporters were the Hindu trading and banking classes, plus zamindars and Hindu rajas. Besides being bigoted Hindus, these people had interest in the land, too, and it is possible that the threat which cow killing posed to agriculture made them worried. Moreover, religious enthusiasm perhaps rose because of their long standing rivalry with some Muslim zamindars and weavers.[27] The upper castes were, however, more active, for instance the Ahirs, probably because of their age-old business of tending cattle. Some lower castes were 'allowed' to join in and they were happy to join the snobbish upper castes. So a desire for social mobility played an important part. Besides this, 'major cases of rioting are always likely to provide opportunities for plunder, or for settling of old scores by poor and exploited groups'.[28] Many thus joined the movement without any real conviction regarding saving the cow. Among Muslims, the Julahas or weavers were the main group who attacked the cow.

The economic angle could not be ignored. The challenge posed by money-lenders for protected tenants and others of the upper-caste zamindari communities may have encouraged the latter to support movements of religious revival. An identical argument could be put forward in regard to the Julahas, whose economic insecurity, if not impoverishment, grew markedly in the nineteenth century. The local press was no less vocal as the following extract would show.

> The fact is that in all these seemingly religious riots there lies poverty under the surface and religion's only the cloak under which 'badmashes' and the starving commit them . . . unless the government does something to lessen

the number of the hungry riff-raff and alleviate the poverty of the masses, the riots that have been so frequent of late will continue to multiply.[29]

The language newspapers, especially those predominantly Hindu, protested against government's interference or deliberate non-interference in religious affrays. The Azamgarh riots typify government attitudes at the local and state levels. An account of the magistrate's orders before the riots occurred, is given in the *Hindustani*.

At the instigation of some Musalmans the Magistrate asked for a list of the places within the town where the Musalmans intended to kill kine on the day of the Id. On receipt of the list he sent for the Hindus living near those places and forced them to declare that they had no objection, without taking the trouble to satisfy himself that kine had always been slaughtered at the identical places. Some Hindus were even arrested and sent to the lock-up. On the day preceding the Id he issued a proclamation permitting Musalmans to freely kill animals between 9 a.m. and 12 noon, and the result was that hundreds of kine were slaughtered within the town. He was not content with the grant of free permission, but himself attended several places to witness the slaughter . . . .[30]

The Muslim paper, *Gorakhpur* of 25 August 1893 discounted the *Hindustani* story. The establishment of the cow protection societies at Muhammadabad and Sagri in the Azamgarh district was followed by Hindus forcibly taking some cows from Muslims at Bhadra. Because of the continued hostility of Hindus, Dupernex Evans had been inclined to 'repress the men who were bent on mischief, and to take precautions with a view to prevent riots on the day of the Id'. These contradictory views spoke of the way things were with the two communities. Yet, 'divide and rule' was a phenomenon which was stressed by most of the writers of the day. Sir Charles Crosthwaite's speech after the riots of 1893 was a direct assault on Hindus whom he blamed for the occurences. The Hindus, represented by the Hindu press, were horrified. They felt that his comments on the Gaurakshini Sabhas would make the Hindus and Muslims more disaffected towards each other.

On the other hand, Muslims praised Crosthwaite for his 'sagacity' and his declaration of government opinion in unequivocal terms. These two reactions of different sections of the press showed the way government declarations could affect communal sentiments. There were, however, some balanced newspapers who had a foreboding about the way things could develop in future if the two communities continued to allow themselves to be exploited in this way. They advised the people, whether Hindu or Muslim, to keep their cool and not allow sentiments to overrule their better sense.[31] They felt that the British were allegedly under the false impression that ill feeling between Hindus and Muslims was a source of strength to British rule. This was a wrong assumption as the bitter experience of 1857 should have been warning enough that exciting a strong religious feeling could prove disastrous.[32]

The efforts of the British at practising social control often made them resort to ambiguity and evasion. A perfect example of this was Lord Landsdowne's speech after the riots of 1893. He insisted that 'it requires two to make a quarrel'[33] and got away by blaming both sides. Such indifference and ambivalence could not be exonerated as the government knew that there was no basic cleavage between the two communities, and trouble could have been nipped in the bud.[34]

So Crosthwaite with his exaggerated protestations,'If it (the movement) is allowed to grow, it will become a Hindu government beneath, or supplanting, the British government',[35] and Landsdowne with his indecision, formed the stereotypical British reaction to cow killing riots. Both helped in dividing the Hindus and Muslims and strengthening cohesiveness among their respective social groups. The authorities blamed the language press for exciting emotional fervour. The newspapers found this charge unacceptable and protested that the English language papers were the ones creating trouble.

However, as the national movement gained momentum, even as the communal divide became pronounced squabbles over the cow question lessened. There were bigger issues involved which were apparently much more serious. Language newspapers in general were gratified to note that friction between Hindus and Muslims was getting rarer on Muharram and Bakr-Id festivals. This did not mean that the following years were incident free. Cow slaughter continued and Hindu protests did not stop, and the government displayed its studied evasiveness. As Pan-Islamic fervour increased, the government's eagerness to appease the Muslims grew. For example, when one Khwaja Ghulam-us-Saqlain in 1913 questioned the way cow slaughter was banned in Miranpur in the Muzaffarnagar district during Bakr-Id by the Deputy Collector Mahadeo Prasad, he was assured of rectification by the government. Finally, it was decided that Mahadeo Prasad should not be allowed to officiate as Collector as he had 'not acted in good faith'.[36]

The Bakr-Id riots at Ayodhya and Faizabad in 1912 shocked the public out of its complacence. Muslims protested against Hindu complaints at Ayodhya as cow sacrifice had long been held there. They accused Hindu leaders of conspiring to instigate these riots. The Hindus, however, considered cow sacrifice at a sacred Hindu place as sacrilege and claimed that it had never been permitted at Ayodhya.[37] Hindu supporters were pleasantly surprised when Way, the Deputy Commissioner of Faizabad, refused permission for slaughter of cows within the limits of Ayodhya city. Meston's order to release the Ayodhya riot prisoners was regarded as noble and generous and an indication of his desire to promote Hindu-Muslim unity. The Bakr-Id riots at Farrukhabad in 1914 were again indicative of the British penchant for favouring Muslims. Collector Gracey was blamed, and telegrams to the Lt.-Governor evoked no response. The Muslim League in a resolution at Agra on 24 December 1914, on the Farrukhabad riots said that as always it relied upon government, 'for the protection of the Musalman interest in that connection'.[38]

The Clash Over the Celebration of Festivals of Hindus and Muslims

The cow question was not the only cause of Hindu-Muslim bitterness. A major issue during that period became the celebration of Muharram and Dussehra at the same time. Every year these two festivals almost coincided. Muharram was a time of mourning, Dussehra of cheerful celebration.

The approach of the two festivals meant tension in the minds of officers as well as the press, apprehending possible riots. Irreligious behaviour by people of both communities towards one another was stressed by the language press. For example, a certain Muslim paper accused Har Prasad, Municipal Commissioner of Kanpur, of having thrown a piece of pork in a mosque on the ninth day of Muharram. The *Shahna-i-Hind* of Meerut of 1 November 1886 bemoaned the ill-treatment of the Muslims at the hand of the Hindus during Muharram, which led to riots at Etawah.[39] The singing and dancing of Hindus to celebrate their festivals and fairs evoked Muslim objection. To illustrate this point, the report of a Muslim paper of 1888 would be adequate. According to this paper, Hindus were allowed to hold the Nauchandi fair on the sixth day of Muharram, but the Hindu swimmers were told to pass through the streets of the city quietly in five small batches. In utter disregard for this, the last batch of Hindu swimmers made a loud *Jaikara* cry before a *Sabil* (Muslim water-stall). In fury four or five Muslims attacked them. The Hindu and Sikh police overreacted, entered Khwaja Wafa's mosque with their shoes on, arrested those offering their prayers, and insulted them by pulling their beards.[40] The Hindu newspapers approved of the dancing and singing during their festivals, and blamed the Muslims for causing riots. They stressed that Hindus were always adjusting their acitivities to the routes taken by Muslim processions.

A chronological account of the religious riots which broke out, and which greatly vitiated the congenial atmosphere between the two communities, is necessary. Serious riots broke out at Najibabad in the Bijnor district in 1888 during the Muharram and Dussehra period. The Muslims had allegedly accepted that they would not take a certain route for their *tazia* procession. Despite this, they created a riot and were fired upon by Kunwar Bharat Singh, the Joint Magistrate. Two men were killed, Muslim sentiments aroused. The Muslim papers condemned the Kunwar's actions and deemed him to have been reckless. To add fuel to the fire, the Local Government under Sir Auckland Colvin passed a resolution exonerating the Kunwar from blame and bestowing high praise on MacPherson the magistrate, and his juniors. In this, the Hindu papers felt, the Kunwar was justified in ordering firing as otherwise serious confrontations would have resulted between the two communities. The Muslim press was quite chagrined and blamed government partiality to Hindus as the cause of the riots.[41]

Riots in Varanasi occurred as a result of a rumour that the temple of Sri Ram Chandra at Bhadani was going to be demolished to make way for water-works. Although the temple was ultimately left alone, the Hindu papers blamed Colvin for forcing water-works on the people in this manner. What was important was that Hindus were suspicious of the designs of a government that harped on the disturbances being representative of an obsessive religious zeal, without going into the real causes, which were shortage of grain, and poverty. The papers were resentful of the harsh punishment meted out to the rioteers.[42] The government had its own theories to offer about the cause of this outbreak. One was that the *badmashes* had taken advantage of the situation and had aggravated it.[43]

Mutual suspicions were evident in most Hindu-Muslim dealings. The *Naiyar-i-Azam* of Moradabad of 26 December 1892 had an interesting news item:

> . . . if Ajodhya is considered sacred by the Hindus on account of its being the birth-place of Ram Chandra, it is held in still greater estimation by Musalmans, inasmuch as thousands of Musalmans perished in religious wars there, and the place contains several large mosques built by Mohammadan kings and many tombs of holy saints.

The next major Muharram disturbance took place in 1902 at Amroha in Moradabad district. Shias were involved. The issue escalated as after the Muharram procession a wedding took place to which the Muslims objected.[44] The Shias were most unhappy about all this and the question arose as to why disturbances had occurred when Hindus had held marriage celebrations here since 1894. The Shias resented the ill-treatment afforded to them by the authorities and disapproved of Sunni officers being asked to give impartial opinions. What was unique about this particular riot was that it assumed a double dimension—Shias *v.* Hindus and Shias *v.* Sunnis.[45] The *Shahna-i-Hind*, probably a Sunni paper, condemned the role of the Muslims in these riots and questioned their true adherence to the tenets of the Koran.

Mutual hatred between Shias and Sunnis continued even after the Hindu-Muslim enmity had spent itself. In the heat of Pan-Islamism the question arose of the inviolability of the Turkish Khalifa after 1908. This exacerbated the hatred between the two sects. During Muharram they clashed at Lucknow and government impartiality was evident when it regulated that Sunnis could not be allowed to decry Shia religious beliefs though they could praise their Khalifas. The basic question asked by the Sunnis was whether it was right to recite praises of Husain without reciting the praises of the first three Khalifas, as they had been the companions of Mohammad and both sects believed in the Prophet. The Sunnis were poorer and this was an added grievance. There were examples of pamphlets being published by Sunni editors against Shia beliefs. This generally led to a furore as it did when Muhammad Hamid, editor of *Kaiser-i-Hind* of Faizabad, attacked the Shias in 1914. The government as 'honest broker' intervened and pressurized the editor to apologise.[46]

THE COLONIAL APPROACH

The communal problem had become complex. It was not just the relationship between Hindus and Muslims, but the relationship of the two with the British which was important. The cow protection riots and the Muharram riots provided an easy handle for British manipulation of the religious sensitivities to their own advantage. British policy seemed to be aimed at encouraging each community to believe that vehement expressions of its orthodoxy would not only be allowed but also approved and safeguarded.[47]

Inevitably, the language papers blamed the British government entirely for the riots. Some took on a communal bias, but many saw through the British game and advised both communities to avoid confrontations. The *Karnamah* of Lucknow of 2 October 1895 was illustrative of the thinking of the discerning newspapers. It said that since Hindus and Muslims had lived on good terms with each other during Muslim rule, they should not fall apart under British rule. The British engendered economic scarcity and it was necessary for the two communities to live peacefully and bring prosperity to the country.

The colonial approach in general was to foster the Muslims. The British realized the usefulness of favouritism. Dufferin as Viceroy (1884-8) encouraged Muslims to regard themselves as a distinct political entity in India. In the 1890s MacDonnell, the Lt.-Governor of UP, though otherwise pro-Hindu, tirelessly wrote of the danger the Muslims posed to the Raj.[48] Sir Alfred Lyall, described a game of badminton under the Mughal walls of Delhi:

> Near me a Musalman, civil and mild,
> watched as the shuttlecocks rose and fell;
> and he said, as he counted his beads and smiled,
> God smite their souls to the depths of hell.[49]

The British thus tried to appease the Muslims and gave them special concessions. They wanted to reconcile them to British rule, and according to some historians, this unintentionally resulted in encouraging Muslims to operate as Muslims.[50]

Whatever their psychology may have been, the British had it firmly rooted in their minds that Hindus and Muslims were irreconcilable, especially in religious practices.[51] Even in politics, the British realized that the two communities were on separate platforms. Auckland Colvin, the Lt.-Governor openly accused of being pro-Muslim, felt that a 'national movement' was not possible in India as Muslims would never adopt any movement initiated by the Hindus 'and they detest the claim of the Hindu whom they dispossessed centuries ago, to return, in whatever guise, to power'.[52]

The Muslim bias of most of the officers was a known fact, whatever the idea behind it might have been.[53] More than the Hindu-Muslim occasions of confrontation, this bias was evident in the attitude of the British in the management of the Hindu fairs like the Magh Mela or the Kumbh. In 1892, because of a few cases of cholera, the Haridwar fair of the Hindus was dispersed by the authorities. The language newspapers were horrified at the high-handed and tyrannical way the pilgrims were treated by the police. Some even suggested that most of them were Muslims.[54]

However, the officers *were* directed by higher authorities to apprehend trouble and make adequate arrangements to avoid communal confrontation. I do not want to minimize the importance of the theory of 'divide and rule', but the constraints on the government were undeniable. Many decisions had to be taken by district officials that kept one party happy but irritated the other. In 1900, some Hindus of Amroha appealed to the Commissioner of Rohilkhand Division against the magistrate of Moradabad's orders prohibiting Ram Lila celebrations at a certain place. The Commissioner refused as this would be a new practice and would harm the sentiments of the Muslims living there.[55]

The language newspapers too had different stories to narrate. In 1885, a Hindu paper *Nasim-i-Agra* of 23 October criticized the regulation of the Muharram and Dussehra at Etawah, and reported the unjust arrest and dishonour of an illustrious Hindu, Babu Benarsi Das. On the other hand, the Muslim *Najm-ul-Akhbar* of Etawah, praised the tahsildar and sub-inspector of police for maintenance of peace during Muharram, and said that Hindus were hostile. All this set one wondering whether the contribution of the British to the development of divisive forces was intentional.[56]

Rapid developments of the next few years moulded communal responses in particular ways. Already, the growing tide of communal hatred had been stemmed as a consequence of certain events, the plague riots at Kanpur in 1900, and Sir Syed Ahmad's death. There developed a camaraderie between the two communities.

This temporary lull was however soon broken. The advent of Sir Anthony MacDonnell, his Hindu bias and his Nagri Resolution of 1900, renewed the mutual suspicions of the two communities. Curzon's partition of Bengal in 1905 exacerbated tension between the Hindus and Muslims. Whether Curzon engineered this divisiveness is debatable, but his act definitely increased communal inexorability. His successor, Minto, was undoubtedly a supporter of the Muslims. His intransigence regarding the Councils' reforms resulted in the passage of the Morley-Minto reforms in 1909 in which the elective principle was applied predominantly in favour of Muslims. This was the ultimate nail in the coffin of communal amity. While Hindus resented the blatant favouritism, Muslims were not wholly satisfied. Hindu-Muslim-British relationships had entered their most sensitive phase.[57]

The growth of Anglo-Turkish antipathy had its repurcussion on a large section of Indian Muslims. As Pan-Islamism grew, they became more and more disillusioned with the British. The Kanpur mosque incident of 1912 exhibited a certain overreaction on the part of the Muslims. Frenetic efforts were made to discredit the so-called claims to fair play made by the British. A recrudescence of Hindu-Muslim unity was feared by the government. Even though the Lt.-Governor, Meston, was in favour of adopting a firm attitude towards the Kanpur rioteers, Viceroy Hardinge realized the enormity of the repercussions this could have on the Anglo-Muslim relationship. He hurriedly entered into a compromise before the Muslim fervour could mount further. Muslim newspapers published articles condemning the British for their vindictiveness at Kanpur.[58] The closeness generated by the Pan-Islamic fervour was evident in the liaison between the Hindus and the Muslims even if ultimately it did not prove to be permanent.

India was loyal to the British in the First World War. Muslim loyalty was, however, doubtful as it was dependent on the apprehension of a possibility of England waging war against Turkey. There was an abundance of seditious Muslim pamphlets in UP which were repressed by the government. Warnings were given to editors of the language newspapers who propagated rebellion. These newspapers, like the *Rohilkhand Gazette, Asr-i-Jadid* of Meerut, *Muslim Gazette* and *Al Khalil* of Bijnor, reflected a clear Pan-Islamic bias. Nevertheless, the presence of several Muslim newspapers who were loyal to the government and who counselled restraint, cannot be overlooked.[59]

CONCLUSION

The communalization of the religious beliefs of Hindus and Muslims was the culmination of the communalization of almost all educational, social, linguistic and cultural phenomena in the NWP and Awadh. Differences of religion, beliefs and observances escalated as a result of mutual suspicion in other spheres. The reforms made by the British were double-edged, with the balance tilted heavily in favour of making the people aware of their separate communal entities. The colonialists realized the efficacy of playing communities against each other in achieving social and political control. In this effort they were helped by a language press, which was both a collaborator as well as a critic of the regime in accordance with its communal leanings. In fact, the partisan attitude of the language press was nowhere as visible as it was in the sphere of religion. The views of the newspapers framed and also reflected the opinions of the general public. Hence, the breeding ground for communal awareness was prepared by an unsuspecting people (represented by a still evolving language press) and a shrewd government which did not want to loosen its colonial stranglehold. The politicization of the socio-religious-economic factors was, however, the medium to keep a growing political trend in tether.

NOTES

1. Anil Seal, *Emergence of Indian Nationalism: Competition and Collaboration in the later 19th Century*, London, 1968, p. 27.
2. Francis Robinson, *Separatism among Indian Muslims: The Politics of the United Provinces Muslims 1860-1923*, Delhi, Bombay, Bangalore, Kanpur, pp. 24-8.
3. Ibid., p. 28.
4. Seal, op.cit., pp. 27-8.
5. C.A. Bayly, *The Development of Political Organization in the Allahabad Locality, 1880-1925*. Unpublished D. Phil. Thesis, Oxford, 1970, p. 259.
6. Robinson, op.cit., p. 31.
7. S.A.A. Rizvi and M.L. Bhargava, *Freedom Movement in Uttar Pradesh*, Vol. I, Lucknow, 1957, pp. 448-9.
8. Robinson, op.cit., p. 25.
9. Ishwari Prasad, op.cit., pp. 24-5.
10. The festival of Bakr-Id commemorates Abraham's sacrifice. At this festival it is obligatory for every free Muslim who can afford to buy a sacrificial victim, a sheep for one person, cattle or camel for one to seven persons. H.A.R. Gibb and J.H. Kramers, *Shorter Encyclopaedia of Islam*, London, 1961, quoted in Robinson, op.cit., p. 78.
11. Robinson, ibid., p. 78.
12. VNR of NWP&O, *Prayag Samachar*, Allahabad, 29 Sept. 1886. Also of Chief Secretary to Govt., NWP to Commissioners of all Divisions, 22 July 1898, Judicial of 1893.
13. *Hindi Pradip*, Allahabad, Nov. 1886.
14. VNR of NWP&O, *Almora Akhbar*, 19 March 1888.

15. Gyan Pandey, 'Rallying Round The Cow—Sectarian Strife in the Bhojpuri Region 1888-1917', in *Subaltern Studies II, Writings on South Asian History and Society,* edited by Ranjit Guha, Delhi, 1983, pp. 78-83.
16. VNR of NWP&O, *Godharm Prakash,* Kanpur, Oct. 1888.
17. Ibid., Dec. 1889.
18. Ibid.
19. Gyan Pandey, op.cit., p. 80.
20. VNR of NWP&O, *Gosewak,* Varanasi, 31 Aug. and 7 Sept. 1893.
21. Gyan Pandey, op.cit., pp. 82-3.
22. From Abdul Majid's diary at Mubarakpur—cited in 'Rallying Round the Cow', Gyan Pandey, p. 78. Mau was a famous cloth manufacturing centre where after the British rule was established, Hindu elite were on the ascent while the hitherto Muslim dominance was threatened.
23. VNR of NWP&O, *Riaz-ul-Akhbar,* Gorakhpur, 16 July 1893. '. . . Twenty or twenty-five thousand Hindus gathered together at Mhow (Mau) early in the morning on the day of the Id, and made two unsuccessful attempts to plunder the town. Only two shots from a gun frightened the crowd, which proceeded to Chandpur, where it grew to about 125,000 men, while the Musalmans who turned out to oppose the enemy did not exceed 125 men. Hundreds of Hindus were killed and wounded; but the number of Muhammadan martyrs was six, who were shot by the Hindu police, and five Musalmans were wounded. The Hindus retreated in the evening with five kine, surrendered to them through the District Superintendent of Police. A Hindu Deputy Collector was present at Mhow. He sometimes desires the Musalmans to surrender their arms, sometimes advised them to make a declaration never to kill kine, and sometimes asked them to settle the dispute amicably, but the Musalmans did not accede to his wishes. Jagdeo Singh, Ghansham Misra and other big landholders, who were accompanied by eight or ten thousand men each, took part in the riots.'
24. VNR NWP&O, *Godharm Prakash,* Farrukhabad, Sept. 1893.
25. *Hindustani,* Lucknow, 12 July 1893; *Rafi-ul-Akhbar,* Varanasi, 28 Aug. 1893.
26. VNR of NWP&O, *Najm-ul-Akhbar,* Etawah, 28 Aug. 1893; *Awadh Akhbar,* Lucknow, 30 Aug. 1893.
27. Home Progs. Confidential, 1919, Vol. 52, No. 1583 S.B. D.I.G.'s letter of 10 April 1919.
28. This resume has been prepared by me from Gyan Pandey's *Subaltern Studies,* op.cit., pp. 98-109 and the vernacular newspapers of 1893.
29. VNR of NWP&O, *Hindustani,* Lucknow, 13 Sept. 1893.
30. VNR of NWP&O, *Hindustani,* Lucknow, 18 July 1893.
31. VNR of NWP&O, *Azad,* Lucknow, 1 Sept. 1893; *Sitara-i-Hind,* Moradabad, 20 July 1893.

32. VNR of NWP&O, *Rahbar*, Moradabad, 31 July 1893; *Sitara-i-Hind*, op.cit.
33. VNR of NWP&O, *Hindustani*, Lucknow, 15 Nov. 1893.
34. S. Gopal, *British Policy in India—1858-1905*, Madras, 1965, p. 194.
35. Crosthwaite to Landsdowne, 1 Sept. 1893 sent by Landsdowne to Kimberley, 5 Sept. 1893, Kimberley Papers, Vol. E/18C.
36. GAD File No. 567/1913.
37. VNR of UP, *Kaiser-i-Hind*, Faizabad, 28 Nov. 1912, 26 June 1913; *Rahbar*, Moradabad, 28 Nov. 1912, *Abhyudaya*, Allahabad, 5 Dec. 1912.
38. GAD File No. 577/1914; VNR of UP; *Leader*, Allahabad, 24 Oct. 1913; 13 Nov. 1914; *Albashir*, Etawah, 1 Dec. 1913; *Arya Mitra*, Agra, 16 Nov. 1913; *Mashriq*, Gorakhpur, 17 Feb. 1914.
39. VNR of NWP&O, *Shahna-i-Hind*, Meerut, 1 Nov. 1886. 'They (the Muslims) cannot quietly bear to see their mosques desecrated by pigs and cow-dung and their women dishonoured.'
40. VNR of NWP&O, *Mufid-I-Am*, Agra, 20 Sept. 1888. The other Muslim papers who reported this were *Agra Punch*, 20 Sept. 1888; *Surma-i-Rozgar*, Agra, 24 Sept. 1988.
41. VNR of NWP&O, 1888: *Tahzib*, Moradabad, 19 Oct.; *Jubilee Paper*, Lucknow, 1 Nov.; *Tohfah-i-Hind*, Bijnor, 28 Oct.; *Almora Akhbar*, 29 Oct.; *Mashir-i-Qaisar*, Lucknow, 1 Nov.
42. *Bharat Jiwan*, Varanasi, 20 April 1891; *Hindustan*, Kalakankar, 22 April 1891; *Awadh Akhbar*, Lucknow, 30 April 1891; VNR of NWP&O; *Hindustani*, Lucknow, 22 April 1891; *Rahbar*, Moradabad, 12 June 1891; *Hindustani*, Lucknow, 27 May 1891.
43. GAD, UP, 1891, File No. 255B, The Benares Riots.
44. GAD,UP, 1903, File No. 255 (Letter from the Commissioner of Rohilkhand Division to Impey).
45. Ibid.
46. GAD, File Nos. 591/1908; 366/1911; 480/1914.
47. Ishwari Prasad, op.cit., pp. 26, 61.
48. MacDonnell to Elgin, 16 July 1897 (confidential) and 22 Aug. 1897; Confidential Elgin Papers (71), MacDonnell to Curzon, 18 May 1900, Curzon Papers (201).
49. Studies at Delhi 1876 II, *Badminton*, in Sir Alfred Lyall, *Verses written in India* (London, 1889), p. 47. Cited in Robinson, op.cit., p. 127.
50. Robinson, op.cit., p. 132.
51. Home Public A., Aug. 1887, pp. 205-6. Mr. Woodburn, the Chief Secretary to Govt. of NWP and Awadh wrote on 9 July 1887 that the Hindus and Muslims were divided intrinsically.
52. To Dufferin 24 May 1888, Dufferin Papers, Reel 533.
53. 'There is a bias in favour of Mohamedans on the part of my officers which must not be allowed to appear'—MacDonnell to Landsdowne, 4 Aug. 1893, Landsdowne Papers, Series VII, Vol. 10, Part 1, No. 86.

VNR of NWP&O, *Hindustani*, Lucknow, 23 March 1892, 'In his speech on the occasion of laying the foundation stone of the Muhammadan boarding house at Allahabad, Sir Auckland Colvin expressed himself as a true friend to Musalmans.'

54. *Bharat Jiwan*, Varanasi, 23 May 1892.
55. GAD, UP, 1900, File No. 496C.
56. Strachey, *India*, p. 241. Dufferin told the Editor of *Pioneer* in 1887 that 'diversity of races was there when the British came to India, and denied that government would be so diabolical as to emphasize or exacerbate race hatreds among the Queen's Indian subjects for a political object' Dufferin Papers (Reel. 531) quoted in Gopal, op.cit., p. 160.
57. A detailed account of the 1905 Partition and the Morley- Minto Reforms of 1909 has been given in Chapters 6 and 7.
58. VNR of UP, *Al Shahid Urf Ahl Sonnat*, Allahabad, 20 Aug. 1913. The Pan-Islamic fervour and the Hindu-Muslim relationship has been discussed in Chapter 8.
59. GAD, File Nos. 283/1910; 360/1914, 589/1914. Warning given to the Editor of the *Rohilkhand Gazette*. Extracts from the confidential Annual Reports on the language press of 1908 in Bengal, Bombay, Punjab and UP.

PART IV

National Awareness as Reflected in the Press

6. Nationalism at its Nascent Stage

Social, economic and cultural developments in the NWP and Awadh went *in tandem* with the growth of nationalist feeling. Pride in one's culture engendered a feeling of pride in the concept of one's nation. The growth of educated classes worked as a catalyst in creating a spirit of resistance to all injustice, social, political or economic.

The progressive spirit soon began to manifest itself in an ardent eagerness for political reform. A conviction about the efficacy of nationalism gradually grew among the thinking Indians. Nationalist ideologies can best breed in an atmosphere of cultural and ethnic cohesion, which was sadly lacking in India. In soldering the disparate elements of society, and in adapting modern institutions of representative government to traditional societies, political parties have always played a decisive role.

The Indian National Congress was the party which endeavoured to be an important channel in bringing about the growth of national feeling. It initiated the national movement which attained mammoth proportions, and culminated in the transference of power to Indians. The period between 1885 and 1905 was a comparatively quiescent period, but the seeds of the subsequent turmoil were sown and would be tended and fostered later as the movement gained momentum.[1] The presence of other associations and parties helped in carrying on the political agitation, but the Congress party was definitely the keystone of the future political developments.

FACTORS IN THE GROWTH OF NATIONALISM

When delving into the reasons for the growth of nationalism, it is not enough to define nationalism. An understanding of the inherent pysche present in ardent nationalism is necessary. The ideology of nationalism is always present and needs only the appropriate atmosphere and situation to assert itself practically.[2] In India this ideology of nationalism took a long time to manifest itself as homogeneity and cohesion in the social scenario were sadly lacking.

In UP itself, the Congress movement was initially one of upper middle-class people. It was only gradually that it flowered out into an effective movement of the masses.[2]

Growth of Education

It cannot be over-emphasized that the concept of nationalism finds fruition when material motives are present. The growth of Western learning and education were responsible for discontent among the 'English' educated when they did not get employment.[3] Between 1881-2 and 1901-2, there was a three-fold increase in the number of students being taught in English at high schools and colleges.[4] They looked to the government to provide them jobs; government employment was considered prestigious, and also carried a certain amount of power. Although gradually state employment opportunities rose, Indians found themselves manning only the poorly paid and humble posts. Europeans and Eurasians occupied half the posts and in the higher rungs at that.[5]

Similarly, the fast turnover of professional men, mainly lawyers, resulted in supply outstripping demand, and government dealt with this problem by raising standards. When one considers that leading Congressmen were lawyers and part-time politicians, it lends credence to the view that the disgruntled middle class joined the Congress bandwagon to ventilate its grievances.[6] The growing political consciousness among them naturally worried the authorities, and officials like Lyall, endeavoured to dispel the idea of a 'general disciplined organization' from the minds of the people.[7]

Education and contact with the West also engendered a religious revivalism. People became aware of the existing degradation and humiliation they were facing[8] as colonial subjects. National consciousness was implicit in such awareness and it was argued that 'Indians must not abandon their religion and must not forget their past history, if they again wish to rise in the world'.[9]

Consequently, associations brought nineteenth-century India across the threshold of modern politics. Gradually minor caste and religious cliques gave way to a more broad-based nationalism wherein common education, common goals and common grievances, acted as the binding forces rather than religious affiliations.[10] Early nationalists stressed on secularism and a natural consequence of this changed approach was the endeavour to develop a unified language press.[11]

The emergence of famous playwrights, poets, dramatists and writers had a positive effect. The leading figures of Hindi literature, Bharatendu Harishchandra, Pratap Narain Misra and Pandit Badri Narain Upadhya 'Premghan', dwelt on the maladies of the country in their work even if they were cautious in their approach. For example, in a poem, Pratap Narain Misra, called the British rule *Ramrajya* but was elsewhere, quick to express his disgust at the spectacle of India 'grovelling at the feet of the . . . . foreigner'.[12] Harishchandra's appeal to his countrymen to unite to uphold the dignity of 'Mother-India', and Pratap Narain Misra's labelling all Indians 'women' who to become 'men' must cultivate patriotism, provoked many to think.[13] The common man, incidentally, also had access to their ideas, as most of these writers started newspapers in the regional language.[14]

Political Measures

Most of the administrative measures of the government had a negative effect on the minds of the people. Ripon's Ilbert Bill created a furore. The Arms Act, which disarmed the Indians, resulted in a volunteer movement and created a fertile ground for future Indian dissatisfaction.[15] The Vernacular Press Act of 1878 angered Indian editors as a purely discriminatory measure that did not apply to the English language press.

To add insult to injury, the treatment meted out to the 'natives' was prejudiced and high-handed, and instances of abuse and physical assault were not infrequent. These were time and again emphasized upon by the Indian journalists who, to a large extent, were responsible for the political moves launched in 1885-6.[16]

Social Reform

This period witnessed sincere efforts to effect a reform of society by the government, by educated Indians of all classes, and by Christian missionaries. To mobilize support against the imperialist government, social and national reformers sought to remove distinctions of caste, religion or sex, and unite the people as a cohesive whole.[17] What resulted was the Hindu and Muslim orthodoxy struggling against the onslaught of the reforming zeal of educated Indians, who realized that having pride in one's own culture did not mean adhering irrationally to retrogressive social practices.

The Economic System

The repressive economic measures of the British were crippling the Indian economy. Communications had to be improved to enable the British to pursue uninterrupted trade. To facilitate this, and to meet the expense incurred in paying high salaries to the British officials, taxation was indiscriminate.[18] Besides, English goods were loaded on Indian markets, while raw materials were speedily taken out to meet the requirements of British manufacturers.[19] The 'drain' continued, but writers like Bharatendu Harishchandra blamed it also on the mentality of those who clamoured for imported goods.[20]

Probably the major economic breakdown was in the field of agriculture. The British introduced the zamindari, mahalwari and ryotwari systems in northern India. The economic relations underwent a change and the most hard-pressed were the tillers of the soil. Indian agriculture was used only for the benefit of the rulers. Their aim was to extract land revenue to meet growing expenditure in other fields. Famines occurred frequently and the agriculturists found themselves in an impossible situation. An element seething with discontent emerged. It would be correct to say that, '. . . the very transformation needed to make India a paying colony endangered colonial rule' for it produced 'the social forces of nationalism that organized a struggle against colonialism'.[21]

Moreover, the colonial rule in itself was unity generating. There was a common administration, more or less uniform systems of law and government. National consciousness was thus being generated by identical aspirations and frustrations among the populace. 'Even in the North-West Provinces and Punjab, the backwaters of political awakening in India, a hidden but deep undercurrent of political feeling flowed beneath the surface of apathy and despair.'[22]

THE GRADUAL DEVELOPMENT OF THE CONGRESS MOVEMENT—CHARACTER AND AIMS AT THE INITIAL STAGE

The National Congress was initially an organization formed to provide a 'safety valve' to the growing discontent among the educated. The government, unperturbed, regarded it as a link between the people and itself, and never doubted the loyalty of the people. For, according to Alfred Lyall, the Lt.-Governor of NWP and Awadh '. . . we represent peace and a firm government whereas anything else leads to unfathomable confusion'.[23] The colonial contempt towards the early Congress leaders is well-reflected in D.A. Low's work. He regards them as underlining of their British rulers who wanted to forge a new elitist society and culture for themselves, but who would be inextricably influenced by the ideas and ideals of the British aristocracy and the British middle-class.[24]

The Congress was regarded as a vehicle for the expression of Indian public opinion so that the British government could tailor its policy accordingly. A reform to make the Legislative Council more representative was desired, Indians were being deprived of their justifiable claims in the administration, and the Congress sought remedies. It was sought, among other things, to make Indian entry into the Civil Service easier. The age for entry into the Civil Service had been reduced from twenty-one to nineteen, which meant an almost total exclusion of Indians from the Covenanted Civil Service. The Congress demanded the raising of the age limit. The holding of the Civil Service examination only in England was an obvious impediment for most Indians and the Congress thus put forward the demand of simultaneous examinations in England and India. The condition of the masses was pitiable and the Congress wanted a better deal for them, though for many years it did not involve itself with social questions. To fight the demon of poverty and starvation, fiscal reforms were considered necessary. A redistribution of money had to be decided upon. Justice would be rendered more effective, if a separation of the judiciary and the executive was effected. These demands were based on the proclamation of 1858.[25]

The early nationalist leadership believed that the arousal of national feeling was very important. The fundamental objects of the Congress were the promotion of the Indian nationalism; the social, moral and political advancement of the Indian people; and the 'consolidation of the union between England and India' by securing the modifications of such of its conditions as may be unjust or injurious.[26] Its aim was to basically unite all the people of India, irrespective of religion, caste or region. For the purpose of bringing about a unified public opinion, Congress leaders held meetings periodically in most major cities. These provided a forum for passing resolutions, enumerating demands, and delivering impassioned speeches, which were pieces of high-class literary and intellectual expositions.

THE ROLE OF THE LANGUAGE PRESS

Memorials and petitions were carefully drafted and sent to the government. Arguments and counter arguments were carefully enumerated in these and distributed among Congress members. However, to reach all sections of society, a more universal and simple medium was required. This was provided by the language press which published continuously the conditions prevailing and the views of the Congress. The tone was one of loyalty. The *Bharatendu*, (Brindaban), of March 1885, for example, advised the government to remove false notions regarding the actions of the British government, which put it in a wrong light in the eyes of the Indians. As the Congress movement progressed, the press also grew vociferous and more expressive. Language journalism had come to stay, and political consciousness, national consciousness, evolved out of its columns; so too the other way around: the language press received a tremendous boost from the growing national consciousness. The importance of the press was realized in the early stages of the national movement itself, and one feels that the British were nervous of it right from the beginning. In 1886 itself, Dufferin the Viceroy, harassed by the press, called it a 'foul torrent of abuse' and 'a great river of calumny'.[27] The days were over when it could be 'loftily ignored' because 'the press does undoubtedly express the ideas of the educated class'.[28] Many historians too accused the language press of readily employing agitation to preach sedition. According to them, it did not believe in British fair play and justice and only valued the Congress programme as a means of inciting people against the administration. This view is perhaps extreme, as future events would show. The language press gradually became divided over the Congress, but the papers cannot be accused of 'using' it to practice sedition.

The NWP and Awadh was regarded by most historians as slow in catching up with the national movement. This was true to an extent, but when one considers the various overtones of the movement in UP, it is undeniable that rumblings of future developments causing political upheaval in the twentieth century were heard here in the late nineteenth-century. Brass was correct, when he said that 'the roots of many developments in twentieth century Indian politics lie not in nineteenth century Calcutta and Bombay but in nineteenth-century Benares, Allahabad and Agra'.[29] What little effect it had in NWP and Awadh in its incipient years was evident in the complete disregard of the Congress sessions of 1885-6 by the language newspapers of those years. They probably considered it a stooge of the government, and did not attribute to it the importance of a viable national forum.[30]

There were several factors which influenced the Congress movement in UP and did not accord to it the cohesiveness which was being engendered in the other provinces. The root cause was the difference of concepts in every sphere in the provinces. Diversity was the most important environmental factor in UP politics.[31]

After the Rebellion of 1857, the overhaul of the administration had been much less drastic in NWP and Awadh than in Bengal. Muslims held their own in the public services, while towards the second half of the nineteenth century the Hindus were making valiant efforts to have more preponderance in these services. Muslims were predominant in the professions too. In Lucknow, the bar was almost totally Muslim. In the Allahabad High Court, Bengalis and some local Hindus had gained entrance forcibly, but most lawyers were still Muslims. In 1886, of a total of 9 Indians who were advocates of the High Court, 5 were Muslims and 3 were Bengalis. Muslims, though disgruntled by British educational policies, were definitely not discriminated against in province, and had an edge over the others. One cannot help agreeing—if partially—with a remark in the Report of the Director of Public Instruction (Awadh) in 1875 that in Awadh, the political danger was because of there being too many educated Muslims.[32] Congressmen realized later how important it was for the movement to have Muslim support.

This phenomenon—the importance of Muslim support for the success of the national movement in NWP and Awadh—was realized only gradually. It was then that Muslims endeavoured to overcome their sectional interests and bring cohesion in their ranks.[33] The representation of Muslim needs and interests was undertaken by Sir Syed Ahmad Khan, the self-styled leader of the educated Muslim community in the province. Two facets of his beliefs were clear. Firstly, he did not want to dabble in politics and repeatedly stressed the loyalty of the Muslims towards the British. Second, he was not against Hindus and their eagerness for reforms until the birth of the Congress. He founded a branch of the British Indian Association at Aligarh, urging both Hindus and Muslims of the NWP to take greater interest in their affairs and to speak up for their rights, while assuring them that this was compatible with perfect loyalty to the Raj.[34] He spoke in glowing terms about Hindu-Muslim unity. 'The word Hindu does not denote a particular religion, but on the contrary, every one who lives in India has the right to call himself a Hindu. I am sorry that although I live in India, you do not consider me a Hindu.'[35]

However, the birth of the Congress in 1885 meant a volte-face in the attitude of Sir Syed. He opposed it tooth and nail, and felt India was not prepared for a national movement. Congress was regarded as a Hindu body, for the poor Muslims attendance at its sessions was stressed. He advocated that Muslims keep aloof from the Congress.[36] He feared the exclusion of Muslims from higher services and the Legislative Councils if the Congress demands were met. This would adversely affect community interests in comparison to the majority and its aspirations.[37] Sir Syed's objection that M.As. and B.As. did not come from the landlord or the richer classes, so they were not fit to occupy seats in the Viceroy's Legislative Council or join the covenanted civil service, is indicative of his arrogance and contempt for the deprived sections of society. Consequently, his anti-Congress campaigns had an effect on only a certain section of the society, aristocrats and the upper middle-class. Despite the fact that many Muslims refrained from identifying with Sir Syed, his influence in raising anti-Congress feeling among an important section of Muslims, was undeniable. He realized the necessity of some sort of a Muslim organization to nullify the effect of the Congress.

In 1886, Sir Syed held the first Muslim Educational Conference. It was not much of a political body. His real answer to the challenge of the Congress was the United Patriotic Association which he formed in August 1888.[38] Its membership was open to all communities. Muslim nawabs, rajas, titled gentlemen and some Englishmen joined it. This heralded a positive campaign against the Congress in the shape of pamphlets, papers and journals. The Aligarh group exhorted Muslims to reaffirm their loyalty to the British. Loyalty to the Raj meant the possibility of big returns from the government. Syed went to the extent of sending envoys to other parts of India to persuade Muslims to repudiate the Congress.[39] The Aligarh opposition gained strength from Theodore Beck, the English Principal of the College. He was allegedly the architect of Muslim separatism, the stereotype of a typical colonial officer who found the effectiveness of the Congress movement unacceptable and contemptible.

Besides the important factor of Muslim disaffection, another phenomenon which influenced the national movement was the preponderance of the elite in the province. They were rabidly loyal to the government and had nothing to do with the Congress. As a result, Congress received its support here from smaller zamindars and bigger peasants in the countryside, supported financially by the textile and sugar mill-owners and the big cloth traders.[40] It was thus essentially a middle class movement and in towns and cities was led by lawyers and part-time professionals.[41] Muslim separatism on the other hand, did not have that middle-class base. It was led by Muslim aristocrats and government servants.[42] The absence of elite—Muslim or Hindu—support was a retarding factor in the progress of the Congress in UP.[43]

Writers have stressed the importance of the fact that there was no great metropolis in the province as the dominant locus of social change. Bengal had Calcutta but UP was polycentric. There were at least five towns of equal pre-eminence, Agra, Lucknow, Allahabad, Varanasi and Kanpur. Their character varied and not one of them could hope to lead the whole province in a new direction.[44]

The growth of local interest groups based on religion, caste, professions or political consciousness was rapid in the latter half of the nineteenth century. Regional organizations sprouted. The Hindu Samaj led by Malviya was to encourage the uplift of Hindus, to nurture their self-dependence, and to present a strong face to their enemies. It played a major role in the Hindi issue. The Madhya Hindu Samaj of Allahabad was established in 1884 and its meetings were presided over by men like Mahabir Prasad Dwivedi, who later edited the high quality literary Hindi journal, *Saraswati*. Its patrons were men of eminence like the Raja of Kalakankar, the owner of the *Hindustan*, which was supportive of the Congress movement.[45] The Magh Mela and the organizations connected with it provided for a whole range of religious associations from cow protection to eclectic theosophy which formed the political undergrowth in Allahabad in the 1880s.

Some organizations were not traditionally Hindu and preached 'bhakti', like the Arya Samaj. The Radha Swami Sect of Agra, started by the son of a banker, was also important. An example of caste affiliation was the Kayastha Conference, organized in November 1887 by two Lucknow pleaders, Munshi Har Govid Dayal and Sri Ram, both graduates. Its aim was to take 'decisive measures for the amelioration of the condition of their race'.[46] The low social standing of the Kayasthas made them eager to join the Congress bandwagon and improve their position by associating themselves with people outside the province, especially the Bengal Kayasthas, who were of a considerably higher status.[47]

Then there were several secular organizations which took the form of specific and localized pressure groups projecting the interests of the service communities. A Kashmiri Brahmin, Ajodhianath Kunzru, leading pleader in Allahabad during the 1880s and very active in the Congress movement was responsible for the involvement in political activities of the young Nawab Abdul Majid and Sayyid Abdul Rauf, his subordinate colleagues on the criminal side of the Bar.[48] Two other notables of the professional aristocracy of Allahabad contributed to the secular political traditions that were present in the NWP and Awadh Association in 1885. These were Bishambar Nath, a pleader, and the Srivastava Kayastha, Munshi Hanuman Prasad, the first President of the Kayastha Pathshala.[49]

These groups and associations of all hues and shapes had some common features—'a viable ideology, publicists, printers and patrons'. The importance of the early Congress movement was not only its all-India expression of constitutional grievances. Its importance was also because it was capable of linking up with organizations and leaderships at the regional and district levels.[50] Associations thus brought nineteenth-century India across the threshold of modern politics. This naturally sped the growth of the 'native' press.[51] Adding together the registered editors of Allahabad's long-lived journals between 1885-95, and men who appear in the press or in official reports as lecturers, or men who were active propagandists for three or more public movements over these years, the conclusion would be a 'mixed bag' of forty-one men who could be labelled as publicists. Fourteen of them were connected with local broad-sheets, ten were frustrated lawyers or teachers, nine were religious lecturers, and six others had connections with anti-liquor, caste, or cow protection movements. These were easily incorporated into the Congress bloc.[52]

THE CONGRESS MOVEMENT IN THE UTTAR PRADESH IN THE EYES OF THE PRESS

As stated earlier in the chapter, the importance of the NWP and Awadh for the context of the Congress cannot be minimized. The tempo was slow initially but within a few years it established a foothold in this province. Incidents elsewhere had repercussions here, as it endeavoured to become part of the mainstream of the Congress movement. Sometimes biased, sometimes neutral, sometimes casteist, sometimes secular—the language newspapers gradually became a force to be reckoned with as they were the media through which the common man became aware of what was going on elsewhere.

The Congress Session at Allahabad in 1888

In 1888 preparations were made for the fourth session of the Congress at Allahabad. This was the first time that the province was hosting a session and naturally there was tremendous excitement all around. The Allahabad session proved to be an extremely important session indeed and many latent forces came into the forefront. To express sympathy with the National Congress, public meetings were held at Lucknow and Kanpur, where supporters like Raja Rampal Singh and Pandit Ajodhianath delivered speeches on the aims and objects of the National Congress.[53] In fact, meetings of the Congress were held in most major cities. At Agra and Aligarh, for example, the speeches of Pandit Ajodhianath impressed the participants considerably. What was interesting was the eagerness on the part of the Congressmen to emphasize their loyalty to the government. The meeting at Agra ended on a typical note, 'The meeting came to a conclusion with three cheers for Her Majesty, three for the Congress and three for the President.'[54]

However, there was no dearth of opponents who identified the Congress with disloyalty. The *Aligarh Institute Gazette* became the spokesman for Sir Syed Ahmad. He said 'The Congress is nothing more or less than a civil war without the use of arms.'[55] Thus the situation in 1888 was full of ominous portents. The future turmoil could not be visualized or prophesied, but seeds of disaffection had begun to sprout. Muslims were divided into the Aligarh group, others who opposed the Congress and Sir Syed, and followers of the Congress.

The Congress session scheduled for Allahabad in 1888 was a jolt for the Muslims. Several anti-Congress meetings were held to nullify the effect of Congress meetings all over the province. The *Aligarh Institute Gazette* reported an anti-Congress meeting at Shahjahanpur on the same day as a Congress meeting was held there. Resolutions to the effect were passed, that if any Muslim from Shahjahanpur attended the Congress at Allahabad, he would not represent the whole community.[56] Meetings were held at other places too, and the invective also found its way into the pages of those language newspapers which were anti-Congress. A meeting was reportedly held at the Kaisarbagh Baradari at Lucknow which was attended by 20,000 people. Under the chairmanship of Munshi Imtiaz Ali, resolutions were passed expressing opposition to the Congress and condemning Ajodhianath's speech.[57] This meeting had allegedly 'convinced all classes from the princes of the ex-Royal Oudh Family to chandu smokers of the mischievous character of the Congress. . . .'[58]

Besides Muslim opposition, many Hindu taluqdars too came out openly against the Congress. Perfect examples were the Maharaja of Benares (Varanasi) and Raja Shiva Prasad, C.S.I. The latter doubted the integrity of the delegates elected at Varanasi. The language newspapers condemned him as a selfish man, interested in forwarding himself in the name of patriotism.[59] Newspapers owned by taluqdars too took an anti-Congress stance, and they were as vociferous in their condemnation as the Muslims. The *Oudh Akhbar*, owned by Munshi Nawal Kishore, called the movement seditious and warned the government that if educated people were allowed to preach sedition and denounce the government, a general rebellion was sure to break out throughout the country.[60]

There was no better space for the volley of accusations and counter-accusations regarding the Congress than the pages of the language press. While the opponents were trying their utmost to prove the limited following of the Congress movement, the followers were stressing upon its wide following. By continuously pointing out the cosmopolitan membership of the Congress, they were trying to prove its national character.

It was in this atmosphere that the Congress held its fourth session at Allahabad in 1888. Pandit Ajodhianath was the President of the Congress Committee and Raja Rampal Singh its Secretary. Already expenses had begun to bother the delegates.[61] The government was sceptical about the sincerity of the delegates and explained away the interest taken by important men like Raja Rampal Singh, owner of the *Hindustan* and taluqdar of the Pratapgarh district, as being motivated by selfish interests. The Deputy Commissioner cryptically wrote about him, 'His intense vanity and a wish to render himself conspicuous by some means or other, are at the root of all his Congress vapourings.' He believed the Raja to be well disposed to the English. 'His marriage with a European wife has placed him in an isolated position, and his restless vanity needs some outlet. . . .'[62]

The previous goodwill displayed by Dufferin to the three Congress sessions underwent a change. Writers have blamed the language press for spreading rumours about Dufferin trying to create a rift between Hindus and Muslims, which infuriated him. His stance towards the Allahabad session changed completely. Colvin, the Lt.-Governor, was also responsible for this change. Hume's report of the third session was circulating and was winning a lot of support locally. Colvin warned Dufferin that the pamphlets were seditious and would create distrust in the minds of the people towards the British. He was convinced that the Muslim leaders were considering the Congress as synonymous with Hindu supremacy and the taluqdars of Awadh were regarding it as a threat to landed interests.[63] To an extent Colvin was justified in his views, though he miscalculated the Muslim interest and saw it only in terms of Sir Syed and Beck.

At the Allahabad session, held after Dufferin's departure, the atmosphere was so charged that people feared this session would be the death-knell of the Congress. Some writers have given the credit for the thumping success it proved to be to Ajodhianath's efforts.[64] There were 1,248 delegates while at Madras there had been only 607. The administrarion of the NWP under the directive of Colvin played the undignified role of obstructing the holding of the session at the proposed site. However, there was so much enthusiasm that local people made arrangements for the needs of the delegates and it was held in a private building to beat the obstructionist actions of the government.[65]

A special feature of the Allahabad Congress was the association of Anglo-Indians[66] and Muslims with it. It was attended by 965 Hindus and 221 Muslims, at Madras the attendance had been 492 Hindus and 81 Muslims.[67] Hamid Ali Khan, the eminent barrister of Lucknow, was effective in stopping the torrent of Muslim opposition, and there was a feeling of camaraderie between the two communities. George Allen, the editor of the *Pioneer*, too was there and supported the resolution for the expansion of the Legislative Councils. There was a definite shift among the ranks of even henceforth antagonistic Muslims like Ameer Ali, in favour of the Congress. Ali professed sympathy with Congress, but before any positive result could emerge out of this, the government allegedly bought him over by appointing him a judge in place of Justice Romesh Chandra.[68] In the Congress membership, besides aristocrats and landowners were many of the middle-class consisting of 'native' lawyers, school masters and news paper editors who formed its base. The average peasant kept away from it, which provided its critics with a handle. The language Press was growing more and more vocal and the success of the Allahabad Congress gave it a boost. The boldness of the press was exemplified in the interesting observations of the *Hindustan* of 12 January 1889 on the anti-Congress memorial presented by some Muslims and Hindu taluqdars. The Raja of Bhinga and Munshi Newal Kishore were singled out for criticism. About the Raja, it wrote,

> The word 'bhinga' means a worm, and a worm looks for a hole even in a golden pillar, but in vain; similarly the Raja of Bhinga endeavoured to find out some faults in the National Congress, but when he could discover no fault, he got up the memorial above referred to.[69]

Munshi Newal Kishore was accused of desisting from joining the movement for selfish reasons despite his liking for it. 'Munshi Newal Kishore says that he receives two lakhs of rupees from government every year on account of printing work done by him for it . . . .'[70]

All this reaction seemed rather intense as Congress had only stuck to its earlier stand and even its protests were rather innocuous. Protests were made about certain recommendations of the Public Service Commission, which were considered injurious to 'natives'. A reduction of public expenditure was desired, particularly in the military department.[71] Pro-Congress papers like the *Hindustan* urged the holding of a Provincial Conference at Lucknow or Varanasi to take steps towards redressal of the grievances in NWP and Awadh, and promotion of prosperity. These provincial matters were presently beyond the purview of the National Congress.[72]

THE CONGRESS MOVEMENT BETWEEN 1888 AND 1898

In November 1886 a Legislative Council had been established for the NWP and Awadh. The Lt.-Governor and Chief Commissioner of Awadh was now the Lt.-Governor of the provinces.[73] Most of the members of the Provincial Legislative Councils were reappointed, including Pandit Ajodhianath, and Colvin was hailed for his justice and fair play by the pro-Congress press. Sir Syed's reappointment was naturally resented![74]

Delegates were elected at many places in the NWP and Awadh for the next Congress at Bombay. Enthusiasm was great and delegates were elected at Kanpur, Jhansi, Shahjahanpur, Meerut, Saharanpur,

Aligarh, Varanasi, Mirzapur, etc. The names which stood out were of Pandit Prithvi Nath of Kanpur, Babu Sita Ram of Jhansi, Maulvi Muhammad Sakhawat Hussain of Shahjahanpur, Pandit Madan Mohan Malviya, Pandit Kashi Nath, Babu Sri Ram and Babu Ram Kali Choudhari. The loyalty of the Congress was repeatedly stressed, the presence of Muslims in good number was publicized. At Shahjahanpur, twelve Hindu and ten Muslim delegates were reportedly elected.[75]

In the meanwhile, another crisis arose, when Hume threatened to sever his connections with the National Congress if the Provincial Congress Committee did not make adequate arrangements for providing thirty to forty thousand rupees a year to meet the expenses of the agency of the Congress in England. The newspapers termed this 'temporary insanity' and haste on Hume's part.[76] Hume stuck to his demand as he felt all Congressmen to be 'the creation of Great Britain—of British learning, history and literature, and with British rule you stand or fall'.[77]

In the meanwhile Lord Cross proposed a bill in Parliament for the expansion of the Legislative Councils. It was purely according to official appointment, and additional members increased, very few. The Congress was not satisfied and wanted Bradlaugh's Bill to be implemented.[78] Meetings were held all over NWP and Awadh to discuss this. The anti-Congress papers alleged that at these meetings, Muslim Congressmen were still insisting on their demand that an equal number of Hindu and Muslim representatives should be present in the Councils.[79] The Congress was accused of misrepresenting facts regarding Muslim delegates. Mirza Garami Qadar Bahadur, a member of the ex-royal family of Delhi, was represented by the *Advocate* of Lucknow as a supporter of the Congress. This gentleman allegedly denied any such affiliations, at the same time accepting that the Congress made all efforts to win him over by giving expensive gifts![80]

With the growing Hindu-Muslim acrimony, the government too became more rigid and suspicious. A major section of the press, however, still loudly proclaimed Congress loyalty to the government. The spirit of the Congress was aptly illustrated by the *Oudh Punch* in a cartoon in which a 'native' lady called Jamuna was shown to be pouring water marked 'loyalty, wealth and greatness' and a European lady called Ganga pouring water marked 'education, protection and peace'—both streams uniting as the Indian National Congress.[81] However, the spirit of rebellion was evident in the columns of a section of the language press. They highlighted the miserable economic condition of the people, but still stressed the desire of Indians to make British rule in India permanent if the government complied with their demands.[82]

Besides pestilence and deprivation, the racial discrimination practised by British officials and the denial of proper access of the Indians to law, were matters resented by the Congress and presented time and again in their supportive newspapers. Pandit Hriday Narain's case at Kanpur was one that created a furore and the language newspapers were divided in their opinions on it. I must mention the fact that though the Congress had earlier decided not to subsidize language newspapers, there were papers which were definitely supportive. This was because many Congressmen were also editors of some papers, Raja Rampal Singh of *Hindustan* and Babu Ganga Prasad Verma of *Hindustani* among others. On the other hand, the major Congress antagonists, the *Oudh Akhbar* of Munshi Nawal Kishore and *Aligarh Institute Gazette* of Sir Syed Ahmad, were subsidized by the Local Government. These would naturally highlight the misdemeanours and mistakes of the Congress.[83] Papers like the *Azad*, which opposed the national movement on account of its identification with Hindus, opposed any matter supported by the Congress.

The Congress Movement at a Low Ebb

Interest in the Congress started to wane after this, as was highlighted by the 'anti' papers.[84] The protagonists of the Congress, naturally denied any such development. The *Zarifu-l-Hind* of Meerut of 15 November 1890 had a thought-provoking cartoon showing the National Congress as a strong and robust child, attacked by a number of Anglo-Indian editors who were ready to stab him, while it appealed to Her Majesty for protection.

The signs of depression were evident. The laxity of the province's Congressmen in collecting funds, and sympathy for the Congress session was evidence of this. Writers like Pratap Narain Misra in their impassioned works like *Suchal-Shiksha* (1891), made pleas for recovering pride in being Indian as this realization of self-respect was a prerequisite for national regeneration. In all his songs, poems, plays, essays or folk ditties, the emotion of pain is always present—pain at the subjection of Indians to the British, at Indians grovelling before the foreigner.[85]

The Allahabad session of the Congress in 1892 was hardly the success the 1888 session had been. Only 625 members came, of which 520 were Hindus and 87 Muslims.[86] The Congressmen who had tried to hold the Congress together by mobilizing funds for its 1892 session, however, expressed satisfaction at the success of the eighth session.[87] They went to the extent of explaining the lower number of delegates by accusing Mr. Crooke, District Magistrate, of having made secret enquiries to find out the names of the donors to the Congress fund and the probable delegates to the Allahabad Congress.[88]

The identification of the Congress with cow protection, which made many local philanthropists patronize the Congress without really understanding its motive, completely anatagonized the Muslims. 1893 saw the outbreak of serious riots on Bakr-Id in Bareilly, Azamgarh and other places. Cow protection societies were held responsible, and Crosthwaite, the Lt.-Governor, hinted that the Congress was involved.[89] The Muslim press approved of Crosthwaite's sagacity. It advised Muslims to keep aloof from all political movements, and accused Congress of throwing 'the apple of discord among the people'.[90] The *Nizam-ul-mulk* went to the extent of saying, 'The Hindus who have made pretty good progress in English education have established the National Congress, of which the movement for protection of cattle is but one off-shoot.'[91] These papers felt that Muslims were really not represented in the National Congress, and only those who were opposed to Sir Syed or were selfish had joined it. Feeling insecure, Muslims made all sorts of protestations to declare their faith in the government with renewed vigour. With the encouragement of Theodore Beck and under the auspices of Sir Syed, was formed the Muhammadan Anglo-Oriental Defence Association of Upper India, in Aligarh. This was meant as a bulwark of English and Muslim people against the devious designs of Hindus and the Congress, whose ultimate aim was expulsion of the British.

The Congress, unhappy with all this Muslim ill-feeling, tried to convince them that the intentions of the nationalists were clean. They desired cohesiveness, which had been broken as a result of the manipulations of the British. The pro-Congress papers completely denied any involvement of the Congress in the riots, or that every Congressman was a member of a Gaurakshini Sabha. These had sprung up only as a reaction to the British mode of administration. 'It might be urged that the Congress is an offspring of these very causes that have given rise to the Sabha in question. Steam is the motive power of all engines, but some of them do useful and others destructive work.'[92] It is interesting to note the presence of some Muslim papers who were against Sir Syed. Some of the Muslim newspapers, who were anti-Congress initially, by 1894 had become neutral if not positively supportive. This could have been because of their contempt for Sir Syed. The *Azad*, a land-owners' paper, was a striking example.

There was opposition to the Congress movement by some orthodox elements who saw it as the epitome of the modernism engendered by the revivalist movements. Orthodox Hindu journalists found fault with educated Hindu youths who maintained the Congress movement.[93] Considering this, how convincing was the accusation that the Congress was associated with pure religious movements like cow protection?

The nationalist leadership too began to disintegrate. Pandit Ajodhianath died in 1892, which was a serious blow. The pro-Congress papers took it as a national calamity.[94] Rampal Singh, with all his fiery invective in his paper, was ambivalent from the start and did not have the calibre of Ajodhianath. He was probably disillusioned with the anti-landlord stance of the Congress and made a volte-face in 1901, completely severing connections with the Congress.[95]

THE REFORM OF THE LEGISLATIVE COUNCILS

The India Council Act of 1892 was a travesty of what Congress had expected from the British. Lord Landsdowne was initially sympathetic with the demand of the Congress for some sort of elective system in the Provincial Councils, but was not in favour of introducing direct election. He felt that even if some Congressmen were elected to the Councils, it would be beneficial to the government, as they would be a means of contact with the people, and would be less harmful within than outside.[96] But the mode of elections as finally emerged in the Provincial Council was hardly acceptable to the discerning classes. The Congressmen feared that the membership could easily be manipulated by the District Collector.

The newspapers gave the example of Deputy Commissioner Mulock, who got himself nominated as an elector by the Lucknow Municipal Board. Hamid Ali Khan, who was being backed by the Congress, had now to contest Babu Sri Ram, Rae Bahadur, the protege of Mulock. When Munshi Jagan Prasad, the Agra delegate, arrived at

Lucknow, Munshi Nawal Kishore and Babu Sri Ram persuaded him to vote for the Babu. Munshi Thakur Prasad, the Bareilly delegate, was all for Hamid Ali Khan when he arrived at Lucknow, but among others, Kunwar Kamta Prasad, tahsildar, put pressure on him, and he finally agreed to vote for Babu Sri Ram. Ultimately, Babu Sri Ram was elected by a majority of one vote. This sort of manipulation was resented by the Congress and the language press appealed to Crosthwaite to prove government's goodwill by avoiding such devious tactics.[97] However, the Congress candidate, Raja Rampal Singh, was elected, and later there were examples of other Congress sympathisers being elected to the Provincial Council. These manipulations, however, resulted in the Muslims getting disaffected. They blamed the Hindus and the elective system propagated by the Congress.[98] Muslim papers were generally taking up isolated cases and incidents in their endeavour to identify Congress as an anti-Muslim organization. The nomination of Muhammad Ismail Khan by government was hailed by the Muslim newspapers, though they did feel disappointed at his neglect of Muslim interests in the Council. The government's design to discourage Muslims from joining the Congress, and brand it as a Hindu organization, was obvious. The Muslim candidate, Hamid Ali, was unable to get himself elected as he had Congress leanings, while the sycophant Ismail Khan was nominated by the government! The pro-Congress papers felt that Muslims were themselves responsible for their lack of representation in the Council. They had always pandered to the whims of the Anglo-Indian officers, while educated Hindus had had the guts to oppose them and try for the elective system to be introduced. The time was ripe for them to put forward able, energetic and independent men of their community as candidates, and they would surely succeed.[99]

THE CIVIL SERVICE QUESTION

The raising of the age for the Covenanted Civil Service examinations and the simultaneous examination were taken up by the Congress. Ultimately, a resolution was passed in the House of Commons to hold simultaneous Civil Service examinations in England and India. Even when faced with this resolution, Landsdowne refused to yield as he felt that British supremacy in India would be endangered if there were an insufficient number of British Civil Servants to effectively control the administration.[100] His successor, Elgin, also went along with this as he was convinced that Indians were as yet unsuited to manning high posts.[101]

The Muslims were generally happy with this. Haji Muhammad Ismail Khan of Aligarh forwarded a draft resolution to the President-elect of the Calcutta Congress, which affirmed that the Congress considered that half the elected members of the Legislative Councils and the Municipal and Local Boards in British India should be Muslim, and, therefore, called upon Hindus and Muslims to return members to these bodies accordingly in future.[102] The Muslim papers treated this resolution as a yardstick of the good intentions of the Congress towards Muslims.[103] The Hindu papers found this preposterous as elections to Legislative Councils ought to be according to ability and not religion.[104] Perhaps the slow working of the Anglo-Muhammadan Defence Organization made the Muslims desperate for some sort of concession to Muslims, and the ardent support by Sir Syed and his clan resulted in this manifesto.

The outbreak of famine in 1897 and plague between 1896 and 1900 further enervated the Congress movement. The neglect of the social aspect by the Congress was stressed by the opponent pressmen. Moreover, it became evident that Congress supporters were dormant during the year and were neglecting the important task of imparting political education to the people. In fact, the session at Madras had poor attendance by UP Congressmen on account of the plague. However, a Social Conference in connection with the Congress was established in 1898, with the objective of attempting social reform. This progressed as feebly as the political one.[105]

THE CONGRESS SESSION AT LUCKNOW IN 1899

The death of Sir Syed Ahmad in 1898 probably gave a boost to the Congress. The presence of Anthony MacDonnell as Lt.-Governor in the province was also a morale booster. The 1899 Congress session was held at Lucknow. It met with a lot of local official opposition on the plea that delegates from the plague infested areas would spread the dreaded disease to Lucknow. The meeting was ultimately allowed on the Shahmina ground, but delegates were not allowed to go into the city.[106] For this, the Chairman of the reception committee gave full credit to MacDonnell.[107]

Despite this, the local Muslims formed a Committee under the leadership of Mirza Muhammad Abbas, who tried hard to dissuade

FIGURE 1: THE PARTICIPATION OF MUSLIMS IN THE CONGRESS SESSION OF 1899 AT LUCKNOW

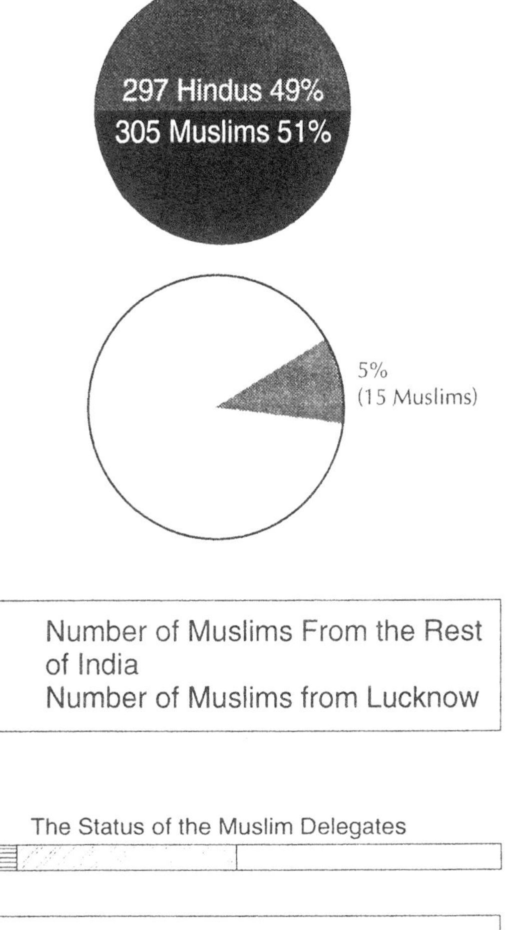

GAD (U.P.) Report of the 15th Indian National Congress held at Lucknow on 27, 28, 29 and 30 December 1899

the Muslims from joining the Congress. But the agitation was unsuccessful in injuring the Congress cause, and reportedly drew more Muslims to the Congress camp. It was a fact that Lucknow had always been free from Hindu-Muslim acrimony, hence the opposition of Muslims could not stand its stead. Congressmen at Lucknow were enthusiastic, and reaffirmed their faith in the British government. The appeal of this meeting was the zeal of the organizers who enthused the audience with emotion-filled oratory. The Chairman assured the members, 'No hostile forces can arrest the march of the Congress movement. It has lighted its beacon on a high rock, against which the waves of opposition will beat in vain.'[108]

However, the taluqdars and the moneyed upper classes remained indifferent to the Congress, and this was attributed to their lack of education as compared to the richer classes in other provinces. Steeped in ignorance, they were 'in constant dread of an inquisitional officialdom'. The financial question, therefore, presented problems to the committee, so it had to raise money by taking small contributions from its sympathisers. The Congressmen hailed the tremendous success of this session. Mr. R.C. Dutt was the President. He professed that 'The Mahrattas and the Bengalis, the Sikhs and the Madrasis, Hindus, Mahomedans, Christians, Parsis—all races, religions, interests were represented there. . . .'[109] Besides the usual political and governmental demands, the Congress bemoaned the condition of the peasantary.

The reaction of the language newspapers to this Congress was, as always, according to their approach towards the national movement. The Muslim papers insisted that 99 per cent of the Muslim community was opposed to it.[110] Another paper emphasised on the low status and still lower incomes of the Muslim candidates.[111] They insisted that it was vainglory on the part of the Congress to attribute the late expansion of the Legislative Councils to their agitation. The Congress movement had resulted in the people losing their privileges rather than gaining them. The new Sedition Act was allegedly the result of the irresponsible outpourings of the Congress newspapers. These papers insisted that the Muslims who attended the Lucknow session were disillusioned with the Congress.[112] When we consider the statistics after studying the attendance list carefully, we may wonder about the depth behind the tall claims of the Congressmen of Muslim support and being a national body. The Muslim delegates were local men and there was a possibility that they had been rounded up by

Congress workers to show numbers. The status of the local Muslim delegates lends credence to the view that they could have been lured by offers of money .[113]

However, the Muslim papers realized the ineffectiveness of the policy of opposing only the Congress. A more mature, though dangerous, outlook took shape. Only those policies of the Congress should be opposed with which Muslims disagreed and which would affect Muslim (rather than national) interests.[114] The presence of MacDonnell and his support to Hindi and finally the Hindi Resolution in 1900, troubled the Muslims and many of them realized the need to depend on their own resources rather than the benevolence of the government.[115]

Disaffected Congress protagonists like Hamid Ali Khan held meetings to decide the steps needed to safeguard future Muslim interests. The need to establish a separate association for Muslims for satisfying their political and social needs was realized.[116] The Hindu papers were not happy with this development and were rather clairvoyant when they said, 'The only mischief likely to be created by the Association will be kindling of the baser feeling of race and class hatred . . . .'[117]

This alienation of Muslims as a whole was miscalculated. MacDonnell was definitely not wholeheartedly for the Congress and considered it a movement of 'an oligarchy of a few thousand persons'. He felt that if neglected ' . . . the government will find itself confronted by an agitation which aims at subverting the present form of government and bringing about a revolution'. MacDonnell compared the Congress to the Estates General in Versailles which had caused such havoc. The latter had also professed loyalty to the government. He feared that the Congressmen would stimulate an uprising playing upon the ignorance of the masses.[118]

MacDonnell's fears appeared to be realized when the Congress undertook to limit its field of discussion to the few vitally important problems relating to the economic and material conditions of the masses. This way, the movement could reach out to all and disabuse the public of the idea that Congress stood for the richer and educated classes.[119]

However, a new kind of leadership was emerging in the Congress and there were constant squabbles between the old and newly-emerged leaders. Two kinds of language newspapers sympathetic to the Congress had cropped up. One believed in the moderation propagated by the established leaders; the other thought a more firm and vigorous policy was required.[120] The attacks of these extremists on the established leadership was unacceptable to many newspapers, who felt these rifts within the ranks would harm the Congress cause. To revive the Congress in UP, a Provincial Political Association was established with headquarters at Lucknow in 1904. Pandit Bishambhar Nath was elected as its President. The Vice-Presidents, including Pandit Sunderlal, as also the Chairman of the committee, belonged to different parts of the country. Pandit M.M. Malviya, who had recently become a member of the Legislative Council, and Dr. Satish Chandra Banerji were appointed secretaries.[121] This body would be a feeder to the National Congress and its British Committee. Much of its activity would be confined to provincial matters—education, administration, industry, etc. It would be non-sectarian and act as a sort of an institution for the representation of the aims and aspirations of the public, at the same time imparting political education. Ten years ago organizations like the Anjuman-i-Rifah-i-Am at Lucknow, the Anjuman-i-Tahzib at Faizabad, the Kashi Arya Samaj and Sarvajanik Sabha at Varanasi, and the Hindu Samaj at Allahabad had cropped up, but only to wind up later. This new organization was stated to be an organized central body.[122]

The Muslims took this development as a design to eliminate them from the scheme of things. The time was ripe for them to form their own political association. It would aid government in apprising it of the needs of the repressed minority[123] and would have complete confidence in the government. The result was the joining up of the Aligarh School and other UP Muslims, who undertook a journey to Dacca, where in a session chaired by Viqar-ul-Mulk, the All-India Muslim League was founded on 30 December 1906.[124].

The Partition of Bengal

Curzon's partition of Bengal in 1905 sparked off a wild reaction all over India. It precipitated an emotional outburst, and gave a fresh lease of life to the Congress movement. It is one of the pleasant ironies of history that he who criticized his predecessors for patting infant nationalism on the back, left behind a 'formed opposition', strong and violently stirring.

By the time the Congress met in December 1905 at Varanasi, the agitation had spread like wild fire. The Varanasi session was presided over by G.K. Gokhale who condemned the partition, but in temperate language.[125] Congress leaders like Gokhale and S.N. Banerjea were apparently gratified at the success of the method they had been recommending; but a new brand of agitation creeping into the Congress was threatening to displace earlier liberalism. The year 1905 marked an epoch as far as the Congress movement was concerned as the rise of the extremist element in its ranks became obvious and pronounced, culminating in the Surat Split of 1907, where S.N. Banerjea, 'the hero of a hundred platforms, grey-beard, son of thunder', was disgraced and humiliated.[126]

Two important movements resulted from this partition—the Boycott movement and the Swadeshi movement. Government posts and foreign goods had to be boycotted, and goods made in India had to be used. The government accused the Congress of using Swadeshi as a political weapon, and the turmoil was described as 'the popular agitation which began in Boycott and ended in Swadeshism'.[127] The government view was upheld by some Indian newspapers. Muslims considered Swadeshi an economic and not political movement.[128] They wanted its complete dissociation from the anti-partition movement which they refused to join.

The Congress denied that Swadeshi had been encouraged as a ploy to make the agitation against the partition more forceful. The language newspapers were vehement in their disclaimer of this connection. At Allahabad, Malviya reminded people that Swadeshi had begun in the seventies and eighties. It was not against any government policy, but a genuine effort to improve the economic condition of the people, and to find work for people who, owing to decay of their industries, had reverted to agriculture.[129]

THE COLONIAL CONCEPT OF DIVIDE AND RULE

The responsibility of the government in driving a wedge between the two communities by its policy of misrepresenting the motives of the National Congress was again and again repeated by almost all the newspapers supportive of the Congress. It insidiously motivated Muslims to consider the Congress a Hindu body fighting for administrative, political and social gains calculated to benefit Hindus. The appointment of Auckland Colvin as Lt.-Governor meant the presence of an officer with clear pro-Muslim leanings. His studied anti-Congress actions—instigating Sir Syed Ahmad and Munshi Newal

Kishore to check the movement; instructing district officers to prevent men from joining the Congress; pandering to the Muslim whims; convincing Dufferin of the deviousness of Hume and the Congress—contributed to making the Congress claims of a 'national' movement questionable.[130] Taluqdars were won over by offers of special privileges and they chanted anti-Congress slogans obligingly.[131] The incitement of emotions on religious grounds was done in an unobstrusive manner.

Crosthwaite was witness to the terrible riots in 1893 which swept away rational thought. His speech at Ballia, where he blamed Hindus, swept aside all expectations that Hindus would get a better deal at his hands.[132] Consequently, the suspicion of deviousness behind every move of the government became firmly entrenched in the minds of the Congressmen, even as they never desisted from professing their loyalty.

Even a compassionate Lt.-Governor like Sir Anthony MacDonnell, whom the Congress hailed as a true friend, created turmoil—this time in the minds of the Muslims—his Hindi Resolution of 1900. He observed:

> The people at large may be contented or at least not discontented, but we should be blind indeed not to see that there is a large number of people, collectively a great population, who hate us and our rule, who would welcome the excitement of insurrection or invasion, and who are ready to show what they feel if they get the opportunity. These dangerous classes are now scattered and disunited; ours will be the fault if we give them the means of coming together under pretext of taking part in a political agitation.[133]

CONCLUSION

The colonialists, thus, by following a policy of repression, constriction, social management, evasion and communal jugglery were able to keep the people confused and uncertain as to the real motives of the government or even their own countrymen. The language press was the constant feature from beginning to end which reported and evaluated the prevalent social, political, economic, educational and cultural phenomena. Sometimes deliberately, sometimes coincidentally, it dwelled upon the interdependence of these seemingly heterogeneous factors. The politicization of non-political issues created a variety of socio-economic permutations, the genesis of which might have already existed and only required to be emphasized and articulated. This was done by the government, and, inadvertently, by a still-evolving language press which was wrought with innumerable problems and had to keep itself afloat against heavy odds.

NOTES

1. D.A. Low (ed.), *Soundings in Modern South Asian History*, Berkeley, 1968, p. 4.
2. Ravinder Kumar, *Essays in the Social History of Modern India*, Delhi, 1983, p. 2.
3. Ibid.
4. Anil Seal, *Emergence of Indian Nationalism: Competition and Collaboration in the later 19th Century*, London, 1968, pp. 20-2.
5. Ibid., pp. 115-17.
6. Low, op.cit., p. 1.
7. A.C. Lyall to Dufferin, 4 June 1885. D.P. 47 (Reel 528).
8. Sudhir Chandra, *Dependence and Disillusionment: Emergence of National Consciousness in the Later 19th Century India*, New Delhi, 1975, p. 43.
9. *Arunoday*, in G.W. Kurkaray's report, 24 June 1880; Home Deptt. Public Proceedings, B, July 1880, No. 181.
10. Seal, op.cit., p. 255.
11. Ibid., p. 256.
12. Sudhir Chandra, *Literature and the Colonial Connection (Occasional Papers on History and Society)*, New Delhi, 1983, pp. 30-1.
13. Ibid., pp. 4-6 and 30.
14. Harish Chandra started the *Kavi Vachan Sudha* from Benaras in 1868, Radha Charan Goswami named his monthly journal *Bharatendu* (1883-6) published in Brindaban, Pratap Narain Misra started the monthly *Brahman* from Kanpur, Balkrishna Bhatt started the *Hindi Pradip* from Allahabad.
15. Sudhir Chandra, op.cit., *Dependence and Disillusionment*, pp. 1-17.
16. Seal, op.cit., pp. 172-7.
17. Ibid., p. 28.
18. Ibid., pp. 10-16.
19. Bipan Chandra, Amalesh Tripathi and Barun De, *Freedom Struggle*, New Delhi, 1972, p. 9.
20. Sudhir Chandra, op.cit., *Literature and the Colonial Connection*, pp. 4-16.
21. Bipan Chandra, op.cit., pp. 16-35.
22. Special Report on the Civil Service Question—S.N. Banerjea, p. 14.
23. Sir Verney Lovett, *A History of the Indian National Movement*, London, 1920, p. 33.

24. S.R. Mehrotra, *India and the Commonwealth*, London, 1965, p. 16; Low, op.cit., p. 1.
25. Prem Narain, op.cit., p. 47.
26. Mehrotra, op.cit., p. 16, cited in Dr. Padmasha.
27. Dufferin to Kimberley, 17 May 1886, D.P. 19 (Reel 517).
28. Dufferin to Cross, 18 Jan. 1887, D.P. 29 (Reel 518).
29. Paul R. Brass, *Factional Politics in an Indian State: The Congress Party in U.P.*, Bombay, 1966.
30. The Vernacular Newspapers Reports of NWP and Oudh, 1885-6.
31. Brass, op.cit., p. 20.
32. RDPI, Oudh, 1875, p. 10, cited in Anil Seal, op.cit., pp. 306-7.
33. Ibid.
34. Syed Ahmad Khan, A speech on the Institution of the British India Association, NWP, Aligarh, 1867, pp. 3-7.
35. Tarachand, *History of the Freedom Movement in India*, New Delhi, 1967, Vol. 2, p. 358.
36. Ibid., p. 11.
37. Ram Gopal, op.cit., cited from Proceedings of the Council of the Governor-General in 1883.
38. Seal, op.cit., p. 328.
39. Ibid., p. 335.
40. Brass, op.cit., p. 229; Raghuraj Gupta, op.cit.
41. Low, op.cit., pp. 1-8.
42. Gupta, op.cit., p. 39.
43. Low, op.cit., pp. 1-8.
44. Ibid., pp. 9-12.
45. Bayly, op.cit., pp. 108-10.
46. A short account of the Kayastha Conference, Part I, pp. 1-16.
47. Ibid., p. 328.
48. Bayly, op.cit., pp. 117-33.
49. Ibid., p. 135.
50. Ibid., pp. 122-3.
51. Seal, op.cit., pp. 250-6.
52. (a) Press Memorandum for Upper India—Home Public B, March 1886, 122-4; April 1887, 201-3; Sept. 1891, 129-35; (b) Home Public A, Oct. 1894, 143-6; (c) Cited in Bayly, op.cit., pp. 120-1.
53. *Hindustan*, Kalakànkar, 26 April 1888.
54. VNR of UP, *Nasim-i-Agra*, 15 Oct. 1888.
55. *Aligarh Institute Gazette*, 4 Feb. 1888.
56. *Aligarh Institute Gazette*, 13 Oct. 1888.
57. VNR of UP, *Azad*, Lucknow, 11 May 1888.
58. VNR of UP, *Alam-i-Taswir*, Kanpur, 25 May 1888.
59. *Bharat Jiwan*, Varanasi, 23 July 1888; VNR of NWP&O, *Bharat Bandhu*, Aligarh, 27 July 1888.

60. VNR of NWP&O, *Oudh Akhbar*, Lucknow, 28 June 1888.
61. *Hindustan*, Kalakankar, March 1888.
62. Home Public B, June 1890; 126-8. Report on Vernacular Newspapers of Upper India for 1889.
63. Briton-Martin, Jr., *New India 1885, British Official Policy and the Emergence of the Indian National Congress*, Bombay, 1970, pp. 327-8.
64. S.P. Sen, Editor of *The Indian Press*.
65. Prem Narain, op.cit., pp. 24-5.
66. Lovett, op.cit., puts this number at 6 consisting of the discontented, non-official class who claimed they were disfranchised in India, pp. 42-3.
67. K.K. Aziz, *Britain and Muslim India*, London, 1963, Chapter II.
68. Prem Narain, op.cit., pp. 26-8.
69. *Hindustan*, Kalakankar, 12 Jan. 1889.
70. Ibid.
71. *Hindustan*, Aug. 1889.
72. Ibid.
73. Home Judicial A, Nov. 1886. Nos. 256-9.
74. VNR of NWP&O, *Najm-ul-Hind*, Moradabad, 1889.
75. VNR of NWP&O, 1889: *Nasim-i-Agra*, 7 Dec.; *Bharat Jiwan*, Varanasi, 9 Dec.; VNR of NWP&O, *Nasim-i-Sahar*, Mirzapur, 11 Dec.
76. *Hindustan*, Kalakankar, 16 Nov. 1889.
77. Ibid.
78. *Hindustan*, Lucknow, 14 March 1890; VNR of NWP&O; *Hindustani*, Lucknow, 9 March 1889.
79. VNR of NWP&O, *Azad*, 25 April 1890, referred to the Congress meeting at Lucknow, saying Munshi Hidayat Rasul passed a motion saying that the representation in the Council should be of both Hindus and Muslims in equal number. The paper alleged that great confusion resulted.
80. VNR of NWP&O, *Oudh Akhbar*, Lucknow, 27 May 1890.
81. *Oudh Punch*, Lucknow, 2 Jan. 1889.
82. VNR of NWP&O, *Tohfa-i-Hind*, Bijnor, 27 May 1890.
83. *Hindustan*, Kalakankar, 23 May 1890.
84. VNR of NWP&O, *Akhbar-i-Alam*, Meerut, 15 July 1890.
85. Sudhir Chandra, op.cit., *Literature and the Colonial Connection*, pp. 29-30.
86. Aziz, op.cit.
87. Malviya, Bishambar Nath, Babu Charn Dhunder Mitter, Ajodhianath and lecturers from Delhi, Bareilly and Meerut; Bayly, op.cit., pp. 140-1; *Hindustan*, Kalakankar, 3 Jan. 1892.
88. VNR of UP, *Khichri Samachar*, Mirzapur, 7 Jan. 1892.
89. Crosthwaite to Landsdowne, 18 Aug. 1893, Landsdowne Correspondence, Microfilm at NAI.

90. VNR of NWP&O, *Najm-ul-Akhbar*, Etawah, 24 and 28 Aug. 1893.
91. VNR of NWP&O, *Nizam-ul-mulk*, Moradabad, 16 Sept. 1893.
92. *Oudh Punch*, Lucknow of 31 Aug. 1893.
93. VNR of UP, *Nagri-Nirad*, Mirzapur, 14, 21, 28 Feb. 1895.
94. VNR of UP, 1892: *Prayag Samachar*, Allahabad, 14 Jan.; *Hindustan*, Lucknow, 13 Jan.; *Bharat Jiwan*, Varanasi; *Cawnpore Gazette*, *Sitara-i-Hind*, Moradabad, Jan.
95. Bayly, op.cit., pp. 146-7, *English Hindustan*, Kalakankar, 12 Aug. 1901.
96. Landsdowne to Harris, 10 June 1893. Landsdowne Papers Series VII, Vol. 9, Part 2, No. 345. Also Landsdowne to Wenlock, 22 July 1893, Landsdowne Papers Series VII, Vol. 10, Part 2, No. 35.
97. VNR of NWP&O, *Hindustani*, Lucknow, 3 May, 14 June; *Hindustan*, Kalakankar, 4 May 1893.
98. VNR of NWP&O, *Najm-ul-Akhbar*, Etawah, 28 Sept. 1893.
99. VNR of NWP&O, *Hindustani*, Lucknow, 8 May 1896.
100. S. Gopal, op.cit., p. 191.
101. Letters to Rosebery, 7 July 1895, Elgin Papers. Correspondence with People in England, Vol. 2, Part. 2, No. 51 and to Hamilton 23 Dec. 1896; Hamilton Correspondence, D 509/3 for. 439ff.
102. VNR of NWP&O, *Azad*, Lucknow, 27 Nov. 1896.
103. VNR of NWP&O, 1896: *Nur-ul-Anwar*, Kanpur, 25 Nov.; *Aligarh Institute Gazette*, 28 Nov.; *Police News*, 1 Dec.; *Akhbar-i-Alam*, Meerut, 1 Dec.; *Dabir-i-Hind*, Agra, 1 Dec.; *Naiyar-i-Azam*, Moradabad, 5 Dec.; *Mufid-i-Am*, Agra, 1 Dec.
104. VNR of NWP&O, *Hindustani*, Lucknow, 9 Dec. 1896, *Jami-ul-Ulum*, Moradabad, 7 Dec. 1896.
105. VNR of NWP&O, 1898: *Jami-ul-Ulum*, Moradabad, 28 Jan.; *Bharat Jiwan*, Varanasi, 14 Nov.; *Hindustani*, Lucknow, 30 Nov., 21 Dec.
106. GAD, UP, File No. 385C, 1899.
107. GAD, UP, Report of the 15th Indian National Congress held at Lucknow on 27, 28, 29 and 30 Dec. 1899, p. 15.
108. Ibid., pp. 16-17.
109. Ibid., p. 19.
110. VNR of UP *Liberal*, Azamgarh, 1 Jan. 1900.
111. *Indian Daily Telegraph*, Lucknow, 1900.
112. VNR of UP, *Riaz-ul-Akhbar*, Gorakhpur, 4 March 1900.
113. See diagram on p. 185.
114. VNR of UP, *Al Bashir*, Etawah, 16 July 1900.
115. Ibid., 12 Aug. 1901.
116. VNR of UP, *Hindustani*, Lucknow, 30 Oct. 1901.
117. VNR of UP, *Advocate*, Lucknow, 31 Oct. 1901.
118. MS English History C 355, BPD 6368, MacDonnell Papers.
119. VNR of UP, *Kayasth Samachar*, Allahabad, Dec. 1902.

120. Ibid., Nov. 1902.
121. VNR of UP, *Indian People*, Allahabad, 23 July 1904.
122. VNR of UP, *Advocate*, Lucknow, 16 April 1903.
123. *Advocate*, Lucknow, 20 Aug. 1903.
124. Robinson, op.cit., pp. 148-9.
125. VNR of NWP&O, *Indian People*, Allahabad, 4 Jan. and 28 Dec. 1905; *Advocate*, Lucknow, 4 Jan. 1906.
126. Prem Narain, op.cit., pp. 56-64.
127. Home Public B, June 1906, Nos. 102-4, Vernacular Newspapers in 1905, p. 920.
128. Vernacular Newspapers in 1905, p. 21.
129. VNR of NWP&O, *Advocate*, Lucknow, 10 Sept. 1905; 'Swadeshism means ill-feeling towards nobody, no rousing of hatred or class-feeling towards anybody or class of persons. It means a desire to supply our own needs by manufacturing them in the country and to husband the country's resources; and has thus no political significance. The Swadeshi movement is one of those few movements which ought to bring people of all classes and of opinions on one common platform and rouse in them the feeling of patriotism.'
130. VNR of NWP&O, *Hindustani*, Lucknow, 20 July 1892.
131. VNR of UP, *Rahbar*, Moradabad, 9 Aug. 1892.
132. VNR of UP, *Godharm Prakash*, Farukhabad, Sept. 1893.
133. MS English History C 355, BPD 6368, MacDonnell Papers—From the Bodelian Library, Oxford, Confidential-Congress.

7. The Nationalistic Upheaval

The possibility of catharsis in any socio-political-psychological scenario is always looming in the background of any polity. The actions of men, the events that follow, and more important, the conducive environment that exists, all generate such a cornucopia of feeling that the professed innocuousness of the action or the event is belied. The ideological conviction present in the minds of the people since time immemorial, however dormant, receives a fresh impetus. The partition of Bengal, engineered by Lord Curzon in 1905, was one such event.

The simple nationalism that had emanated out of patriotism and had been the prerogative of the Congress party, gradually eroded old beliefs and became more communal and political. Amidst all this change, the British could not be expected to remain quiet. They had got used to relatively quiescent subjects and found it rather tiresome to handle the new querulousness.

If the partition of Bengal had spurred on nationalism, it had definitely given a new life to the language newspapers. The latter suddenly found that they had no dearth of opportunities to ventilate national grievances. Almost all leading luminaries of the national movement were owners, or editors, or patrons of the language papers. The efficacy of the latter was at no time in the past felt so strongly as now. They became a means through which national regeneration could be effected.

NATIONALISM REJUVENATED

The confusing socio-political-economic forces that were let loose baffled the British government. Mahatma Gandhi in his *Hind Swaraj* in 1908 explained neo-nationalism and its effectiveness very clearly.

> The shock the British power received through the partition has never been equalled by any other act. . . . Hitherto we have considered that, for the redress of grievances, we must approach the throne and if we get no redress we must sit still except that we may still petition. After the partition, people saw that petitions must be backed by force and that they must be capable of

suffering. This new spirit must be considered to be the chief result of the partition.[1]

Radical Nationalism

A group of people emerged who believed in forcibly securing their rights from the government. Though these sections, both outside and inside the Congress, were reportedly not very effective in the United-Provinces, they still perpetrated radical ideas that had an enormous influence on the public mind.[2]

While moderate factions called these forward thinking men extremists, the latter preferred to call themselves nationalists. The radicals considered their mission noble and praiseworthy. 'The word "nationalist" . . . does not denote one who belongs to a nation strictly so called, but it simply signifies a person whose mission in life is to create and foster ideas of nationalism among the people and thus contribute towards the growth of the nation.'[3] The fiery Tilak felt that the words 'moderates' and 'extremists' had 'a specific relation to time. The extremists of today will be moderates of tomorrow, just as the moderates of today were extremists yesterday.'[4] The moderates regarded their more impatient brethren as anarchists, not loyal or law-abiding.[5] The Muslims, though lukeworm in their opposition to the government, had a revolutionary section among themselves, who felt that the men labelled as anarchists were just free thinkers. They asserted that the time was fast approaching when the self-seeking leaders of the present day would be discarded and 'when the suggestions of those who at present styled carping critics, will mould the policy of the community'.[6] Although the British accepted that all extremists were not violent, they still felt that 'The distribution of the least violent form of sedition is, as might be expected, very much the same as that of the terrorist movement, and there is no doubt a close connection between the two. . . .'[7]

Causes of the Growth of Radical Nationalism

That this period saw the perpetuation of a tremendous patriotic fervour is undeniable.

1. The *psycho-spiritual* aspect lay behind the particular idea of revolutionary nationalism that gripped the mind of a generation of Indian leaders in the last decade of the nineteenth and the first decade of the twentieth centuries. Spiritually, it countered the threat to

traditional Hindu religious ethics and social values posed by Christianity and utilitarianism, and Brahmanism, which was influenced by both. Believers in this form of nationalism were repelled by the inferiority complex of the anglicized Indian, but propagated the equally unhealthy superiority complex of the conservative and orthodox Indian. While the old guard preached secular nationalism, the revolutionaries took their source from neo-Vedantism. It led to the particularization of Hindus as a religious and political community. Consequently, many joined the Hindu Mahasabha and other communal organizations.[8]

Bankim Chandra, Vivekananda and Aurobindo Ghose were the luminaries on whose philosophical and spiritual convictions the revolutionary movement was based. Bankim extolled the virtues of Sri Krishna and his emphasis on Dharamrajya and Dharmayuddha was not missed by the revolutionary nationalists. Dharamrajya was equated with Swarajya and passive resistance with Dharmayuddha.[9] Aurobindo was not a pacifist and in his essays on the *Gita* he said that Dharmayuddha was necessary to kill enemies. Vivekananda's philosophy emphasized the corrosion from within by the canker of materialism of the West. Inner richness had been sacrificed for wealth and glory. Dayananda Saraswati's stress on the dogma of 'Vedic infallibility' was used by these radicals to counter and challenge the Christian and Islamic dogma of supernatural revelation. Most of these revolutionary nationalistic philosophers brought out their own newspapers to express these ideas. The *Karmayogi* started at Allahabad in 1909 on Janmashtami day was to further the cause of these forward-thinking men. It insisted on fighting oppression and felt that the country's regeneration was only possible if a true balance between materialism and spiritualism was maintained. People should look back to the Vedas and Hindu beliefs for encouragement and should not depend for their progress on the methods of the foreigner.

The ideology of nationalism was stressed by these philosophical revolutionaries. Freedom, in the sense of political liberty, was not the consequence but the pre-condition of freedom in the sense of liberation of the soul. The language press championing the cause of these revolutionary nationalists emphasized this connection between politics and spirituality. The latent desire for nationalism could be aroused by appealing to the emotions of the people.

2. Another reason for the advent of radicalism was the basic identification of the Indian National Congress with slackness, torpidity,

tameness and quiescence. Language papers with moderate leanings extolled the Congress and its achievements. 'The Indian Congress has not existed in vain these twenty years. It has been doing great work of schooling the Indian heart in self-forgetting patriotism ever since it was started into being.'[10] The moderates followed constitutional methods. Popular sovereignty was fraught with the danger of possible violence and terrorism, and the moderates thus regarded it as morally and politically repugnant. Extremists, however, considered the existing Congress policy 'emasculating'. As Aurobindo said, 'We do not want to develop a nation of women who know only how to suffer and not how to strike.'[11] As a language newspaper gleefully affirmed, 'The moderates maintained that even walls have ears, while the extremists would not mind crying from housetops.'[12] The faith of the moderates in the Liberal Party in England seemed incongruous to the extremists who saw the British, however liberal, as colonialists who may dole out palliatives but would never willingly surrender power.

There was a wide discrepancy in their aims too. The issues were similar but both perceived them differently. This was enough to incite the revolutionary nationalists into reacting strongly and imprudently. Both held the British responsible for poverty in India, but the extremists felt that economic regeneration was only possible after the overthrow of colonial rule. Gokhale, a moderate, agreed that Swadeshi was laudable, but felt uneasy about boycott of foreign articles, especially British goods, as he felt it would be politicizing an economic issue. He found the giving up of government jobs by Indians acceptable, but highly theoretical.

The extremists felt differently. They saw the necessity to streamline their own special brand of Swadeshi, Boycott and Swaraj, to counter moderate pessimism and an overoptimistic regard for British benevolence. To Tilak and Lajpat they meant a moral training in self-help, determination and also a weapon for political agitation. Swadeshi meant preference for one's own people and for articles manufactured in one's own country. Love for one's own country was the chief tenet of Hindu belief. All imported articles should be boycotted, especially British goods and institutions, to revive the dying arts and industries. National education was a symbol of patriotism, and education would be under national control.[13] Boycott was an assertion of the will of the nation against the economic, political and spiritual oppression that the dominant nation universally inflicts on its subjects. Tilak was precise in enunciating the dream of the nationalists. 'Swadeshi is the first step, Boycott is the means, and Swaraj is the end.'[14] Boycott and Swadeshi were inseparable and it was necessary to restrict boycott to a limited number of foreign imports in order to make the Swadeshi movement an enormous success.

The economic background of the extremists is the reason given by the communists as the main cause of their severance from the moderates. They equate the moderates with those of the bourgeoisie who had ties with British capital, and the fuedal lords, and who simultaneously favoured the development of native capitalist enterprise. They were the money-lenders, the commerce wizards, industrialists, lawyers, and public servants. They predictably identified Swadeshi with 'economic autonomy'. The extremists were petty landlords, the small commercial bourgeoisie, lowly paid clerks, craftsmen and artisans, and unemployed students. These were generally penurious, trying to eke out a living somehow.[15]

3. The Congress regarded the growth of the extremist consciousness as a natural consequence of the turmoil created by the partition of Bengal, thus implying its temporary character. Pandit Motilal Nehru, remarked 'Extremism is only the natural outcome of the present condition of things in Bengal.'[16] The pro-moderate papers also attributed the rise of the radical group to the partition but felt that 'moderates can become extremists in times of extraordinary calamity and extremists are not necessarily wedded to their extreme views under all circumstances'.[17]

4. Hindu revivalism, whether political or religious, upset upper class Muslims. Their reaction had a heightened emotional fervour. At Aligarh, Viqar-ul-Mulk said, 'God forbid, if the Hindus will lord it over; and we will be in constant danger of our life, property and honour.'[18] The advanced party in the Congress resented Muslim arrogance. The Congressmen saw in the partition a victory of Muslim communalism with the benign support of the British. Hindu chauvinism, as projected by extremist leaders, was a reaction to Muslim chauvinism born of the Wahabi movement and nurtured at Aligarh. Though Bankim's 'Hindutva' was not pronounced, Tilak's anti-Muslim bias was not so detached.[19]

Muslim opinion veered in favour of Swadeshi, but perceived it purely as an economic issue. It was laudable and would improve indigenous industries. But Muslims were not prepared to associate it in any way with the anti-partition agitation or with Boycott. While the Swadeshi propagators regarded it as 'deep intense, passionate, all absorbing love of one's country', the Muslims refused to attend meetings of Swadeshi clubs constituted by the Congress. Swaraj or self-government, so dear to the radical element, was completely rejected by the Muslims, who preferred the continuation of British rule to becoming mere tools in the hands of wily Bengalis.[20] *Bande Mataram* which inspired Hindus appeared offensive to many Muslims.[21] The revolutionaries reacted violently to this Muslim complacency; the more aggressive among them resorted to widespread looting and spoilation of Muslim citadels.

5. The French revolution and the Italian nationalist struggle were held up as models. The Russian revolution of 1905 was fresh in the minds of those revolutionaries who were not averse to resorting to violence if the need arose.

6. The attitude of the colonial government was undoubtedly the force behind the fruition of all these cataclysmic ideas. British equivocation, with underlying favouritism for Muslims, infuriated the radicals. The endeavour of the British to keep the two great communities divided seemed to have culminated in the partition of Bengal. The psychosis of evil religiosity afflicting the minds of both Muslims and Hindus was to a large extent the handiwork of the British. Curzon's dislike for Indians and the Congress contributed to the growth of extremism. Colonial disdain in the matter of jobs for Indians, had, by 1905, tested the patience of many.[22] Government repression, in the garb of firmness and condemnation of extremist excesses, revitalized the revolutionary movement.

7. The influence of the language newspapers in inciting revolutionary ideas was the catalyst that affected and detonated the already simmering disaffection. The government too became extra wary and accused the language papers of deliberately trying to 'inflame the minds of the people, to encourage ill-will among classes and to promote activity hostile to government, and to disturb public tranquility'.[23]

CHARACTER AND ORGANIZATION OF THE NATIONALISTS

Alhough the nationalists were roughly divided into two classes, those inside the Congress and those outside it, there were actually four Schools of militant nationalism. These were

(1) *Centrist activists*—extremists within the Congress party. They

generally did not believe in the cult of violence, and sometimes cooperated with the moderates. They did not deny the utility of constitutional movements. Tilak, Lajpat Rai, Bipin Chandra Pal were all professed Congressmen. In the UP the leading members were Shanti Narayan, Ram Hari, Nand Gopal, Ganga Ram, Tahal Ram, Ladha Ram. Shanti Narayan established his Desh Sewak Press in Allahabad. Earlier he had been editor of the *Hindustan*, Lahore. Nand Gopal, an associate of Ajit Singh was editor of *Inquilab*, Lahore before becoming editor of *Swarajya*, Allahabad. Many of them were Arya Samajists. There were some prominent Muslims too who were members, Hasrat Mohani (Unnao), Mauzal Ali Sokhta (Allahabad) and Raja Ghulam Hussain (Aligarh).[24]

(2) *Political Missionaries*—who considered the Congress a *sarkari majlis*. They wanted to spread revolutionary propaganda by way of religious propaganda. They cared for the end and not the means employed in fighting the British. Rebellion, anarchy created through bombs, strikes, refusal to pay taxes, and even taking help from other countries, were all political weapons that could be employed. They believed in widespread dissemination of ideas in the language of the people, and what better medium than the language press! The perpetrators of this school of militant nationalism in the UP were Sufi Amba Prasad, Moti Lal Varma, Hardayal, Ram Sarup, Keso Ram, Amir Chand and Sundar Lal. They seemed to have some connection with Shyamji Krishna Varma, a close disciple of Dayananda and a friend of Tilak.

(3) *The Sanatanist Extremists*—very orthodox, for whom the nationalistic fervour was only an extension of their obsession to superimpose Indian culture on established organs. They believed in rekindling national spirit through hardship and self-sacrifice. To them nationalism was synonymous with spiritualism. Their leading activist and spiritualist was Aurobindo Ghose, who was certainly not averse to the use of violence to excite national emotions. Varanasi and Allahabad were the centres of extremism in the UP. Balkrishna Bhatt (editor of *Hindi Pradip*), Jitendra Nath Sen (editor of *Citizen*) of Allahabad and Shri Krishna Varma (editor of *Bharat Jiwan* of Varanasi) were all of this school. Of them only Kashi Mohan Ray was a lawyer; Shiva Prasad Gupta and Bhal Chandra were not professional men; and Bidhu Bhushan Chatterji, Jogeshwar Mukherji and Mohshda Charan Samadhyaya were all active workers of 'Bharat Dharam Mandal' of Varanasi.

(4) *The Mahatma Nationalists*—with headquarters at Gurukul Kangri at Haridwar. The regenerative force for the moral upliftment of the people could only be released through service, love and non-violence. They considered terrorists unscrupulous.[25]

Despite the fact that the extremists can be divided into those within the Congress, who did not believe in violence; and those outside it, who wrought terrorism in the country by their violent actions, 'the line of division is not a sharp one nor of a permanent character'. The Congress adherents were not ordinarily believers in violence. The terrorists directed their fury not only against public servants, European or Indian, but also against those assisting the cause of justice and giving evidence. The government was suspicious of the connection between extremists and terrorists.

> The distribution of the less violent form of sedition is, as might be expected, very much the same as that of the terrorist movement, and there is no doubt a close connection between the two, for the persistent preaching of sedition has a marked effect upon the youth of the country and thus creates a favourable recruiting ground for the party of revolutionary violence while there are some reasons for suspecting that the real leaders of the party of violence conceal themselves under the cloak of more moderate opinion.[26]

They had no mature leadership. Theirs was a secret organization so they could not work with deliberation and mutual consultation. They were always under stress and strain, and nervous tension.

Such extremists (or nationalists, or radicals, or revolutionaries) had little mass appeal and their effectiveness was limited to provincial capitals and some district headquarters. Although the rank and file were recruited from the lower middle-class and could have reached the nerve of the masses, but, probably because of lack of resources and comprehension of the main issues, they remained dominated by the middle-class which was wealthy and educated. The men of the lower income groups were superior in caste hierarchy and consisted of office assistants, school masters and hospital assistants. Though economically deprived for years, the economic factor was eclipsed by the cultural obsession of their leaders.[27]

These youthful terrorists were banded together in societies but how far these associations were under any central control is not clear. The two main revolutionary organizations in Bengal were (1) the Anushilan Samitis and (2) the Yugantar Group. The first was puritantial and stressed religiosity and rigid vows; it had several societies at district and village levels too. These hoped to establish a Hindu government with Muslims as subjects. Anushilan broke up in 1909 but secretly continued its activities, collecting money through daring dacoities. The Anushilan was started by B.C. Pal and P. Mitter, and Aurobindo Ghose reinforced it. In the UP, Sachin Sanyal founded the Anushilan Samiti at Varanasi.[28] The Yugantar was inaugurated by Aurobindo's brother, Barindra K. Ghose in November 1906. Anushilan was parochial, narrow-minded and disciplined, while Yugantar was more open and flexible, but both wanted a general rising, and were not averse to bombs, dacoities or rioting to achieve their aims.

The revolutionary journalists wrote provocatively, 'We would stop only when we have shaken (as by an earthquake) the earth and when we have lifted the world on our shoulders. Anybody may gag our mouth a 100 times, but we would not keep quiet.'[29] However, most journalists did not advocate violence. They felt that law and order were necessary for carrying out revolutionary propaganda and they denounced in unrestrained terms the murderous attempts of false patriots.[30]

THE GROWING COMMUNAL TANGLE

Communal consciousness grew during this period, and national loyalties became entangled with communal loyalties. This development was more discernible in Muslim attitudes, as they had entered the nationalistic arena quite late. While some newspapers wanted a total dissociation between religion and politics, the more radical stressed the natural interdependence of the two.[31] The Hindu-Muslim cleavage had, by now, become a recognizable social and political feature. The causes of the development of this during the period of study were diverse and many.

As stated above the partition of Bengal in 1905, created a cataclysm in the country. It was a move in favour of the Muslims, and sowed the seeds of jealousy and ill-will between the Hindus and Muslims. The Muslim upper class countered Swadeshi with Swaraj, urging purely Muslim commerce, industry and education. It aimed at boycott of Hindus.[32]

The growth of extremism in the country, especially inside the Congress itself, incited the Muslims racially. As it is, the Congress was considered a Hindu body. The revolutionaries outside it made no secret of their racial superiority and stressed their 'Hindutva'. The Hindu revolutionaries unwittingly gave the pro-government Muslim faction a handle by the forcible imposition of Boycott in rural areas. Hindu landlords, servants, pleaders, law agents, and volunteers enforced the use of Swadeshi goods and Boycott of foreign goods. Shopkeepers, often Muslim, retaliated by attacking their aggressors, sometimes entering Hindu temples and destroying the image of the gods. This caused serious communal tension.

The Muslim leadership also feared that their youth would join the Congress. This danger had always been present, kept alive by such newspapers as Sajjad Hussain's *Azad*, Jamaluddin's *Hamdard*, and particularly by Hasrat Mohani's *Urdu-i-Moalla* of Aligarh. In 1905, young Aligarh Muslims such as Tufail Ahmad and Hasrat Mohani attended the Congress meeting at Varanasi. What alarmed the conservative Muslim leadership was the passing by overwhelming majorities of motions advocating joint action by Hindus and Muslims in politics, by the Aligarh College Students' Union in May 1906.[33] The eagerness to gain a political base led to the establishment of the Muslim League on 30 December 1906 in Dacca. The influence of the Dacca Muslims was superseded by Aligarh and the UP men. Mohsin-ul-Mulk and Viqar-ul-Mulk returned to Aligarh as joint secretaries. The secretaryship and power of the League were to remain in the hands of the UP men for most of its existence. The League's leadership remained in the hands of the landed aristocracy and found a fertile field for its growth. In the UP, especially in Awadh, the traditional landholders were the most powerful. The League established a number of provincial branches. The headquarters of the All-India Muslim League and the provincial branch were at Aligarh. The Muslim League enumerated its objectives as loyalty to the British government, protection and advancement of the political rights and interests of Muslims in India and representing their needs to government, and the prevention of the rise among the Muslims of any feeling of hostility towards other communities 'without prejudice to the other aforementioned objects of the League'. It was the last objective which was rather ambiguous and could be interpreted to suit Muslim interests.

The desire of Muslims for adequate representation in the Imperial and the Provincial Legislative Councils had always been present. They feared that if government introduced elections on a more extended scale in the imminent reforms, they would get few seats. Their fears were not baseless as, for example, in the UP no Muslim had succeeded in winning an election between 1893 and 1906. The Aga Khan, until now veering towards the Congress, joined Mohsin-ul-Mulk and other

Aligarh leaders in taking a deputation to Lord Minto, Curzon's conservative successor. At a meeting in Shimla they demanded a separate and communal electorate on a numerical basis as well as on the basis of political importance. Minto was very encouraging. He praised them for their loyalty and gave them assurances of favoured electoral representation. This was a wily way to dissipate Hindu predominance. Newspapers with Congress leanings protested at the possibility of the election of Muslim candidates by Muslim voters being granted. Christians, Brahmins, Kayasthas, and Banias, etc., they felt, could also then claim separate representation.[34] Thus, the question of greater representation in the Legislative Councils had become graver and filled with more ominous portents than before.

The responsibility of the colonial masters in effecting communal divisiveness has been considered. Besides the obvious bias in favour of the Muslims, Minto apprehended serious trouble if Muslim interests were flouted. 'Muslim electorates are absolutely necessary, if we retract from that view, we shall have an infinitely worse trouble than anything that can arise from Hindu opposition.'[35] Morley welcomed the emergence of a third party which would lessen the weight of the Congress in British public opinion and give government room for manoeuvre. The Lt.-Governor of the UP, Hewett, though not racist, veered towards the Muslims. The attitude of the British bureaucrats if not antagonistic was certainly suspicious of Hindus. Hence different psychological pressures worked on the colonial power in determining its communal policy while maintaining social and political control.

The slaughter of cows was an age-old issue of strife. But after 1905 the cow became a political issue. Besides, peasants were dependent for their livelihood on cows and cow killing was anathema to them. They did not respond to the Swadeshi movement as they were basically suspicious of the educated classes. For them the cow was the most important factor and its killing would create agrarian trouble sooner or later.

Alhough Muslims were divided among themselves, the ulema formed an important link between various Muslim groups. They were responsible for education of a religious nature. They were especially effective in small towns and villages, where the local Muslim population was more susceptible to religious impositions through local mosques and Madarsas.[36] There were several instances of Maulvis giving discourses in mosques which would endanger Hindu-Muslim unity.[37]

TABLE 7.1: HINDU AND MUSLIM MEMBERSHIP OF THE LEGAL PROFESSION IN THE UP (1873-1929)[38]

	1873	*1889*	*1899*	*1909*	*1919*	*1929*
Hindu	88	608	890	1222	1620	1847
Muslim	98	335	402	455	453	460

The Muslims had all along been conscious of their minority status and grudged Hindus their better employment avenues and better education. As the number of educated Muslims grew, the need for increased employment avenues became obvious. Jobs were few and many Muslims sought a livelihood in law. Mounting communal tension and MacDonnell's Nagri resolution had made the people wary of sending briefs to Muslim lawyers. Table 7.1 is self-explanatory.

In the early twentieth century, the UP contained a large number of educated Muslims with 'high aspirations' and 'low expectations'. Meetings were held at Varanasi and other places of the Muslim Political Association to discuss how Muslim rights and privilages could be protected. The only way out seemed to find a vocation that would enhance prestige and boost financial condition. Politics seemed to be the most propitious and accessible profession, especially with the steadily growing political consciousness. This stimulated political journalism. Hasrat Mohani who brought out the *Urdu-i-Moalla* from Aligarh, and Syed Shabbir Hasan of the *Muslim Gazette* from Lucknow were two such budding journalists.

The Muslims had always been divided in their religious beliefs. Shia-Sunni riots periodically occurred, but gradually political divisions also sprouted. These divisions were based on envy of deprived Muslims of the social, economic, cultural self-sufficiency of their more fortunate co-religionists. One group was from either the rich land-owners and aristocratic class or belonged to the successful professional or service class. It was not very particular about higher education. The government to instal them as the actual Muslim leaders, generously doled out Rajaships, Knighthoods, etc. The Rajas of Mehmudabad, Jehangirabad, Pirpur and Qizilbaksh were typical examples of Awadh taluqdars. Among the successful professional men, Sheikh Abdullah and Bashir-ud-din were educationists and Asghar Ali Khan and Mufti Haider Hasan, Vice-Chairman of the Bareilly and Jaunpur Municipal Boards, respectively, were examples of powerful local leaders. These professionals were not puppets of the government but certainly preferred to act in accordance with its wishes. They formed the primary leadership of the Muslim League. Conservative journalism had more staying power and stability than revolutionary outpourings. *Al Bashir* of Etawah and *Mashriq* of Gorakhpur were the foremost conservative Muslim newspapers and the colonial government encouraged them to voice their pro-Muslim opinions which often bordered on being anti-Hindu.[39]

This conservative group was disconcerted when the other young group, less important, with less employment, penurious, belonging to the middle classes, more educated and less loyal to the British government, distressed with the underdog treatment meted out to them by their co-religionists and the powers that be, started looking for other affiliations than those primarily based on caste. Politics seemed to have limitless allure and associating with the new revolutionary trends in the Congress seemed a way out of their dilemma. The Muslim papers in general reflected the views of most Muslims, who felt that these young firebrands should refrain from aligning themselves with the Congress. They argued that it was only due to lack of government patronage that this section was acting uncharacteristically. The Muslim deputation to Minto at Shimla in 1906 and the formation of the Muslim League the same year, were measures which had appeasement as their base.[40]

EVENTS INFLUENCING THE NATIONALISTIC AND COMMUNAL REACTION IN THE UNITED PROVINCES, 1905-10

The partition of Bengal evoked extremism in nationalism, and though the worst affected provinces were Bengal, Bombay, Central Provinces and Bihar, and Punjab, the United Provinces did not remain untouched. While it was not prominent on the national scene,[41] 'there are danger spots in . . . these provinces which require very careful watching'.[42]

The Congress session at Varanasi in 1905 showed clearly the rift between the moderate and extremist elements. The ultimate aim of the moderates, as laid down by Gokhale in his presidential address, was that of colonial self-government. The Varanasi Congress revealed the disjunction between extreme and moderate elements in the Congress. The nationalists staged a walk-out over a resolution welcoming the Prince of Wales. The newspapers favouring them gave Bal Gangadhar Tilak, Babu Bipin Chandra Pal, Lala Lajpat Rai, etc., the credit for reviving the Congress and for reawakening an interest in it of the English press.[43]

Muslim reactions went according to political biases. The conservatives of Aligarh had most papers behind them. They put forth arguments to errant young Muslims as to why they should refrain from joining Congress. They viewed the Congress as a Hindu body concerned only with Hindu affairs trying diabolically to use Muslims to identify them as anti-government. The resolution passed at Varanasi against quarantine on Mecca pilgrims was regarded as a 'dodge' of the Congress to 'wheedle Muslims into joining the movement'.[44] The newspapers representative of the forward group in the Muslims agreed with the Varanasi resolutions but asserted that both in the extension of Councils and in administration Muslim interest should be preserved. They encouraged Muslims to join the Congress. The *Urdu-i-Moalla* (Aligarh), of May 1906 reasoned that if a handful of Parsis like Dadabhai Naoroji and Pheroz Shah Mehta, could enjoy such power in the Congress, so could Muslims. It requested fellow Muslims to refrain from being guided by the short-sighted views of *Al Bashir*, *Wakil*, *Watan* and *Riaz-ul-Akhbar*.[45]

The moderate element in the Congress felt extremely threatened after the Varanasi session. They were reassured by the coming of the Liberal Party to power in England, with so obviously broadminded a man as Morley as the Secretary of State for India. Gokhale met Morley in 1906 and felt the Liberals would value the liberty and independence of every man.[46] Gokhale visited many places in northern India—Allahabad, Agra, Lucknow, Meerut and Aligarh—to revitalize the Congress and dissipate extremist support in it. Giving impassioned speeches, he clarified the Congress goals to the people. The Muslim League endeavoured to maintain cordiality with him. Nawab Mohsin-ul-Mulk met him at Lucknow and Aligarh. Gokhale declared that national progress was not possible until Hindus and Muslims came together. They would fight for equality with the ruler in the higher rungs of the national ladder, the uplifment of the masses, particularly of the so-called depressed classes, and for the improvement of the position of women in the lower reaches.[47] The old guard among the Muslims did not wholeheartedly respond to Gokhale's overtures. *Al Bashir* of 19 February 1907 accused Congressmen of employing subterfuge to advocate the views of their leading members by only presenting the brighter side of the picture.[48]

However, many Muslims belonging either to the radical group or the Shia community, desired no truck with the Muslim League, considered the stronghold of the rich and the important and professedly a Sunni organization. Either subtly or openly, they declared it undesirable and extolled the virtues of the Congress.[49]

The Calcutta Congress session in 1906 had a large contingent of delegates from the UP. On 14 April 1906, S.N. Banerjea, the great moderate Congress leader, was arrested for shouting *Bande Mataram.* This produced sensation in Allahabad, Kanpur, and Varanasi, and UP leaders considered it 'a blatant interference with primary rights of the subjects'. Protest meetings were held and La Touche, the Lt.-Governor, unwisely sent policemen in plain clothes to such meetings. Banerji was accused of playing to the gallery by the government, but this incident infused fresh vigour in the national movement and questions were raised about the right of public meeting and freedom of speech.[50]

At the same time that Gokhale had been visiting places in the UP, extremist leaders Tilak and B.C. Pal, full of uncertainty after the patch-up at Calcutta, visited Allahabad (1907). Tilak's speech on 'Our present situation' drew a large crowd of mostly students. Pal's speech had an audience unparalleled in history and people listened to him in breathless excitement. The government overreacted and had him constantly watched. 'The more they smelt sedition and adopted drastic measures, the more they fed the flame of the enthusiasm of the people.' The Congress triumvirate at Allahabad—Gokhale, Pal and Tilak—enthused Swadeshi in the hitherto dormant province.[51]

LaTouche left, and Sir John Hewett became Lt.-Governor in December 1906. The year 1907 was a year of political turmoil—the nerve centres being Bombay and Bengal. The UP also felt the rumblings. Following Minto's instructions, Hewett tried to draw the moderates towards government so that Congress unity moves would not succeed. He followed a policy of repression which would stifle any sort of extremist activity. Congressmen organized the Provincial Conference at Allahabad in March 1907 under the presidentship of Motilal Nehru. Luminaries like Satish Chandra Banerji, Tej Bahadur Sapru, Ishwar Saran, Brij Narain Gurtu were the honorary secretaries. The language papers attributed the conference to growing political awareness in the province. Its predominantly moderate character was undeniable. Muslims were ignored. The extremists insinuated that a definite bias had been practised against them when selecting the participants, while the moderate supporters praised it for its high aims and success. Motilal bemoaned 'the somewhat embarassing situation created by a division in our own camp'.[52] Unity was of primary importance without which self-government was not possible. The *Hindustan* of Kalakankar of 10 May 1907 acerbically remarked that worthy aims were useless when there was such disunity—Sikhs and Hindus were squabbling over the Golden Temple, Shias and Sunnis in Lucknow, and Hindus and Muslims were 'fighting like Kilkenny cats in East Bengal'.

The deportation of Lala Lajpat Rai in May 1907 created a furore in the Congress camp. The incongruity of charges of subversion against him lent credence to the journalistic view that government was employing a dramatic and despotic method which might 'shatter the poor nerves of a moderate and strike terror into the heart of the extremist'.[53] There were protest meetings at Allahabad and other centres, but along with these the old guard among Muslims and the Hindu landlords, bankers and merchants, held loyalty meetings at Aligarh. No serious government action was taken in the UP probably because there was no major unrest here.[54]

At the Surat session in 1907, the Congress finally split. It was in effect an expression of polarized interests and ideologies, and created an independent nationalist group as the extremists wanted to be called.[55] The moderates objected to the extremists using the term 'nationalist' to describe themselves as 'surely those who have been in the fold of the National Congress for twenty-three years have a stronger right to that name than those who have put a spoke in the wheel of the Congress'.[56] The second Provincial Conference held at Lucknow had Madan Mohan Malviya as its president. Famine had broken out in the UP so the main discussions in this moderate conference were on famine and plague relief, Indians in high posts, and expansion of the Viceroy's and Provincial Councils. Pandit Gokaran Nath Misra eulogized Sir John Hewett for the prompt action he had taken to battle famine. The Convention Committee meeting at Allahabad severed whatever connections had been left between the moderates and extremists. Unlike Bombay and Bengal, the UP leaders felt a reconciliation with extremists was impossible as peaceful work was not possible if they were included.

With rampant famine conditions in the province, Hewett was disturbed by the threat of extremist culture being transported to the UP from Bengal. He heard alarming reports from the Magistrate of Moradabad that Samnyasis at the Haridwar fair were predicting the fall of British rule in six years. Hewett had taken Minto's warning to Morley about the 'extreme danger of the attempts to tamper with the native army' very seriously.[57] The news that a pay havildar of the 9th Bhopal infantry had delivered speeches on Swadeshi in Allahabad upset him. Besides, Gokhale had been approached by two army officers from Meerut who had told him that if he wished their regiments were ready to take up arms. Students appeared to be the most affected, and had been so audacious as to attack the statue of Queen Victoria at Varanasi. These students were members of the Anushilan Samiti's branch at Varanasi.[58] The Government of India passed the Seditions Meetings Act in 1907. This Act was extended to the UP in 1910 and worked as a deterrent to terrorist activity.

What discredited the extremists completely in government eyes were the Muzaffarpur bomb outrage (in which two ladies were killed instead of Kingsford, the District Judge of Calcutta), and the Calcutta Conspiracy Case (wherein secret arms were discovered at Manikatala). The 'Bomb' had electrified India and government got a rude shock when Tilak wrote a series of articles in his paper, *Kesari*. He was deported to Mandalay for six years for these inflammatory articles. Aurobindo was tried for complicity in the Conspiracy Case and was imprisoned in 1908. He was released in 1909, but seemed a new man and went into seclusion responding to the call from above. The government had no alternative but to practice further repression. In June 1908 the Explosives and the Newspapers Acts were passed. The Newspapers Act empowered magistrates to prosecute and punish all journalists whom they regarded as opponents of the policy of the government.

The language newspapers in UP were carefully watched. *Swarajya*, representative of extremist journalism, became the permanent target of British repression. Though subsequently its first editor, Shanti Narayan, was arrested for eulogizing the courage of the Muzaffarpur revolutionaries, he fearlessly wrote, 'We would stop only when we have shaken (as by an earthquake) the earth and when we have lifted the world on our shoulders. Anybody may gag our mouth a 100 times, but we would not keep quiet.'[59] The truth behind this contention is revealed when one considers that after him seven subsequent editors of the *Swarajya* were imprisoned! All this repression seems rather like an overreaction because the *Swarajya* never actively supported terrorism or violence. It advocated peaceful means of agitation and felt that bombs should be used only as a last resort, as history had shown that this method never succeeded.[60]

Hewett was further alarmed by a paper found at Aligarh in which it had been endeavoured to arouse vile thoughts in the minds of schoolboys. He said the instigator at Aligarh had already preached incendiary doctrines at Meerut, Agra and Moradabad. Besides some newspapers in the UP propagating the revolutionary methods of Bengal, Hewett affirmed that clubs and associations had been formed in the UP to spread sedition among the people here.[61] Hewett also feared the infiltration of instigatory articles from abroad. Hewett's fears were not unfounded. In 1908, the government discovered a truly seditious and incendiary leaflet from England that had been sent to a gentleman at Pratapgarh. The leaflet was titled *Ghadar Movement in UP.* Its passionate appeal was enough to disturb the government and believers in non-violence—people like Madan Mohan Malviya. It wrote, 'For the bones of Bahadurshah are crying for vengeance from their grave; for the blood of the dauntless Laxmi is boiling with indignation . . . your blood, Oh martyrs, shall be avenged!'[62]

Hewett ordered house-searches of prominent men at Allahabad, Varanasi, Agra and Aligarh. Of these, the arrest of the editor of *Swarajya*, Hoti Lal Verma, evoked tremendous response from all the language newspapers. Even the adherents of moderation found Hewett's policy an overreaction. Hoti Lal was an ex-student of Agra College but had only recently returned from Europe. He had been arrested on suspicion, without a formal trial, and having committed no punishable offence. His mere presence in Agra did not mean that he was involved in a terrorist conspiracy. Actually, his impulsive writings had long been an irritant to the government, as his previous position as correspondent with the *Bande Mataram* of Calcutta; and his contacts with Bombay, Poona, and particularly with Tilak, had been rankling with Hewett for sometime now. Hoti lal and his associate Ram Swarup of Vedic Ashram, Aligarh, were consequently sentenced to long terms of imprisonment. The newspapers insisted that no bombs or unlicensed arms were found anywhere, '. . . but a number of peaceful and probably loyal subjects have been subjected to unnecessary humiliation and will swell the ranks of discontented'. These people could fall easy prey to designing and seditious people.[63] The *Indian People* of Allahabad of 14 June 1887 sarcastically commented, Sir James LaTouche was wrong when he said there was no unrest in the United Provinces. When such precautions were being taken, there must be serious unrest! The Muslims of the old school agreed with Hewett's directive that schools should not become hot-beds of sedition—the handiwork of Hindu teachers. 'If by an unfortunate combination of circumstances the British occupation of India comes to an end, the Muslims will find themselves at the mercy of an oppressive Hindu majority.'[64]

THE MORLEY-MINTO REFORMS OF 1909

Fresh shock waves were felt by the passage of the Morley-Minto Reforms in 1909. In the Imperial Legislative Council, out of 60 members, 27 were to be elected and 33 nominated, of which no more than 28 could be officials. One must be from the Muslims, and one from the landholders of the Punjab (likely to be a Muslim). Thus at the Centre, an official majority was maintained. The UP had to have 4 elected members in the Imperial Council, of which 2 would be elected by non-official members of the Provincial Council, one by landholders and one by Muslims.[65]

The Provincial Legislative Councils were also enlarged, and the number of members in the UP was settled at 50. A non-official majority was assured but there were to be only 20 elected members. Of these 4 seats were to be filled by separate electorates established for the Muslims; 16 were to be filled by representatives of landholders (one in Agra and one in Awadh), district and municipal boards (8—one from each division excluding Kumaun), large municipalities (4), Allahabad University (one), and the Upper Chamber of Commerce (one). The government made it clear, that special seats having been reserved for Muslims did not debar those who were otherwise qualified, from 'voting or becoming candidates for the sixteen seats'.[66] 2 seats were allotted to Indians in the Viceroy's Executive Council.

These reforms were very disappointing to the Hindus, whether moderates or extremists. In a nutshell, they disapproved of communal electorates that had been established to please the Muslims, the preponderance of hereditary aristocracy and the non-establishment of the Executive Council in the UP. The double election rights granted to Muslims—along with other communities in joint electorates, and as believers in Islam in separate electorates—rankled with the other communities who regarded it a deterrent to national unity. The newspapers protested,

> This attempt to alienate Musalmans from the Hindus is most insidious, and if separate electorates are provided at all stages, the real object of Lord Morley's scheme will be hopelessly defeated, for racial bitterness will continue to grow and the cleavage will become a public danger.[67]

Even the rules framed for joint electorates were discriminatory, because while Muslim constituencies would be able to return popular representatives, the electorates in which Hindus would participate had been so framed (on account of different standards set for minimum land revenue fixed for eligibility of landlords, and the graduate status of Hindus and Muslims) that none but territorial magnates would find their way into the councils. These rich landowners were generally uneducated, and desirous of gaining a prestigious place on the Councils without being driven by any great patriotic fervour.[68]

Loud protests were made against the power reserved with the Governor-General to pronounce any man disqualified whom he may regard unworthy of sitting in the Councils. The danger was of the Governor-General using this power to sift out a competent and good man who had been a thorn in his flesh. Several men even suspected of having a liaison with the extremists could be studiously left out. The existence of the loudly proclaimed non-official majority in the Provincial Council was only a myth and had a very meagre salutary effect on the working of this body. The reason was that non-official members were either nominated by the Lt.-Governor, or elected by the landlord and Muslim constituencies. The nomination by the government of the Nawab of Rampur, the Maharaja of Varanasi, the Raja of Tehri, the Nawab of Pahasu and Farquhar Mackinnon proved the point of the critics. The men sent up to the Council by the electorates of Municipal and District Boards were generally pro-establishment as the composition of these boards had been very carefully scrutinized.[69] However, some competent and popular men were elected. M.M. Malviya, Ganga Prasad Verma and Motilal Nehru were elected as representatives of educated classes. Sir Sunder Lal represented the Allahabad University; Raja Rampal Singh, Brajnandan Prasad, Lala Ramanuj Dayal, Sukhbir Singh and Munshi Narsingh Prasad were some other luminaries. Abdul Majid, Mohammad Nasim and Aftab Ahmad were the best among the Muslim representatives in the Council in the UP.[70] The language press regarded the above elections as nothing to be jubilant about. It asserted,

> . . . it is with a maximum of difficulty, that a minimum number of independent representatives can get into the Council. . . . Their voice will, we apprehend, be drowned in the votes of the officials, and the nominated non official element, backed up . . . by a section of the elected members.[71]

This was confirmed by the working of the Provincial Council. Between 1909 and 1916, 20 Bills were passed. Of these 15 received little opposition from non-official members, 4 were contested bitterly, and the fifth, the Awadh Civil Courts Amendment Bill, was opposed at the introductory stage itself. There were only 4 occasions on which members introduced their own measures. Of these, 2 were carried with the support of the government, the third was rejected, and the fourth withdrawn.[72]

The reforms were a betrayal of moderate aspirations. Discrediting of moderate opinion proved critical for the British. Moderates could have been used to nullify extremist influence and subsequently annihilate extremism and terrorism. The British would have achieved a lot by yielding little; instead, they unwisely prepared the ground for Mahatma Gandhi's movement by creating a permanent suspicion among the populace of their good intentions.

The Morley-Minto reforms did not satisfy all Muslims. They catered to only the rich Muslims. Second, even in the much favoured Muslim League, two schools of thought had emerged. Ameer Ali and Aga Khan wanted a larger number of seats for Muslims, all based on separate electorates; they felt mixed electorates should be boycotted, as even those Muslims elected in the latter would be Muslims in name 'but really mandatories of Hindu electors'. Besides, they wanted collective voting at all centres instead of separate candidates in separate centres. This was not acceptable to Hewett as it would benefit only Lucknow candidates. Hewett seemed to be slightly uncertain about the desirability of government fostering the Muslims to this extent. The headquarters of the All-India Muslim League and the Provincial Muslim League were at Aligarh but Hewett, forever cautious, persuaded Aga Khan to have the All-India League office shifted to Lucknow and the Provincial League office to Allahabad.[73]

The aftermath of the reforms spelt an increased circulation of seditious and revolutionary pamphlets. Hewett felt that the tone of the language newspapers had deteriorated in the UP and that errant editors should be punished. The language newspapers, though not necessarily pro-extremist, felt anarchism could not be suppressed by repressive measures, as anarchists worked secretly. Muzzling the press would only increase bitterness and defiance. Yet government passed the Press Act in 1910 as the need for more repressive power was considered imperative. In this the Local Government was given powers to summarily stop the publication of seditious matter. Errant newspapers were to give a surety for future good behaviour. Heavy money securities were demanded from them, and in case of persistent seditious and inflammatory articles, they could be closed down. Besides this arbitrary system of warnings, securities being impounded, editors being imprisoned, the system of a press or paper existing only if government gave it a license and considered it fit to be registered, made complete the stranglehold of government. The *Advocate* (Lucknow) of 10 February 1910, wrote that the government was playing into the hands of anarchists by destroying that very agency—the language press—that had brought to its notice their machinations and had honestly commented on the actions of the government. The government, however, blamed the press for extensive revolutionary propaganda. It was stated that the theory of the safety-valve could not be applied to the Indian press without qualification — 'discontent can be fanned into the white heat of fanaticism by the calculating malevolence of newspaper writers'.[74]

All newspapers in the UP considered in any way capable of arousing sedition were dealt with firmly. A security of Rs. 9,000 was demanded from the *Karmayogi* and *Hindi Pradip* of Allahabad and they were subsequently ordered closure. After seven editors were imprisoned or deported, the *Swarajya* of Allahabad was closed down in February 1910.[75] The editor of *Urdu-i-Moalla* of Aligarh had already been imprisoned.

The stringent policy of deportation, imprisonment, virtual press censorship and anti-sedition laws affected the revolutionary movement. Its force was scattered, its best leaders imprisoned or underground. The nationalist movement lost its bite. Many nationalists because of vicissitudes of time, joined the moderates and reluctantly declared themselves loyalists.[76]

Many nationalist leaders secretly left the country in an endeavour to seek foreign help or to organize Indian revolutionaries abroad to overthrow British rule. In England Shyamji Krishna Verma was active. He considered revolutionaries in India like Bipin Chandra and Lala Lajpat Rai too effete.

The UP had been affected by the nationalists and anarchists, but organizationally they had little standing here, and whatever existed was an extension of Bengal. There was an Anushilan Samiti formed at Varanasi whose leading personage was one Sachin Sanyal. He had direct connections with the Dacca Anushilan. His was a secret organization but did not take definite shape on account of internal dissensions, and ceased to exist after 1913. This ineffectiveness could have been because of its active member, Bibhuti, turning out to be a government informer. Besides this, the UP did feel the indirect rumblings of the Indo-German conspiracy, when Rash Behari Bose was hunted from place to place for his complicity in the Delhi and Lahore conspiracy cases and subsequently revealed connections with revolutionaries in Germany in collaboration with the Jugantar group and the Ghadar group of Punjab. He came to Varanasi in 1914. Varanasi was considered '. . . an important centre a sort of clearing house between Dacca and Punjab'.[77] Bose with Sachin planned an armed uprising at Varanasi; 21 February 1915 was fixed as the date for a mutiny of Indian soldiers stationed at the local cantonment at Meerut but a soldier betrayed them and the main conspirators, Vishnu Ganesh Pingley and Sachin were arrested. Rash Behari escaped and subsequently went to Japan. One of his followers, Vinayak Rao Kaple continued to work secretly in the UP but was finally murdered in 1918 by his own colleagues, who suspected him to be a government informer. Among the accused in the Banaras Conspiracy Case, only one Damodar Swarup, a school teacher, showed promise, and later played a prominent role in the non-cooperation movement in the UP. Besides these, Raja Mahendra Pratap, son of the Raja of Hatras, kept in touch with the political developments in the country, but he never joined any revolutionary group. He started the Prem Mahavidyalaya at Brindaban for moral and technical education of young men. When World War I broke out he went to Germany to establish contact with the Germans, and returned to India only after World War II.

CONCLUSION

The extremist movement did not touch UP as effectively as it did Bengal. Yet its presence on the periphery of the province was enough to affect the nationalist psychology there. Nationalism encompassed a large canvas with social, economic and communal hues affecting the nationalist moves as well as the colonial counter-moves. Moderation in politics became a matter of the past, though extremism was spent by the time the Great War broke out in 1914. Every move that the government made to effect control over the language press, which became a symbol of the varied parameters of nationalistic enterprises, made it more intriguing to the people. UP seemed to be resting before Mahatma Gandhi and Nehru were to storm into the national scene.

NOTES

1. Arun Chandra Guha, *First Spark of Revolution: The Early Phase of India's Struggle for Independence, 1900-1920,* Bombay, Madras, Calcutta, New Delhi, p. 36.
2. VNR of UP, *Indian People,* Allahabad, 17 Jan. 1907.
3. VNR of UP, *Karamyogi,* Allahabad, 20 Dec. 1910.
4. O.P. Goyal, *Studies in Modern Indian Political Thoughts—The Moderates and the Extremists,* Kitab Mahal, Allahabad, 1964, p. 93.
5. VNR of UP, *Oudh Akhbar,* Lucknow, 13 March 1910.
6. VNR of UP, *Muslim Gazette,* Lucknow, 24 July 1912.
7. GAD, File No. 137/1910, Letter from Sir Harold Stuart, Secretary to the GOI Home Deptt. (Pol.) to Chief Secretary, UP
8. Amales Tripathi, *The Extremist Challenge: India between 1890-1910* Bombay, Calcutta, Madras, New Delhi, 1967, p. 1; Goyal, op.cit., p. 93.
9. Tripathi, op.cit., p. 14.
10. VNR of UP, *The Citizen,* Allahabad, 1 Jan. 1906; B.B. Misra, *The Indian Political Parties—A Historical Analysis of Political Behaviour upto 1947,* Delhi, 1976, p. 141.
11. Goyal, op.cit., p. 61.
12. VNR of UP, *Citizen,* Allahabad, 4 Feb. 1907.
13. VNR of UP, 1909: *Karmayogi,* Allahabad, 8 Sept.; *Swarajya,* Allahabad, 14 Aug. and 9 Oct.
14. VNR of UP, *Advocate,* Lucknow, 17 Jan. 1907.
15. Tripathi, op.cit., pp. 141-2.
16. VNR of UP, *Advocate,* Lucknow, 31 March 1907
17. VNR of UP, *Abhyudaya,* Allahabad, 26 March 1907.
18. Ganeshilal Verma, *Party Politics in UP (1901-20),* Delhi, 1978, p. 102.
19. Ibid., pp. 118-19; Tripathi, op.cit., pp. 61-8.
20. This resume has been taken from the following: VNR of UP, 1906: *Nizam-ul-Mulk,* Moradabad, 24 Jan. resented that boycott was only being done of British goods and not of all foreign goods. *Zamanah,* Kanpur, Jan. and April; VNR of UP, 1907: *Naiyar-i-Azam,* Moradabad, Feb., *Rohilkhand Gazette,* Bareilly, Feb. *Abhyudaya,* Allahabad, 5 March.
21. V.K. Saxena, *Muslims in the Indian National Congress,* Delhi, 1985, pp. 103 and 104.
22. Curzon to Secretary of State 1900. Eur. MSS D.510/1, p. 216.
23. Motilal Bhargava, *Role of Press in the Freedom Movement,* New Delhi, p. 1.
24. Verma, op.cit., p. 114; GOI Home Pol., Aug. 1910, Nos. 81-95A.
25. Ibid., pp.133-40; GOI Home Pol., File No. 313/1925; VNR of UP, 1909; *Karmayogi,* Allahabad, 4 Feb., 5 Dec. 1910.

26. GAD, File No. 137 of 1910, Letter from Sir Harold Stuart, Secy. to the GOI, Home Pol. to Chief Secy. UP
27. GAD, File No. 137/1910, op.cit.; Misra, op.cit., pp. 100-1; Minto to Morley, 23 June 1908 1.0 MSS Eur. D. 573(16), p. 45.
28. Misra, op.cit., pp. 145-8; Home Pol. Prog. 21, Aug. 1909; p. 20. Guha, op.cit., pp. 307-10.
29. VNR of UP, *Swarajya*, Allahabad, 9 May 1908.
30. Ibid., 7 Oct. 1909.
31. Ibid., 2 Oct. 1909.
32. VNR of UP, *Al Bashir*, Etawah, 3 April 1906; *Oudh Akhbar*, Lucknow, 6 Aug. 1907; Tripathi, op.cit., p. 148.
33. Home Pol. B, Aug. 1912, pp. 120-1. Weekly report of the Director of Central Intelligence, 24 Aug. 1907. Home Pol. B, Aug. 1907, pp. 135-45; VNR of UP, *Indian People*, Allahabad, 24 May 1906; *Agra Akhbar*, 28 Feb. 1906; *Rohilkhand Gazette*, Bareilly, 19 Feb. 1907; *Union Gazette*, Bareilly, 7 Feb. 1907.
34. VNR of UP, *Hindustani*, Lucknow, 5 Sept. 1906.
35. Minto to Moreley, 15 July 1909. Minto papers (21) 10L.
36. Mushirul Hasan, *Communal and Pan Islamic Trends in Colonial India*, New Delhi, 1981, pp. 2-8.
37. VNR of UP, *Hindustani*, Lucknow, 22 May 1907, reports that 5 Maulvis at Varanasi were delivering lectures in mosques and trying to create a rupture between Hindus and Muslims. *Bharat Jiwan*, Varanasi, 27 May 1907, however, says it cannot corroborate this.
38. Ibid., Calculated from Thackers Indian Directory.
39. Robinson, op.cit., pp. 194-200.
40. VNR of UP, *Riaz-ul-Akhbar*, Gorakhpur, 1 Jan. 1906, tries to disabuse its co-religionists of the growth of pro-Congress tendencies in the young Muslims. 'The Muhammadans can in no way be said to have any sympathy with the Hindus so far as politics is concerned.
41. *Freedom Struggle in Uttar Pradesh*, Vol. IX, *Uttar Pradesh Swatantrata Sangram Itihas*, Lucknow, 1885-1909.
42. GAD, File No. 137/1910, letter from Sir Stuart Harold, Secretary to the GOI, Home Pol. to Chief Secretary, UP.
43. VNR of UP, *Rahbar*, Moradabad, 7 Dec. 1906; *Advocate*, Lucknow, *Agra Akhbar*, 28 Jan. 1906.
44. VNR of UP, *Al-Bashir*, Etawah, 6 Feb., 1906; *Agra Akhbar*, 28 Feb. 1906.
45. These were all loyalist papers holding conservative Muslim views.
46. VNR of UP, *Advocate*, Lucknow, 31 Dec. 1906.
47. VNR of UP, *Indian People*, Allahabad, 17 Feb. 1907; *Kanauj Punch*, 1 March 1907; Verma, op.cit., p. 50.
48. VNR of UP, *Al Bashir*, Etawah, 19 Feb. 1907, gives an example of how Madan Mohan Malviya tried hard to persuade Mufti Abdul Majid and

Mr. Abdul Raoof of Allahabad to take the Chair during Gokhale's last lecture, but was unsuccessful.

49. VNR of UP, *Zamanah*, Kanpur, Dec. 1907. This paper changes its stance as earlier it published anti-Congress articles. *Gauhar-i-Shahwar*, Lucknow, 30 Jan 1907; *Israr-i-Alam*, Allahabad, 14 Jan. 1907; *Surma-i-Rozgar*, Agra, 1 Feb. 1907.
50. Verma, op.cit., pp. 108-9, VNR of UP, 1906: *Oudh Akhbar*, Lucknow, April 1906; *Indian People*, Allahabad, 19 April; *Bharat Jiwan*, Varanasi, 23 April.
51. VNR of UP, *Mohini*, Kanauj, 8 Feb. 1907; *Citizen*, Allahabad, 14 Jan. 1907; *Gauhar-i-Shahwar*, Lucknow, 30 Jan. 1907.
52. VNR of UP, *Advocate*, Lucknow, 31 March 1907; *Bharat Jiwan*, Varanasi, 25 March 1907; *The Citizen*, Allahabad, 1 April 1907; *Abhyudaya*, Allahabad, 2 April 1907; Minto to Hewett, 7 March 1907; Minto Papers, No. 81, p. 41.
53. VNR of UP, *Citizen*, Allahabad, 20 May 1907.
54. VNR of UP, *Indian People*, Allahabad, 23 May and 30 June 1907.
55. Misra, op.cit., pp. 106-15; VNR of UP, *Citizen*, Allahabad, 5 Jan. 1908; *Indian People*, Allahabad, 5 Jan. 1908; *Advocate*, Lucknow, 9 Jan. 1908.
56. VNR of UP, *Indian People*, Allahabad, 12 Jan. 1908.
57. Home Pol. A, July 1907, Nos. 178-80.
58. GOI, Home Pol., July 1907, No. 34 (Dep.).
59. Ibid., 9 May 1907.
60. Ibid., 22 Aug. 1907.
61. GAD, File No. 424, 1908, Speech delivered by Hewett at Lucknow, Allahabad and Agra in connection with sedition.
62. Home Pol., Dec. 1908, No. 19.
63. VNR of UP, *Indian People*, Allahabad, 7 June 1908; Verma, op.cit., pp. 60-1, Guha, op.cit., p. 307.
64. VNR of UP, *Aligarh Institute Gazette*, 29 July 1908; *Al Bashir*, Etawah, 4 Aug. 1908.
65. Tripathi, op.cit., pp. 200-4; Saxena, op.cit., p.140; GAD. File No. 58/1909, Council Reforms.
66. GAD, File No. 442/1909, Council Reforms.
67. VNR of UP, *Indian People*, Allahabad, 7 Feb. 1909, *Advocate*, Lucknow, 4 Feb. and 14 Nov. 1909. The above were moderate papers.
68. *Advocate*, Lucknow, 18 Nov. 1909; *Leader*, Allahabad, 17 Nov. 1909; *Naiyar-i-Azam*, Moradabad, 12 Nov. 1909; *Rahbar*, Moradabad, 14 Nov. 1909 and *Leader*, 17 Nov. 1909 all referred to the nomination of Raja Krishna Kumar, as a member of the UP Council and called him a sycophant of the government. Tripathi, op.cit., pp. 206-9.
69. VNR of UP, *Leader*, Allahabad, 16 Nov. and 12 Dec. 1909.
70. Verma, op.cit., pp. 80-9.

71. VNR of UP, *Leader*, 12 Dec. 1909.
72. Verma, op.cit., pp. 89-90.
73. GAD, File No. 449/1909. Proposal made at the UP Conference relating to Council Reforms, Hewett to Minto, 14 Feb. 1908 and 3 Feb. 1910, No. 48 A, p. 58.
74. GAD, File No. 320/1909, Control over the Newspaper press in India.
75. VNR of UP, *Abhyudaya*, Allahabad, 28 April 1910; *Musafir*, Agra, April 1910.
76. VNR of UP, *Karmayogi*, Allahabad, 15 April 1910; *Urdu-i-Moalla*, Aligarh, July 1910.
77. Guha, op.cit., p. 310.

8. Pan-Islamism and the National Movement 1910-14

As the extremists became ineffective, the national movement became somewhat flaccid. The moderates in the Congress had been discredited, their impotence exposed, and their supporters were thinking twice about adhering to the parent body. The Congress session at Allahabad in 1910 was a vapid affair and marked by indecision, over cautiousness and an aura of insecurity. Sir William Wedderburn presided over it and impressed upon his Allahabad audience that their future lay in 'hope', 'conciliation' and 'united effort'. The Congress patronized the All-India Shuddhi Conferences, and passed a resolution objecting strongly to separate representation in local bodies. The Congress was, however, desirous of amicable relations with the Muslim League. The language newspapers generally favoured this too, but were apprehensive about the League's stubborn adherence to communal representation and its desire that the government maintain the 1905 partition. A Hindu-Muslim conference was, however, held at Allahabad to devise means for the establishment of better relations between the two. Nothing concrete was however decided and a few days later there were Muslim and Sikh disturb-ances at Allahabad. The Hindus were quite disillusioned with the Muslim stance, and Madan Mohan Malviya spoke against the over-representation of Muslims in the Councils, in his speech before the Imperial Legislative Council. The Hindu press appreciated Malviya's firmness in remaining undaunted in the Imperial Council despite being opposed by his five 'separatist' colleagues.[1]

No less representative of the Hindu mood was the action of those who had earlier founded a Provincial Hindu Sabha to 'do for the Hindus . . . what the Muslim League has done for the Mahomadans'. This was proposed by Munshi Ganga Prasad Verma, Tej Bahadur Sapru, Lalit Mohan Banarji and Lala Parmeshwari Dayal and they hoped for unity among the Hindus. Its work was to ameliorate the condition of the depressed classes as the Muslim League had been demanding that the latter be treated as separate from the Hindus as far as elections were concerned. Basically, it aimed that Hindu interests should not be jeopardized politically. The newspapers were rather pessimistic about the Hindu Sabha as they felt it was 'only a counterblast to the Muslim League'; and where the latter had the sympathy of the bureaucracy, the Sabha would be 'greeted with thunders of official frowns and suspicions'. This organization would in fact encourage sectarianism and would retard the Congress movement.[2] However, the Hindu press welcomed its establishment as it felt that, government policy being what it was, it had become essential to organize the protection of Hindu interests. The rules of the UP Hindu Sabha clearly prohibited an encroachment on the province of the National Congress, by leaving alone general political and administrative questions which affected all communities equally. No religious or social issues would be discussed so that the government would not be embarrassed.[3] Pan-Hindusism had developed on account of the government's unfounded suspicions of Hindu intentions—the Arya Samaj was suspected of having extremist leanings, and the Gurukul Kangri at Haridwar was considered a training centre for future revolutionaries—and its pandering to the Muslims. The Hindu Sabha, however, was rather ineffective in its early years and pan-Hinduism did not catch on. Pandit Motilal Nehru in 1911 bemoaned Muslim unresponsiveness. He blamed the extremist Hindus and the crafty Muslim League for the over-representation of the Muslims in the Legislative Councils. The Calcutta Congress of 1911 was presided over by Bishan Narayan Dar, but it failed to enthuse much vigour into the Congress movement.

THE MUSLIM LABYRINTH

With a lull in the national movement and the Muslims being given the 'favoured child' treatment, they should have been complacent, but this was not so. The political aspirations of Muslim sects complicated the already existing religious discord. The following grouping would give a fair idea of the complex Muslim factor in the country:[4]

Organizations: Muslim League, Deoband Seminary, Firangi Mahal
Sects: Shias, Sunnis
Beliefs: Bigoted, Forward
Political Divisions: Moderates, Extremists
Economic Divisions: Peasants and Artisans—Educated Middle Class, Rich Landed Class

Out of these, the Muslim League was the politically most active. It is interesting to note the types of Muslims generally associated with it:

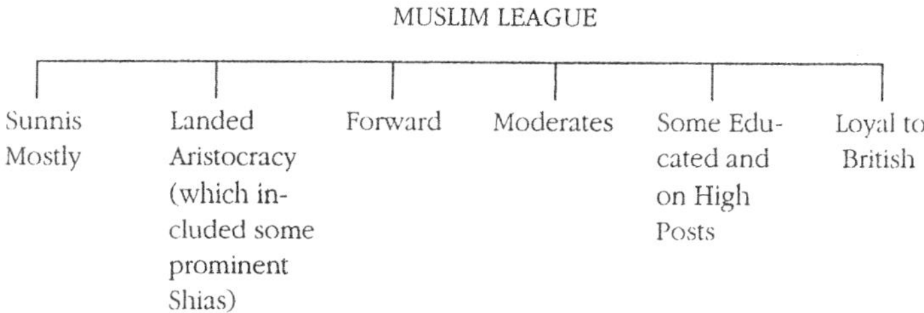

Government patronage to the Muslim League made the Shias disgruntled. A meeting of the Shia Muslims of Lucknow was held on 9 July 1911 in order to demand equal representation with the Sunnis on Legislative Councils and local bodies. Although some newspapers felt 'it was a fine retort to the meeting held by the members of the Muslim League . . .', others gave examples of leading Shia gentlemen like the Nawab of Rampur and Ameer Ali who did not hold the same views.[5] The Muslim League resolved to turn Aligarh College into a Muslim University. In this movement, the province was in the forefront. Out of a total collection of Rs. 16,08,683 its own contribution was Rs. 5,49,962 in 1911. This movement, seen as a politico-communal affair by the government, gave impetus to the rise of the advanced party consisting of not-so-well-placed Muslim sections in the League. The strongest evidence of their rising importance is the rise of the extremist Muslim press. Muhammad Ali in 1911 founded the *Comrade* at Calcutta and later the *Hamdard*. Zafar Ali Khan's *Zamindar* of Lahore, Khwaja Hasan Nizami's *Tauhid* (Meerut), Syed Wahiduddin's *Muslim Gazette* (Lucknow) and Abul Kalam Azad's *Al Hilal* (Calcutta) are some powerful newspapers which enhanced the influence of the advanced group.[6]

THE GROWTH OF PAN-ISLAMISM

Despite all this activity among Muslims, they were fairly united and the majority among them were grateful to the government for its benevolence. Anglo-Muslim camaraderie, however, received a jolt in 1911 and was dissipated to some extent by 1912, because of certain events of far-reaching consequence in India and the world.

The European threat to a Muslim country was felt as early as the Russo-Turkish war of 1876-8. The Koranic belief that of all religions Islam should be the dominant one, was being flouted. The Turkish Sultan was regarded by a large section of Muslims as the Khalifa, descendant of the Prophet. Abdul Hamid II, the Sultan of Turkey, was a true perpetuator of the feeling that the Islamic countries were in danger and had to be protected against European onslaught.

The Turkish victory over Greece in 1897 was hailed by Indian Muslims and the prestige of the Sultan was enhanced. In Kanpur, in 1898, the Sultan was acknowledged by Muslims as a true Khalifa, and their allegiance to him was assured. Their scheme included scholarships for Muslim youths to study in Cairo from where they were likely to return fully imbued with Pan-Islamic ideas. The Macedonian crisis of 1903, the Turko-Egyptian Frontier dispute of 1906, and the British occupation of Egypt, the Anglo-French agreement over Morocco and the Anglo-Russian agreement over Persia in 1907 created suspicion in the minds of Muslims all over the world that the European powers were taking an unhealthy interest in their territories. In India, Muslims protested and even the UP saw several agitations, though not very impassioned. The Young Turk Revolution in 1908 in Turkey converted Turkey into a constitutional monarchy with Abdul Hamid II as the ruler. In 1909 he was deposed by his brother. The removal of Abdul Hamid as Sultan disturbed Indian Muslims who had come to identify him with the venerated Khalifa. The more sensible among them advised discretion and offered convincing rationalizations; Abdul Hamid's exit notwithstanding, the special feeling for Turkey continued. The Turkish Sultan tried his best to muster financial help from Muslims all over, including India. An agent of the Turkish Naval League came to Lucknow in 1910 to solicit subscriptions from the Muslim's to strengthen the Turkish army. Even earlier, Abdul Hamid had sent out propagandists to preach the doctrine of Khilafat.[7]

The invasion by Italy of Tripoli in 1911, which subsequently led to the seizure of the Turkish province in 1912, was interpreted by Muslims as a definite move for the extinction of the power of Islam, both temporal and spiritual. Muhammad Ali in his *Comrade* made it clear that the Muslims in India expected the British government to interfere in favour of Tripoli. The British did nothing to check the invasion of Tripoli, and in addition remained immobile when Russia bombarded Meshed. The belief of the Muslims that the British government was a safe custodian of Islamic interest was fast evaporating.

The Italian attack created a feeling of unity among the Muslims throughout the world.[8] Disaffection with the British was exacerbated by the revocation of the partition of Bengal in December 1911. The Muslim press and the Muslim League were stunned at this, and felt this had been done to please 'anarchists' and 'seditionists'. Government seemed to have sacrificed Muslim interests to Hindu agitation and administrative convenience. The Muslims realized two facts. First, it was futile to expect that 'for all time to come the Government of India will simply set their sail to every passing gust in the Muslim community'. Second, as Muhammad Ali declared, 'agitation is acknowledged by the government to be the only effective method of converting them . . .'.[9]

The third blow fell in August 1912, in the form of government rejection of the Muslims University scheme. The Government of India ordered that the Muslim University was to be localized at Aligarh and not have affiliated colleges elsewhere. This great project on which so much time and money had been invested and which symbolized the projected regeneration of the whole Muslim community, had been repulsed. Young, hot blooded men like Muhammad Ali and Zafar Ali Khan were the most dejected. The loss of faith in British was noticed by the Commissioner of Lucknow in 1912.

> I do not see how any one who is in frequent contact with the Muslims interested in politics, can be of opinion that our prestige with them stands where it did a year ago. At the same time they are well aware that their interests are bound up with ours. What we have to anticipate from them is for more active and persistent agitation to gain their objects than we have ever experienced in the past.[10]

The language press seemed to be divided in its loyalty to the British government. A part of it protested against Hewett's assertion that Pan-Islamism was catching on in India, and the editors affirmed their loyalty to the British Crown. They blamed European journalists for spreading false rumours![11] Yet there were others who published the impassioned verse of men like Maulana Shibli Nomani. Some editors infused with religious fervour wrote, 'This is the time for Indian Muslims to rise up and sacrifice their lives and property in the cause of religion.'[12] The British government was suspected of favouring the European combination against Turkey in the Balkan Wars in 1912-13. The All-India Muslim League met towards the end of 1912 at Lucknow and condemned the attitude of the British government. On the whole the

Muslim press regarded this war as a struggle between the 'Cross' and the 'Crescent' and even the hitherto loyalist newspapers now instigated the Muslims in India to help the Turks. The *Muslim Gazette* of Lucknow of 23 April 1913 quoted Maulvi Saiyid Abdul Wadood of Bareilly, who 'warns Muslims that their condition will be a deplorable one when no independent Muslim Kingdom is left'. Muhammed Ali, Abul Kalam Azad and Zafar Ali Khan reminded Muslims of the Islamic brotherhood. According to Zafar Ali Khan, to the man in the street 'Pan-Islamism was synonymous with a gigantic union of the Moslems of the world having for its cherished object the extermination of Christianity as a living force.'[13]

SOCIETIES, FUNDS AND LEADERS

The young, advanced leadership in the League believed in agitation—instigated by violent articles demagogic speeches and pressing speeches in the press—and in constitutionally capturing all Muslim organizations so that theirs would be the views represented to government. The agitationists were inspired by Muhammad Ali and Shaukat Ali, and the constitutionalists were more subdued and had Wazir Hassan with his lawyer clan from Lucknow to guide them organizationally. Amidst the heightened Islamic fervour, when the Aga Khan resigned in 1912, the Ali brothers, Mohammad Yakub of Moradabad, and Wazir Hassan, succeeded in the contest for leadership in the All-India Muslim League. These leaders were able to muster the support of Nadwat-ul-Ulema chief, Maulana Shibli Nomani, as well as liberal leaders like Syed Raza Ali.[14]

The Turkish relief Fund was instituted and all classes of Muslims contributed to it. Appeals were made by newspapers like *Al Bashir* of Etawah, *Aligarh Institute Gazette* and *Al Mushir* of Moradabad to all prominent men of the UP to devise means for raising subscriptions for the Fund. These were the manager of Madrassa-i-Deoband, the Secretary of the Nadwat-ul-Ulema, Nawab Viqar-ul-Mulk, Raja of Mahmudabad, Raja of Jahangirabad, Honorary Secretary of the Muslim College, Secretary of the Muslim League and the Honorary Secretary of the Muslim League, and the Honorary Secretary of the All-India Muslim Educational Conference.[15] The growing closeness between Aligarh and the Deoband Muslim leaders led to the establishment in 1913 of *Nizarat-ul-Maarif*, or the Academy of Koranic learning in Delhi. Its main object of this was to instruct the Western educated

Muslim youth in the Koran and shake off the ill-founded scepticism about Islamic beliefs.

In order to ameliorate the conditions of their co-religionists in Turkey, Indian Muslims contributed to the Red Crescent Societies that had sprung up all over the country. Two missions of the Red Crescent Societies went to Turkey. The second of these was led by Dr. M.A. Ansari in 1912. Zafar Ali Khan visited Turkey in 1913. On their return to India, Dr. Ansari, in a speech to the students of M.A.O. College, Aligarh, assured them that the spirit of the Turkish nation was not dead, and his mission had achieved a fusion of Turkish and Indian interests.

The necessity of an all-embracing Pan-Islamic organization was felt by most press men. Maulvi Sajid Abdul Wadood of Bareilly, for example, accused the British in the *Muslim Gazette* on 23 April 1913, of conspiring to destroy the independence of Islamic countries. He urged the formation of an organization to preserve the holy places of Islam. A scheme was published by Mushir Husain Kidwai of Gudia, Barabanki for the formation of a society called the Anjuman-i-Khaddam-i-Kaaba, or the society for the servants of Kaaba. It was formed on 6 May 1913 at the residence of Maulana Abdul Bari, head of the theologians of Firangi Mahal in Lucknow. Its members included Shaukat Ali, Muhammad Ali and Mukhtar Ahmad Ansari of Delhi. It contained the advanced party in the Muslim League and some Ulema, but the latter's membership was limited. The Deoband Ulema declared against the Anjuman. Only the Firangi Mahal and Badaun schools of theologians joined it. The subscription, which every member paid, was divided into three parts. One half was to be used for the defence of the Islamic holy places, one quarter was used for administrative expenditure and the remainder would be kept in reserve for use in connection with the *Haj* and other religious duties. The Anjuman was not welcomed by all classes of Muslims, who regarded it as exploitative, futile and impractical. Yet it grew rapidly in membership. There were members in every district of the UP except five, and branches in about eleven.[16]

Despite various allegations hurled against it, the Anjuman stood as a symbol of unity between young, Western educated Muslims and the Ulema, between Abdul Bari of Firangi Mahal and the Ali brothers, between the Muslim League and the masses, and these affiliations were an important phenomenon in the Khilafat movement which was to follow.

HINDU-MUSLIM CAMARADERIE

Disillusioned with the British, both internally and internationally, Muslims felt the need to come closer to the Hindus, whom they had tried to out race politically and communally for such a long time. This was the attitude of the advanced party in the Muslim League which was branded as the extremist group by the conservative elements. Thus the rich, the conservatives, and the Nawabs remained aloof from the political aspect of Pan-Islamism and expressed loyalty to the British. They insisted that it was wrong to say that Muslim states were influenced by Pan-Islamism to combine against a Christian power. Pan-Islamism was not a political or a military movement only a religious movement for the social, moral and religious uplifting of the Muslims.[17]

Nevertheless, the advanced party in the All-India Muslim League, and even the adherents of this group in the local leagues created an atmosphere of an intensifying Hindu-Muslim amity. For example, Saiyid Raza Ali, the Secretary of the Moradabad Muslim League, denounced the separatist policy of the Muslim League and advocated unity with Hindus. The *Kaiser-i-Hind*, Faizabad, of 11 January 1912 expressed its happiness at the greater attendance of Muslims at the last Congress. It counselled that 'Muslims being in a minority cannot work out their regeneration separately, and suggested that they cooperate with Hindus.' The Muslim League conference at Lucknow in 1913 had Shafi as President, who seemed inclined towards reconciliation with the Hindus. Munshi Ehtishan Ali, as Chairman of the reception committee, supported simultaneous examination, creation of an Executive Council for the UP and generally assumed an attitude of gradually 'falling in line with the attitude of the Congress'. The Hindu press was happy at this healthy development, though some papers wondered at the inconsistency of the Muslims.

The Hindu press was justified in projecting Hindu suspiciousness regarding the good intentions of the Muslims, as the latter could not be expected to happily and firmly shrug off their age old grievances, and as said earlier, they themselves were a motley lot. Liberal Muslims wanted to unite with the Hindus politically, and follow the constitutional agitation of the Congress to make self-government a success. The anti-liberal papers were unhappy that overriding the wishes of people like Ameer Ali, Aga Khan and Nawab Viqar-ul-Mulk, the Muslim League had adopted self-government as its ideal.[18] These rumblings notwithstanding, the Muslim League and the Congress joined hands in promoting a meeting of Hindus and Muslims at the Allahabad Mayo Hall. Eminent personages like Dr. Satish Chandra, Dr. Banarji, Dr. Sapru, Maulvi Rahmatullah and Motilal Nehru participated.

In the course of new policy orientations, the Bakr-Id riots at Ayodhya in 1912, the Muharram riots at Agra in 1913, and the Bakr-Id riots at Farrukhabad caused minor aberrations in unity moves.[19] A blatant disregard by the authorities for Hindu sentiments seemed evident. They seemed to be eager to placate the highly excitable Muslims who were on the warpath. The sensible newspapers felt this was not only opposed to 'British traditions and justice', but was also 'derogatory to British prestige'.[20]

At this juncture a unique happening came to pass. It let loose certain forces, and revealed certain subtleties of the Muslim character. The inherent unifying force in the Muslim community was revealed, and the government as well as the other religions realized that no amount of sectarianism would convince Muslims to make compromises in religion for the sake of sound politics. This incident was the Kanpur Mosque case. A small washing place projecting from the Machhli Bazar Mosque at Kanpur was demolished by the Kanpur Municipality in 1913 as a road had to be built. Muslim children and elders collected there and started laying bricks to rebuild the demolished portion. District Magistrate, Tyler and the Superintendent of Police, with a full police force, fired on them and a riot occurred wherein several were killed or injured, or imprisoned. Protests against this were presented by leading Muslims like Shahid Hussain and the Raja of Mahmudabad, but were rejected by Sir James Meston, the Lt.-Governor. There was large scale reporting in the press and the Muslim newspapers outdid themselves in inflammatory and sensational articles. Some orthodox Hindu papers insinuated that the dead were put in gunny-bags and thrown into the Ganga.

The Muslim newspapers accused Meston of being incensed with the advanced party succeeding in the Muslim League and trying to curb them. The Ulema, the advanced Muslims and the Muslim newspapers all protested vehemently. The papers quoted the Shariat and said that every part of a mosque is sacred. Meston attributed the entire conflagration to incendiary articles in the press. He wrote to Hardinge, 'There was next to no excitement in Kanpur itself, and the cry of sacrilege was got up by wire-pullers outside.'[21] He resorted to proscription of newspaper articles which would create trouble. Articles like 'Repeat the Tabir', 'Kanpur Ki Khuni Dastan', 'The Poems of Maulana Shibli' were banned, and certain issues of the *Union Gazette* of Bareilly, banned. This incited the Muslims more, and persons like Sajid Muhammad (Fakhir) from Allahabad gave it a Muslim *versus* Christian colour. Thus 'the Kanpur affair had a greater effect on the feelings of Indian Muslims than the wars of Tripoli and the Balkans'.[22]

Muslim leaders visited Kanpur after the riot. These included Muhammad Ali, Shaukat Ali, Abul Kalam Azad, Zafar Ali Khan, and Mashirul Haq of Patna. They wrote detailed articles in their newspapers, which incited the people. What was remarkable was that all Muslims were united in their condemnation of the government. Even a loyalist newspaper like the *Al Bashir* of Etawah on 16 September criticized Meston. The editor wrote that 'he deplored that the Local Government trusts its Kanpur officials more than it should'. Nawab Viqar-ul-Mulk requested his co-religionists to collect funds to help the afflicted people. Consequently, a Kanpur Mosque Fund was set up. Azad Sobhani, the leading local agitator of the Kanpur affair, discovered, as a result, what fame and money were to be won by pouring vitriol into the columns of the press. The British were impressed by the great Muslim upsurge.

Meston, faced with a fait accompli, went off to England on 'other duty' and in his absence Hardinge visited Kanpur, received a Muslim deputation, and assuaged religious feelings by promising some structural device in the mosque. The riot case was withdrawn and the accused were let off. Muslims were mollified and blamed Meston for their woes. They realized the efficacy of agitation and the advanced party preened itself in victory.[23]

This had a paradoxical effect on Hindu-Muslim relations. On the one hand it engendered unity among the two communities, and on the other, the Hindu papers demanded the release of the Ayodhya rioters and the settlement of the cow slaughter question at Ayodhya. Fearing another upsurge, Meston ordered their release. Hindus had taken advantage of the government's trauma, but the Ayodhya decision was more difficult to take as it involved two sensitive communities, while Kanpur was only an Anglo-Muslim affair and easier to settle.[24]

THE GREAT WAR

The keenness of the British to have peace on the home front was already evident, and with the advent of 1914, this eagerness became an obsession. Meston convened a conference at Lucknow to settle differences between the Hindus and the Muslims in 1914. The conference appointed a conciliation committee with Mahmudabad as its President, but it did not achieve much, basically because of the suspicions of the two communities regarding Meston's good intentions. Besides, this seemed a conference of 'honourables and title holders' and not true representatives of Muslim sentiments. The decision of Mahmudabad to organize a deputation to wait upon the Viceroy was labelled sycophancy, and the advanced party called it 'servile' flattery of officials.[25]

The delegates from the UP at the Karachi Session in 1914, led by Pandit Bishan Narayan Dar, Babu Ganga Prasad Verma and Lala Lajpat Rai, withdrew from the Congress on the third day, as a protest against the disregard for their views shown by the president, Nawab Syed Muhammad. The UP leaders, Pandit M.M. Malviya, Gokhale, Pandit Motilal Nehru, Dr. Satish Chandra and Dr. T.B. Sapru, were conspicuous by their absence. This was because all were dissatisfied with the president who recognized separate representation. The reason for the Congress not evoking much interest could also have been the advent of localized politics. The Hindu Sabhas, the Provincial councils, the local Muslim Leagues, etc., all were platforms where the individual could gain power and prestige. The Hindu newspapers propounded very sound logic. Communal patriotism and provincial patriotism if rightly understood do not conflict with the larger national patriotism, and 'express the belief that Hindu leaders will not allow Hindu sabhas to injure the Congress. . . . Hindu sabhas will deal only with communal questions and these also in such a way as not to jeopardise national interests.'[26] This diversity of interest between the 'main body' and the 'provincial bodies' was most felt in the difference of character of the All-India Muslim League and the UP Provincial League. The former was the seat of power of the advanced Muslims who until 1914 could not gain much power at the local level. For example, the Etawah Muslim League meeting held on 29 May 1914, had the editor of *Al Bashir*, a loyalist paper, as President. This was not liked by the liberals as he was the head of a sycophantic group, and not a true deacon of Muslim interest.[27]

Turkey sent several emissaries to India to fan Pan-Islamic and anti-British feelings here. For example, Tewfik Bey, a journalist of Constantinople, came to India and also attended the All-India Muslim League meeting at Agra in 1914. The post-Tripoli period had convinced even the Turkish government of the efficacy of Pan-Islamism. The advantages of Pan-Islamic hysteria were manifold. Money could be obtained with the 'defence of Islam' as an excuse; anti-Turkish agitators in the Arabic-speaking provinces could be quietened; Turkish and other Muslim subjects of Russia could be won over; the disparate elements of the Ottoman Empire could be coalesced. The Turkish government visualized 'a confederation of the Muslim peoples, with Turkey occupying therein the place which Prussia did in the German Confederation'.[28]

When war broke out in 1914 between Serbia and Austria, Muslim sympathies were with Austria on account of recent hostilities between Serbia and Turkey. When the British entered the war against Turkey, however, the Indian Muslims received a shock. The government tried to show Muslim support by taking affirmative signatures from leading Muslims. The All-India Muslim League, the UP Muslim League, the trustees of the Aligarh College and the Committee of the All-India Muslim Educational Conference were those who passed loyalty resolutions. The Shias, headed by Maulana Syed Naser Husain Mujtahid, were especially loyal. Fatwas were issued by leading Maulvis saying that this war was not based on religion, and it was the duty of Muslims to remain loyal to the British. Only the Ulema could convince the illiterate masses 'that the safety and well-being of the Muslims lie in adhering firmly to their loyalty and devotion to the British government'.[29] Well-known Pan-Islamists like Mazharul Haque, Abul Kalam Azad, and Muhammad Ali stressed the exclusiveness of religious ties with the Khalifa, without any encroachment on the political aspect desired or required.

However, gradually the Pan-Islamists became more belligerent in their writings. Muhammad Ali's article, 'The Choice of the Turks', expressed admiration for the Germans and was objected to by the government. The security of his *Comrade* was forfeited. The Government of India took action against Muslim papers. Muhammad Ali and Shaukat Ali were interned under the Defence of India Act in 1915. The governments of Bengal, Punjab and the UP passed externment orders against Abul Kalam Azad whose connection with the *Hamdard* in UP resulted in its closure.[30]

So much repressive activity was bound to arouse a simmering discontent among the Muslims, especially the radicals. Some of them tried to stir up an armed rebellion in India with the help of the Musalmans of Turkey and Afghanistan. The 'Silk Letter Conspiracy' was engineered by Obeidulla, a converted Sikh, trained as a Maulvi at the Muslim religious school at Deoband in Saharanpur. This aimed at an attack on the North-West Frontier simultaneously with a Muslim uprising in the country. He was, however, caught.[31]

The most alarming result of the War as far as the British were concerned was the coming closer of Hindus and Muslims. In both the Congress and the Muslim League the advanced party was gaining ground. The Maharaja of Darbhanga had complained to Meston that landed gentry were being pushed out and men like M.M. Malviya were dominating the Benares Hindu University. In 1915 the League resumed its activities at the behest of M.A. Jinnah, and the Congress and the League held their sessions simultaneously at the same place. The Lucknow Pact of 1916 was a direct result of this remarkable Hindu-Muslim camaraderie that had intensified during the course of the war.[32]

That they were ill-matched partners, however, is undeniable when one considers the mammoth proportions Muslim separatism took on subsequently leading to the partition of the country. The partition of a province had let off earth-shaking forces that had, after undergoing a variety of transformations, culminated in the partition of India in 1947.

THE ESSENCE OF PAN-ISLAMISM

The ideology of the Pan-Islamic movement as conceived by Muhammad Ali and Maulana Azad touched the nerve of the Muslim people in India, who whether educated or uneducated, saw in it their own subconscious yearning for political and religious freedom. It effectively highlighted the need for an independent centre for the Muslims, for the attainment of which the territorial confines of nationality could be ignored. Pan-Islamist forces and concepts stressed the distinct political entity of the Muslims, which could be achieved through recognition of Islamic brotherhood.

The primary need of the day was to determine the centrifugal force around which Muslims could be expected to rally. The Khalifa or spiritual head could be that centre, for whose protection religious fervour could cross all bounds. The Sultan of Turkey was recognized as the Khalifa by many and Muslim theologians had explanations for this contention. Sultan Salim conquered Egypt in 1517 and obtained the guardianship of Mecca and Medina. He was bestowed the title of Khalifa by a prince of Baghdad, Khalifas, together with a flag, a sword and a cloak, the relics of the Prophet. The present Sultan of Turkey had inherited his title from his ancestor Salim.[33]

The European threat to Turkey was regarded as a threat to the Muslim religion, and Muslims raised the cry of *jehad* against the infidel. The Sultanate in jeopardy was regarded as disastrous by most Muslims and engendered Muslim unity. However, the aberrant to this unity was the basic dispute between Shias and Sunnis regarding the spirituality of the Sultan. Sunnis revered the first four Khalifas, Hazrat Abu Bakr, Omar, Osman, and Ali; Shias believed only in Ali, the last of the four Khalifas, and their priests openly rebuked the first three Khalifas. Consequently, the Shias did not regard the Turkish Sultan as the Khalifa. He was only the head of the greatest Muslim empire at present. This difference of belief led to violent quarrels, but when after 1911 the very existence of Turkey was threatened with extermination, Muslims favoured coming to the aid of the beleaguered country.

Muslim leaders repeatedly stressed the religious aspect of the whole issue. 'In fact, the protection of the Holy places rather than the preservation of the tottering Turkish empire provided the rallying point for virtually all sections of the Muslim community.'[34] The Ulema contributed greatly to Pan-Islamic fervour. These were the interpreters of the Koran and all Muslims looked to them for religious guidance. Besides, they manned the Madarsas, where most Muslim boys were educated. They fiercely advocated the orthodox type of traditional education rather than that offered by the British, and used religion to convince Muslims to adhere to their brand of education. Their word was law, and thus they were an important link between different Muslim groups. The orthodox and the advanced were brought together, and 1912 marked the beginning of the formal participation by Ulemas as religious leaders in national politics.[35]

Whether Pan-Islamism was a religious phenomenon or had political overtones cannot be easily decided. It was a mixture of both. As Azad summed up in 1912, 'There will be nothing left with us if we separate politics from religion.'[36] The Muslims, as a measure of self-protection, and those among them who believed in British benevolence, reiterated their purely religious interest in Turkey, but the political aspect overshadowed the religious as events were to show.

Adherence to Pan-Islamism was also a medium through which Muslims in India could nullify the deprivations suffered by them on account of being a minority. The glories of the medieval Muslim empire were still fresh in their minds, and the

institution of Khilafat therefore provided them with the psychological make-belief against their secondary position in India. In identifying with the Khilafat, Indian Muslims identified themselves with the magnificent achievements of the Turks.[37]

Pan-Islamism was a contravention of the concept of territorial nationality. Muhammad Ali and Azad regarded territorial secular nationalism as a disruptive force. Ali wrote, 'Turkey is almost as much or as less Fatherland of Indian Musalmans as that of the Turks themselves.'[38] The newspapers sponsoring the cause of the advanced party wrote . . . 'it is on account of this feeling of universal brotherhood among Muslims that Indian Muslims treat matters affecting the Muslim world on the whole as of primary importance and relegate Indian affairs to a secondary position'.[39] There were dissenting Muslim papers who advocated that Muslims should understand they were Indians first and Muslims later but these were few, and lost in the Pan-Islamic communal fervour.[40]

This Islamic concept was certainly anti-national and the irony of the situation became clearer when, at the time of the Khilafat movement, the Congress party, a symbol of the national movement, supported the Islamic movement just because it was anti-British. Two concepts are therefore revealed, which affected the turn the national movement later took. One was the politicization of Pan-Islamism, which propounded lofty religiosity, but did not lose much sleep over the advent of Kemal Ataturk in 1924 and the death of the Khilafat. The other was the communalization of the commendable cause of nationalism, so that as politics grew more complicated, Muslim separatism became a palpable, distinguishable force on the national scene.

CONCLUSION

The struggle between nationalism and colonialism had begun tentatively with the latter very much in control. However, as the years passed and the latent communal, cultural, social and economic factors surfaced and became inextricably interwoven in the fabric of the national movement, the struggle became more forceful. Simultaneously and paradoxically it generated disruptive forces which threatened unified nationality itself. The imperial power experienced periods of discomfiture and anxiety but, nevertheless, took advantage of dissensions among the ranks of the enemy and nurtured them. The politicization of almost every aspect of society became sharper and more pronounced, and attitudes—became more compartmentalized. This was clearly evident in the language newspapers, who took emphatic stands in accordance with their sharpened perception of the myriad issues, and became increasingly effective in communication and reflection. The language press gradually assumed great importance as a mouthpiece of the nationalists and communalists, most of whom were owners or editors of newspapers.

NOTES

1. VNR of UP, *Advocate*, Lucknow, 29 Jan. 1911; *Abhyudaya*, Allahabad, 26 Jan. 1911; *Musafir*, Agra, 13 Jan. 1911; Robinson, op.cit., p. 195.
2. VNR of UP, *Leader*, Allahabad, 22 Feb. 1911; *Mashriq*, Gorakhpur, 24 Jan. 1911; *Abhyudaya*, Allahabad, 6 April 1911.
3. Ibid., *Leader*, 20 April 1911.
4. This Table has been drawn up by reviewing the language newspapers and Robinson, op.cit., p. 215. No grouping of this type can be absolutely accurate and I have done this for the sake of clarity.
5. VNR of UP, *Tafrih*, Lucknow, 14 and 28 July 1911; *Mashriq*, Gorakhpur, 14 July 1911.
6. Robinson, op.cit., pp. 201-2.
7. VNR of UP, *Al Bashir*, Etawah, 22 Feb. 1910.
8. VNR of UP, *Naiyar-i-Azam*, Moradabad, 19 March 1912; *Saddharm Pracharak*, Bijnor, 18 Sept. 1912.
9. VNR of UP, *Leader*, Allahabad, 24 Dec. 1911; *Aligarh Institute Gazette*, 20 Dec. 1911; Robinson, op.cit., p. 203.
10. Home Pol. A, June 1912 and March 1913, pp. 45-55.
11. Robinson, op.cit., p. 205. There were several language newspapers in 1912 who denied being Pan-Islamists. These were *Al Mushir*, Moradabad, 4 Oct.; *Naiyar-i-Azam*, Moradabad, 19 Oct.; *Zul Quarnain*, Badaun, 21 Aug.; *Mashriq*, Gorakhpur, 29 Aug.
12. VNR of UP, 1912: *Rohilkhand Gazette*, Bareilly, 8 Dec.; *Tajir*, Meerut, 4 Nov.
13. Bhargava, op.cit., p. 37.
14. VNR of UP, *Rohilkhand Gazette*, Bareilly, 16 March 1912; Verma, op.cit., pp. 215-17; Robinson, op.cit., p. 206.
15. VNR of UP, 1912.
16. Robinson, op.cit., pp. 208-10. Muhammad Ali Papers J.M.I., VNR of UP, *Mashriq*, Gorakhpur, 13 May 1913; *Muslim Gazette*, Lucknow, 21 May 1913; Anti-papers: 1913: *Musafir*, Agra, 6 June; *Zia-ul-Islam*, Moradabad, May; *Al Mushir*, Moradabad, 18 June; *Naiyar-i- Azam*, Moradabad, 19 June; Prasad, op.cit., pp. 15-19.
17. VNR of UP, *Mashriq*, Gorakhpur, 29 Oct. 1913; B.B. Misra, op.cit., p. 161.

18. VNR of UP, 1913; Pro-Liberal: *Muslim Gazette*, Lucknow, 4 June; Anti-Liberal: *Al Bashir*, Etawah, 18 Nov.; VNR of UP, *Leader*, Allahabad, July 1918.
19. VNR of UP, *Advocate*, Lucknow, 24 Nov. 1913; *Musafir*, Agra, 12 Dec. 1913; *Kaiser-i-Hind*, Faizabad, 28 Nov. 1912 and 26 June 1913; *Abhyudaya*, Allahabad, 5 Dec. 1912.
20. VNR of UP, *Azad*, Kanpur, 17 Nov. 1914; *Arya Mitra*, Agra, 16 Nov. 1914.
21. Hardinge Papers, Vol. II, 1913, No. 24. This description has been drawn up from the language newspaper reports of 1913.
22. VNR of UP, 1913; *Al Shahid*, Allahabad, 20 May; *Union Gazette*, Bareilly, 21 Sept.; *Kaiser-i-Hind*, Faizabad, 18 Sept.; Bhargava, op.cit., p. 39.
23. Robinson, op.cit., p. 214; VNR of UP, *Leader*, Allahabad, 15 Oct. 1913.
24. VNR of UP, op.cit., *Leader*, 15 and 24 Oct. 1913; *Anand*, Lucknow, 23 Oct. 1913; *Abhyudaya*, Allahabad, 15 Nov. 1913.
25. VNR of UP, *Muslim Gazette*, Lucknow, 30 April 1914, *Naiyar-i-Azam*, Moradabad, 12 April 1914.
26. VNR of UP, 1914: *Leader*, Allahabad, 22 Feb.; *Musawat*, Allahabad, 15 Jan.; *Zul Qarnain*, Badaun, 13 Jan.
27. VNR of UP, *Musawat*, Allahabad, 11 June 1914.
28. Prasad, op.cit., p. 22; Home Pol. D., July 1916, No. 33, p. 5.
29. VNR of UP, 1914, *Musawat*, Allahabad, 7 Nov.; *Mashriq*, Gorakhpur, 3 Nov.; *Al Bashir*, Etawah, 10 Nov.; GAD File No. 590/1914; Prasad, ibid., pp. 49-55.
30. VNR of UP, 1914: *Al Khalil*, Bijnor, 24 Dec.; *Asr-i-Jadid*, Meerut, 24 Dec.; *Saiyara*, Lucknow, 26 Dec.; GAD, File No. 696/1914, Council Question regarding Turkey Ki Himayat, by Khan Bahadur Qazi Azizuddin; Bhargava, op.cit., pp. 40-4; Verma, op.cit., pp. 65-7; Bamford, op.cit., pp. 118-22.
31. Saxena, op.cit., pp. 157-9.
32. Sir J. Meston to Chelmsford, 4 Sept. 1916. Meston Papers, GAD, File No. 423/1918; Saxena, ibid., p. 92; Verma, op.cit., pp. 164-7.
33. VNR of UP, *Oudh Akhbar*, Lucknow, April 1906.
34. Hasan, op.cit., p. 2.
35. Meston to Hardinge, 25 March 1915, Hardinge Papers (89), ibid., pp. 1-11.
36. *Al Hilal*, 8 Sept. 1912.
37. Hasan, op.cit., pp. 53-5.
38. Quoted in Mihr Ghulam, *Taharukat-i-Azad*, Lahore, 1959, pp. 203-4.
39. VNR of UP, *Muslim Gazette*, Lucknow, 19 June 1912.
40. VNR of UP, *Advocate*, Lucknow, 9 June 1912; *Oudh Akhbar*, Lucknow, 9 June 1912.

PART V

The Agrarian Question as Viewed by the Press

9. The Peasants and Landlords

A variety of social and economic institutions were responsible for evolving a distinctive economic system in the NWP and Awadh. Since the economy of the second half of the nineteenth century and early twentieth century was based primarily on agriculture, the importance of the peasants cannot be minimized. They were the pillars on which the agrarian system rested. The government could encourage them or crush them, but it was impossible to ignore them. As in other spheres, colonial control in the agrarian economy was a highly politicized affair.

The NWP and Awadh or the United Provinces of Agra and Awadh as they came to be known later, was a single Province, under one Lt.-Governor, but the north-western part had certain distinctive features not part and parcel of Awadh. Before dealing with the agrarian economy as a whole, it is necessary to bring out these differences. These made the task of the British more difficult, who found it an uphill task to reconcile these with the psychological and habitual forces that had emerged as a result of historical processes.

REGIONAL DIFFERENCES IN THE PROVINCE

An understanding of the revenue system established by the British and the types of land tenures in both parts of the United Provinces is necessary before we can comprehend the subsequent economic disturbances that lead to agrarian and social unrest.

The North-West Provinces

The British were interested in securing maximum land revenue. They wanted to do away with intermediaries in revenue collection, and maintain direct contact with the village communities who had been bestowed with proprietary rights. Revenue was exacted with great severity from them. Despite official utterances deploring the evil from almost the commencement of British administration, the process of public sale of title for revenue default was prevalent and resulted in proprietors of land losing vast acreages. For example, 31,000 acres were transferred between 1831 and 1841 at Agra.[1] The Rajput village lineages lost their proprietary rights in a large way. At Kanpur, the Thakur's hold on the district had been reduced from 50 to 38 per cent in 1840, to 31 per cent in 1874, to 30 per cent in 1907.[2] Since revenue benefits accrued to those actually cultivating the land, many landowners who had formally let out their lands took to cultivation. By the 1890s W.H. Moreland was reporting from the Unnao District that all Rajputs, except the proud Bais Thakur, had now taken to cultivation with their own hands.[3] The pressure of population on the land, the subdivision of proprietary rights, the rise in prices which benefited the cultivator, and the consequent necessity for land-owning families to rely increasingly on direct exploitation of the soil, helped to make cultivating possession more valuable than rental tribute.

The idea that we get of the NWP was that, on account of a fragmentation of holdings, the growth of petty landlordism took place. There were the village proprietors or the zamindars.[4] Under the prevailing mahalvari system, the local village authorities or zamindars (of one or more, or parts of one or more villages) were recognized as landlords of their mahals or estates, and paid the land revenue directly to the state.[5] Taluqdars or big landlords were not prominent in the NWP and the settlement was predominantly with the zamindars. In most of the provinces, joint proprietorship prevailed, which tended to preserve or reinforce the economic and political dominance of a proprietary lineage. Thus a particular caste group controlled the land and dominated political life in such places.[6] Yet the landed proprietors in the NWP were essentially petty yeomen. An instructive example of peasant proprietary was the subdivision of Kosi, in the Mathura district. Here 55 per cent of the cultivated area was held by Jats, and except a few resident shopkeepers and menial servants, here everyone was to some extent a proprietor. The headman realized the revenue, and not a single landholder could be called large or with any eminent social position. Consequently, there were no cringing menials oppressed by overlords'.[7]

The natural result of this was the even distribution of wealth among the people. Compared to Awadh, the people lived in comfort and there was less poverty. Even during times of natural calamities, the Jat somehow managed to brave the storm. The great advantage of this type of tenure was that incomes was not spent to humour the extravagance of some magnate, who was not always willing to develop the resources of the country to improve the lot of the people. The development of peasant proprietorship to a large extent enabled the growth of interest on the part of the peasant in improving his land and investing money on its betterment.

To understand the advantages accruing to the tenantry in comparison to Awadh, a fair idea of the tenurial system of the NWP is essential. The automatic extension of the Bengal Act X of 1859 to the NWP had established an occupancy right for any cultivator who could show twelve years' unbroken possession, and so, to some extent, had reduced the traditional distinction between 'the non-resident *pahi* cultivator who took up land on a year to year basis and the resident *chapparband* or *khudkasht* cultivator'.[8] The Rent Act of 1873 was exclusively for the NWP and was considered a sort of a complement to the Land Revenue Act which had come into force. This also had a lot of deficiencies, and to amend these, the Act of 1881 was passed as a consolidating measure, the old act being re-enacted with the amendments approved by the Council.

The Rent Act of 1881 seemed to be beneficial for cultivators, landlords and the government. A cultivator with a permanent interest in the land and not liable to eviction at the landholder's pleasure, would be induced to improve the land; the landholder would be sure of getting his rent and would be freed from the trouble and expense of making improvements. The government in turn could claim a share of the increased profits of the cultivator and the landowner at the time of the revision of settlement. This seemed the ideal land-tenure system, but its actual working failed to live up to expectations. It became a fruitful source of discord between landholders and cultivators, and injured agriculture to some extent. The cultivator was always anxious to acquire the occupancy right by completing twelve years' occupation, while the landlord made all possible endeavour to prevent the acquisition of that right.[9]

The reasons are not far to seek. The tenants had definitely gained. Getting rents of occupancy tenants enhanced was difficult, and landlords preferred to let them hold on at low rents from settlement to settlement even if the value of land had risen. Besides, tenants had in many cases established themselves as under-proprietors or middlemen, thus evading the law regarding the non-transferability of their holdings. The result of this was that, while paying low rents to the landlords, they abstained from agriculture, and exhorted rackrents from the actual tillers of the soil. The landlords also could not look on happily while tenants mortgaged or transferred their fields to the money-lenders by some device, consequently paying them (money-lenders) every price above the fixed rents that could be squeezed from the holdings. A mortgagor could not take proceedings to evict a tenant under Section 36 of the Act, so long as the land remained in the possession of the mortgagee; a tenant may, owing to the neglect of the mortgagee to make use of the said section, or in collusion with him, acquire hereditary rights in his tenancy to the great detriment of the real proprietor, the mortgagor.[10]

As long as population pressed lightly on the soil, as long as prices remained low and the standard of living had not risen, as long as landlords were content with customary rents, difficulties remained in abeyance. In fact before 1885 for fifteen years, occupancy rights showed an expansion of about 7 per cent. But probably because of the growth of population, the rise in prices, the increase in the cost of living and in the standard of comfort, landlords' and tenants' interests began to diverge. The landlord endeavoured to deny his tenant the fixity of tenure, while the tenant sought just that, as it gave him protection against the greed of the landlord to arbitrarily enhance rents.[11]

To prevent the accrual of occupancy right to the tenant, the landlord could act directly and legitimately by the grant of leases for however short a term. Shifting of holdings could be done to prevent continuous occupation by tenants. However, the most popular method resorted to by landholders was ejectment. The landlord could exercise this right according to the law by adhering to the restrictions placed by it, but in majority of the cases the landlords abused this right. The tenant was formally evicted according to lawful proceedings, and when it was thought that the continuity of occupation had been sufficiently broken to satisfy the courts in the future, he was quietly allowed to go on cultivating the same land as before. The result was the extreme difficulty the tenants-at-will or non-occupancy tenants experienced in procuring occupancy rights; they were dependent on the caprice of the landlords, insecure, and with the prospect of poverty and pestilence always looming in the background.[12] The *Kashshaf* of Muzaffarnagar of 24 January 1895, aptly said, 'The landholder does not allow a cultivator to occupy the land long; and the latter apprehending ejectment at any time had no desire to improve it at any trouble or expense.'

The large number of suits filed by the landlords to eject their tenants resulted in ruinous and excessive litigation. The only remedy suggested was that the process of eviction should be simplified 'with a view to reduce the number of suits'. It was recommended that landlords first apply for the renewal of the lease with or without an increase of rent. If the tenants disagreed, the landlords may be allowed to file a suit for their eviction.[13]

The NWP Tenancy Act of 1901

Along with the Land Revenue Bill, the government introduced the NWP Tenancy Bill. The government considered the latter a complement of the former. This was widely discussed, both in the columns of the newspapers, as well as in the Legislative Council of UP of Agra and Awadh. The government claimed that it was the perfect remedy to the ills prevalent in the previous bill. It conferred a further measure of protection on the great mass of the agricultural population. It endeavoured to nullify the harassing and expensive devices which were now resorted to merely to evade the law regarding the acquisition of occupancy rights. The landlord had to make a lease of at least seven years with his tenant, for the latter to be disqualified for attaining occupancy rights. Short leases would not interrupt the tenants' progress towards occupancy status. Besides, the bill provided that continuous occupation of the same plot would no longer be necessary for the acquisition of occupancy rights. The right of occupancy may be acquired provided the relation of tenant and landlord had continued for twelve years, although different plots may have been held at different times. The eviction of a tenant had to be genuine, and, if the tenant was readmitted within a year to the tenure of any land under the same landlord, it would fail to interrupt the accrual of occupancy rights.

For the grant of some measure of protection to the tenant-at-will from excessive and frequent enhancement of rent and from arbitrary ejectment by the landlord, certain provisions were made. The Bill provided that, if the new rent demanded by the landlord from a non-occupancy tenant did not exceed the old by one *anna* in the rupee, the tenant had to pay or quit. If it exceeded one *anna* in the rupee, it was left to the courts to determine whether the enhanced rent was fair and equitable, and whether the tenant should be obliged to pay, or be ejected. If the rent was enhanced, then the non-occupancy tenant would hold the land for not less then five years. An important provision of the Act was to confer upon a non-occupancy tenant the right to construct a well for the irrigation of his holding. At the same time, the landholder's right to make improvements was recognized, a preferential right being given to him where the improvement would benefit more than a single holding.

In the case of occupancy tenants, provisions were made for enhancement and abatement of rent. A rise in prices could justify enhancement, and power was given to the courts to allow progressive enhancement where necessary. The evil of rack-renting was also dealt with: tenants sublet their lands to the money-lenders in lieu of payment of debts. These bankers could sublet them again to whoever they liked, while paying rent to the landlords. Hence the original tenant became disconnected with the land and would remain so for decades. If he had heirs, they could not be ousted by the landlords, but in the absence of heirs, at his death (of the occupancy tenant), the holding could be confiscated by the landlord. Another way was mortgage by tenants of their holdings to creditors, and taking them back at rents much higher than those owed to landlords. Large enhancements of rent were thus of no use to landlords: it was money-lenders who benefitted.

The new Bill proposed to solve these difficulties by allowing women, minors and others to sublet, but to prohibit subleases in other cases should their term exceed three years. If the tenants transferred or sublet in contravention of the Act, then landlords could sue for cancellation of the transfers, or for ejectment of tenants, or for both; they could also sue for compensation. The division of tenancies, and distribution of rent payable in respect of such tenancies, by tenants, could only be done with the consent of landlords. Suits for such divisions would be outside the jurisdiction of courts.[14]

After almost three years of discussion, the NWP Tenancy Act came into operation in 1901. The landlords protested. They objected to standing crops being declared immovable property for purposes of attachment in satisfaction of arrears of rent; stoppage of the acquirement and transfer of *sir* right in land in future, the diminution of exproprietary rights; the facility afforded to tenants for acquiring occupancy rights; the liability of the zamindar to be bound by the terms of a contract entered into with an original tenant and a sublessee (in case of the former relinquishing his holding) which would prove a fruitful source of intrigue between tenants and sublessees against the zamindar; the disability of the zamindar to eject a sublessee unless the standing crop was cut; the new restrictions placed on eviction of occupancy tenants; and the need for referring to courts for enhancing the rents of even tenants-at-will. Small landholders would be the worst hit as lands of proprietors who could not continue cultivating after twelve years, or who died leaving minor children behind, who had to lease out the land to tenants, ceased to be *sir* lands under the new law. These landholders were totally dependent for their maintenance on their *sir* lands, paying government revenue from the rent they realized.[15]

The misapprehensions of the landlords seemed well-founded as the Act made concessions to the peasantry. In enacting the Law, the government was prompted by an honest desire to improve the condition of the agricultural population, and was genuinely desirous of providing relief to the peasantry. Sir Anthony MacDonnell, the Lt.-Governor, justified the new rent legislation:

> The Bill, I can well believe is not acceptable to the new-fledged zamindar . . . but as regards the old territorial aristocracy of the country, this Bill will only confirm the existing practice . . . the ryot is also of flesh and blood, and that he had feelings and passions which, if overstrained, lead to results which are unpleasant for the landlord and the government alike.[16]

The language press realized that favouritism had been shown to the peasants, whether rightly or wrongly. Even newspapers which felt the peasants had got their due found the resentment of the landholders justified to an extent. The landlords complained that the value of their lands had been reduced by 25 per cent to 40 per cent. Some papers disagreed with MacDonnell's assertion that only the new-fledged zamindars, namely vakils or banker zamindars, were distressed. About the old territorial aristocracy, the newspapers felt that they gave restrained opposition, but, 'their silent but more serious discontent . . . is akin to sedition'.[17]

The general consensus of the language press was that the noble objective of the government as evidenced by the Act was to improve the material condition of the cultivating classes, but this object could only be secured, and landlords made happy, if government itself pursued a more liberal policy in its assessments of land revenue. Landlords had to be reassured that their lands would not be interfered with without any material improvement in the land.[18]

Gradually the dissatisfaction regarding the working of this major legislative measure became more pronounced. Newspapers requested the government to inquire into the efficacy of the Act.[19] Zamindars and tenants both had allegedly suffered as a result of the passing of the Agra Tenancy Act. The last Revenue Administration Report showed that there had been an enormous increase in the number of suits filed on account of arrears of rent, that agriculture had been neglected, and antipathy had grown between landlords and tenants. Landlords hesitated to readmit tenants before a year had elapsed from the time they had been ejected, as then the tenants could add the former tenure to the new one.[20] Poor tenants had thus to starve for a year while landlords tried to beat the law. On the other hand, landlords resented the clause that allowed rents to remain unpaid until the end of the agricultural year, before filing for recovery. It empowered the court to grant as much as a year's time to the defaulting tenant for paying the rent in arrears. It finally caused another year to pass before all its proceedings were completed. The result was that while the tenant need pay no rent for three years, the landlords still had to pay government the revenue.[21]

It would not be wrong to assume that there was a large number of peasant proprietors in the NWP, and the tenantry in general was not unhappy. Perhaps the absence of big holdings in the NWP meant tenants must fight for their rights. There was no patron to turn to. Yet the absence of paternalism made peasants more self-reliant and conscious of their rights.

Some areas in the eastern region were under the Permanent Settlement, such as Varanasi, Ghazipur and Jaunpur. The permanently settled areas were representative of a comparatively happy and less exploited tenantry. For example, in Jaunpur district, was found a remarkable congruence between high caste tenants and occupancy rights. As 65 per cent of the land was held by privileged tenants, these tenants having privileges of a low rent on account of their 'fixed rate', 'occupancy' and 'expproprietory' status,[22] zamindars could not enhance rents arbitrarily. The privileged tenants derived much benefit from the raising of rents of their *shikmis* or subtenants. But in Jaunpur, these tenants-at-will held only 15 per cent of the land and on the whole 'it was possible for the agrarian structure of the district to contain within it the growing rental'. The zamindars of the area, unable to enhance rents profitably, tried to extend their *khudkasht* holdings to convert these into *sir*.[23] The zamindars too were not overburdened with high land revenue assessments. The bulk of the tenantry not being hard-pressed, high rents which did prevail at the subtenant level, caused little structural economic dislocation. Despite these ideal conditions of lower revenue demand and a good tenant–proprietor relationship, poverty pressed heavily on some of the permanently settled areas—the major reason being population pressure. Consequently, some of the temporarily settled areas like Saharanpur were more prosperous than Jaunpur or Ghazipur.[24]

AWADH

Unlike the NWP, in Awadh the taluqdari settlement was introduced. Local village authorities were generally ignored and the taluqdars, who were responsible for the collection of revenue usually from a number of villages, were recognized as landlords of entire taluqs (revenue collection areas). In their social origin, these taluqdars were a mixed lot. They comprised the remnants of old Rajput lineages, court favourites, tax farmers and *nouveau riche* administrators. Without any social homogeneity, they represented the strongest rural entity and the most important agricultural interest in land.[25] These old rajas had been turned into big landlords with enormous estates. The British had formed this landed aristocracy with the pragmatic view of having a loyal following. The taluqdars, on their part, realized that their continuance was dependent on their loyalty towards the British rule, and strove incessantly towards trying to prove their faith in the British.[26]

By the Awadh Compromise of 1866, the taluqdars agreed to grant special privileges to those cultivators who had lost proprietary rights but still occupied land in their ancestral villages. They agreed to give subsettlement rights to underproprietors on the condition that no right of occupancy would exist in Awadh. It was a way of showing that the taluqdars were not entirely obstinate and were willing to listen to reason. It strengthened their hold on the land considerably.

The Awadh Rent Act of 1868 did not recognize any other tenant right save that tenants who had held proprietary rights within thirty years of the annexation should receive occupancy rights. The Act also debarred the courts from interfering in the matter of rent payable by tenants-at-will. The Awadh landlord had been invested with superior power *vis-a-vis* the tenantry. As against the expected 15 to 20 per cent only 0.5 per cent or one in every two hundred tenants was able to acquire occupancy rights.

By the end of the nineteenth century the typical taluqdari estate was a large one, though sometimes there were smaller ones too. Small estate owners were called zamindars. The zamindar of Awadh was the owner of only one grade of proprietary interest. Generally those estates were called zamindari which were outside the extent of taluqdari areas. However, since the zamindar was a managing landholder, those subproprietors on taluqdari estates who owned the residual proprietary right could also be (and were) loosely called zamindars. Between taluqdari and zamindari tenures, almost the entire *malguzari* or revenue area was covered. Under them were the two classes of underproprietors—those with whom subsettlements had been made as part of the first regular settlement (1860-78), or the *pukhtadars*, those whose proprietary interest was acknowledged but was either not extensive or strong enough to merit a separate subsettlement.

Under these were the tenant-cultivators, of whom only 1 per cent held rights of occupancy under which they paid rents less by two *annas* in the rupee. Below these were the tenants-at-will who were absolutely at the mercy of the landlords. Their rents could be raised periodically and arbitrarily. Besides, the landlord could evict them from their holdings at pleasure. Eviction notices were served freely, but a great many evictions did not result. They were used more as an instrument of arm-twisting; for example in Rae Bareli, out of the 3,506 notices issued 1,153 tenants remained at enhanced rent ranging from 10 to 37 per cent.[27]

The result of all this rent extraction was that tenants were miserable; an evicted tenant had no choice but to work as an agricultural labourer. Tenants had to perforce look to the village bania or mahajan for loans. Among the propertied classes, those who were most in debt were small zamindars—especially the high caste ones, who considered it below their dignity to cultivate themselves—and coparcenary landlords who existed along with the large landlords in the predominantly taluqdari areas of Faizabad, Sultanpur and Rae Bareli.

Tenants desisted from making improvements on their lands, as there was a danger of landlords giving notice of eviction. In such a contingency the unfortunate cultivators could either pay an enhanced rent or vacate the land for other tenants who would enjoy the fruit of their expenditure. The tenants sometimes had no choice but to relinquish their holdings, wholly or partially, thus hoping the landlords would relent and reduce the rent demand. This was especially popular with low caste tenants on whom the frequency of the demand for rent increase was greater. However, landlords still had the upper hand: figures show that the rent was reduced only in a few cases.[28] The system of appointing *thekadars* for managing the estates of taluqdars was full of unhealthy connotations. At the time of the second settlement, 3.9 per cent of the total taluqdari area was under *thekadari*, and as the *thekadars* kept something for themselves after paying off the dues to the taluqdars, this had a harmful effect on the rents in the leased-out area. The management of estates by *thekadars* and *karindas* cut into the profits of taluqdars, but in the long run the latter benefited. There was an all-round demand for reform. The language press was most vociferous. It lamented that although Awadh had long been under the Lt.-Governor of the NWP, Act XIX of 1868, which allowed unjust ejectments of tenants from their old holdings, had not yet been amended.[29] The Awadh Rent Act of 1886 was passed repealing the Awadh Rent Act of 1868. Tenants-at-will were upgraded to statutory tenants. They were secured by statute in the occupation of their holding for a seven-year period. At the end of that period, the landlord could either enhance the rent or evict the tenant. The rent enhancement, however, could not exceed 6-1/2 or 1 *anna* in a rupee of the previous rent. Whether the outgoing (evicted) tenant was reinstated or a new tenant brought in, the rent increase would be the same. Notices of eviction would be liable to the payment of heavy court fee, the maximum being Rs. 25.[30] The orders of the Deputy Commissioner on applications by tenants for permission to make improvements would be appealable to the Commissioner. Landlords would not be liable to payment of compensation for improvements made more than thirty years ago.[31] The newspapers agreed that this Act was an endeavour to curb the power of the landlord.

The Act became operative from 1 January 1887, and resulted in a temporary decrease in evictions. This was, however, short-lived and the landlords started looking for ways and means to evade the legal binding imposed on them. By 1888 it became obvious that enhancements of rent as well as evictions had risen. In 1888, 2,369 ejectment notices were served; in 1889, 4,233; in 1890, 6619 and in 1891, 8,422.[32] Landlords soon found loopholes in the 'half hearted' Act.[33] Sometimes the rent enhancements were so high, as in Barabanki in 1887-8, that tenants had to relinquish their holdings. Often the landlords, to avoid ejectment and its hassles, forced tenants to relinquish their holdings (Hardoi in 1887). In a vast majority of cases, the landlords and tenants entered into contract without going to court. Sometimes ostensible transfers of holdings were made by placing dummy tenants who were actually affiliated to the landlords or their fellow tenants.[34] Another way devised to beat the law was the conversion of grain rents to cash rents or *vice versa*. This was reported from Rae Bareli, Sitapur, Hardoi and Gonda districts, to name a few.[35] Probably the most natural and frequent method of eviction was a landlord's demand for arrears of rent. Another and more effective way in which rents enhancements could be hidden was through the practice of *nazrana*. The landlord contrived to evade the law by taking a premium as a condition for renewing a tenancy or admitting a new tenant. As no accounts were kept of these illegal transactions, the revenue authorities could not estimate them adequately and appropriately. Often even after taking *nazranas* landlords did not desist from ejecting tenants if other bidders offered more. The *nazrana* evil had set in and some tenants were forced to commit the heinous crime of *kanya vikray* or sale of daughters to bribe the landlords. To pay off *nazrana*, Gayadin Dubey, a poor Brahmin, sold his ten-year-old daughter to a man of forty for Rs. 400.[36] A truly morbid form of *nazrana* extraction was *murdafaroshi* or the sale of corpses. When a tenant died, land was let out for a bid much higher than what he had been paying to his death.[37]

The important taluqdars found little difficulty in enhancing rents. Clause 51 of the Rent Act allowed the government in exceptional circumstances to vary the rate of enhancement. The Maharaja of Ayodhya requested the government to invoke this clause for the purpose of enhancing the rents payable by his tenants in 1899. MacDonnell refused, but not a man to be easily stymied, Pratap Narayan began covertly leasing out his estates to *thekadars*, with instructions to raise rents all around. The Maharaja ostensibly enhanced the rents reasonably—by about 25 to 40 per cent—but there was no curb on the *thekadars* to increase the rental by even 75 to 100 per cent. By the time the government found out, in 1902, the process was beyond control. Ejectment notices on the estate had gone up from 132 to 700 a year.[38]

The government paid only lip service to the Awadh Rent Act. Even though rents were enhanced beyond legal limits, the government did not pull up the guilty taluqdars. They were useful for exercizing control over the populace. The Lt.-Governor, J.P. Hewett, said, 'It is far more important to retain the goodwill of the taluqdars than to start an enquiry which may have the effect of putting the whole of Awadh into a blaze'.[39]

The last half-century of British rule in the United Provinces witnessed a sharp intensification of agrarian difficulties and an increasing responsiveness of the land revenue administration to political pressures. Fresh tenancy legislation was made—the Awadh Tenancy Act of 1921 and the Agra Tenancy Act of 1926. These extended rent protection to tenants-at-will, hence naturally eroded landlord interests. With the national movement gaining momentum it became imperative for colonial control to be applied through the landlords. Hence the British found it politic to make concessions to landlord interests. The landlords in turn obliged by accepting the tenancy acts!

NWP *versus* Awadh

It is now obvious that tenants were much more prosperous and contented in the NWP, than in Awadh. The petty yeomen in the NWP were more interested in improving their lands as they would be able to enjoy the fruits of their labour, while the Awadh peasant always had the fear of eviction hanging on his head. In the NWP the proprietary bodies had been formed by a process of evolution, while in Awadh, the sycophant taluqdars had been established by the British for their own use. The taluqdars could be identified with the feudal system. The tenants were like their subjects, for a long time bound to them by a feeling of subjection and allegiance. In times of natural calamities, the Awadh tenants were reduced to serfage and beggary, while the NWP tenants could keep their heads above water. In course of time, the Awadh tenantry came to acquire a socially inferior position to that of the Agra tenants. So much so that the Agra families felt reluctant to give their daughters in marriage to persons who might become 'beggars at the whim of their landlord'.[40] The power of the Awadh landlord was more than the zamindar of the NWP, because besides being a revenue collector, he was also a judge, policeman, and dispenser of loans.

There were differences. Awadh had a quarter of the population, and less than one-fourth of the area of the NWP. In the latter the area of cultivation was 51 per cent while in Awadh it was 60 per cent. However, the extension of cultivation area was more possible NWP than in Awadh where 40 per cent of the land was double-cropped (in

NWP only 20 per cent of the area was double-cropped). The NWP was more prosperous, yielded greater revenues.[41] Yet, from the government's point of view, settlement operations were more easily conducted in Awadh than in the NWP, with its petty landlords and joint tenures, concealment of rent, and falsification of rent-rolls. MacDonnell's observation about this seems quite convincing. 'In Meerut and Badaun and in the other North-western districts . . . the same feeling of honour does not prevail amongst the landlords as I found prevalent among the Taluqdars of Oudh.'[42]

Differences between the Eastern and Western Districts

Striking contrasts in living conditions of agriculturists prevailed between the eastern and western districts of the province.

The population in the eastern districts was much higher than it was in the western districts. A comparison between the figures of the population of some places in both the areas is self-explanatory.

The difference in population was due to several factors. The climate of the eastern districts was more equable, and did not require so high a scale of necessaries as the more rigorous climate of the western districts. There better food, lodging and clothing were necessary to the support of life. The eastern districts had been longer under settled rule and peaceful administration—perhaps 'a whole generation ahead of the west where the memory of war and plunder is still green under the double influence of a firm and peaceable government'.[44] Hence, population multiplied in the eastern districts, leading to lower standards. Because of this population growth, though total wealth had increased under British rule, people felt the pinch

TABLE 9.1: POPULATION DENSITIES IN WESTERN AND EASTERN DISTRICTS[43]

Name of Place	*Persons to a square mile*	*Name of Place*	*Persons to a square mile*
Jaunpur	778	Saharanpur	441
Azamgarh	748	Muzaffarnagar	457
Ballia	805		
The Azamgarh peasant with 1244 persons to a square mile of cultivation had to subsist on about half an acre.		In the Meerut division to the extreme west each person had about an acre and a half.	

much more as there were more mouths to feed. This connection between population growth and lack of comfort was plausible enough, but seems to have been overemphasized by the British.

In the matter of the average area under each plough, the western districts naturally were better off. In Saharanpur, there were on an average nearly 12 acres to each plough, but at Azamgarh only 5-1/2. Increase in the area of cultivation was easier in the less congested western areas, with fewer small holdings, where the cultivator was interested in just looking after his family's sustenance. Many agriculturists followed other occupations too and were often weavers and craftsmen. The western areas being more progressive, the percentage of town dwellers was higher here than it was in the east. In the Meerut division about 19 per cent people lived in towns, in Rohilkhand about 16 per cent, but in the Varanasi division to the extreme east, the proportion fell to 12 per cent, and in half the Awadh districts and Gorakhpur to less than 5 per cent.[45]

This discussion of the diverse agrarian conditions of the UP would not be complete without a mention of the conditions prevailing in Bundelkhand. The alternate niggardliness and overabundance of rainfall here made agriculture permanently precarious, population scanty. There was much arable wasteland, which could not be cultivated easily, so that even though on paper a holding may have been big, for all practical purposes only a small portion of it was cultivable. The system of land tenures was basically the ryotwari system. There existed no proprietary occupancy group between the state and the resident cultivating class. Thus there was no true landlord class except in favoured localities. As late as 1907 the Settlement Officer found in Jhansi that the zamindar promoted from among his fellows by the British was only the first among equals. The distinction between landlord and tenant was more legal than social.

The Bundela Thakurs were zamindars, but too proud to take up cultivation themselves. In 1893, in Jhansi proper, they worked on only a third of the land they owned, and the rest they sublet. Consequently, they were reduced to poverty. As a result, Marwari money-lenders became important. These money-lenders were not interested in gaining proprietary rights over mortgaged land as it was not economically viable. Ownership yielded only management rather than rental profits. The result was that the lands taken up by the money-lenders were neglected; with land freely available, cultivators preferred to abscond than live under an alien landlord. Compared with the gains of non-agriculturists elsewhere in the UP, in Bundelkhand money-lenders gained very little. Between 1864 and 1945, holdings of Marwari Brahmins rose from 20 per cent to no more than 24.7 per cent, and of Banias from 0.2 per cent to 6.3 per cent.[46]

To meet the problem of indebtedness, which threatened to wipe out the Thakur estates, the Jhansi Encumbered Estates Act was passed in 1882. It was not very effective and necessitated legislation for the whole of Bundelkhand. The Bundelkhand Encumbered Estates Act was passed in 1903. It affected private debts and public debts, i.e. liabilities to government. The provisions were to be administered by a special judge appointed by the Local Government. The Act was applicable to any encumbered estate on the application of the proprietor to the Commissioner; or on the motion of an officer especially authorized by the Local Government; or on the application of the manager of the Court of Wards. The language newspapers were grateful to the government for its endeavours to protect the indebted tenantry of Bundelkhand from money-lenders and usurers. However, it would have been better, in their opinion, if government had made efforts to remove the causes of recurrent famine in Bundelkhand. They felt that no sincere effort had been made to reduce the indebtedness of the depleted zamindars and poor tenants. The government had assumed enormous powers while reducing the invincibility of the money-lenders. These could be misutilized.[47] The *Indian People* of Allahabad of 6 March 1903 was against the Act and felt that the establishment of Agricultural Banks, where the zamindar could freely borrow without the fear of the *soukar*, was more desirable. Thus, the agrarian framework of the UP of the nineteenth and twentieth centuries was a loosely integrated one and contained varied interests. It was an ideal situation wherein colonial self-interest could prosper. Divisiveness was rampant and it was not difficult for the government to endeavour to further it through economic jugglery.

THE TALUQDARS

After 1857 Viceroy Canning had *sanads* or patents awarded to principal taluqdars, which confirmed the holders in the full proprietary possession of their estates provided they paid their revenue, remained loyal to the British government, encouraged agricultural prosperity, and preserved the rights of those beneath them on the land. All claims to land in taluqdari possession, no matter how the land had originally been acquired, were forever debarred.[48]

Taluqdars were defined as opulent landholders who paid a revenue of over Rs. 5,000.[49] However, a list of 276 taluqdars was officially promulgated in the *Gazette of India* on 31 July 1869. 'Thereafter a taluqdar was a person whose name appeared on the list, or an heir of such a person; and no one else.'[50] Taluqdars holding this right under the Nawab were generally accepted by the British, but the latter also gave lands and the title of taluqdar to their favourites, whether Sikh, European or Bengali. The British often rode roughshod over Nawabi practices. For instance, there was no precedent in the Nawabi practice that cosharers in jointly held properties should be refused taluqdari status, or that those whose estates were inherited by primogeniture should be accorded preferential treatment. But the British insisted on these practices being adhered to.

The main aim of the British in promoting taluqdars was to establish a class of people who would be loyal to them and stand by them. They would also control the 'fermenting masses'. Harcourt Butler, later Lt.-Governor of the UP, symbolized the support of the taluqdari system. The 'Oudh Policy' was put forward by him emotionally though cogently:

> The raja may be over-bearing, often cruel, but his people live at his gate, where his horses and cattle and elephants are stalled, and there is a strong bond of common humanity between them. It is the old idea 'you shall be my people, and I will be your God.[51]

However, the British could not risk any danger from these big landlords, and completely disarmed them. This effectively deprived the taluqdars of the political and military power they had exercized earlier. They became only landlords, though some of them were bestowed with magisterial powers. Attempts to evade disarmament were dealt with severely. For instance, the attempt of the Raja of Bhinga to conceal several cannons, resulted in the confiscation of one-half of his estate and 138 villages assessed at Rs. 15,400.[52]

British hopes of loyalty from taluqdars were not misplaced. The latter realized that their interests could only be secure as long as they toed the line of the British. This feeling was not limited to the taluqdars. Big and small zamindars and 'respectable' persons of NWP and Awadh displayed, in general, a sycophancy that won the ire of the thinking people.

There were examples of feasts being given to entertain officials. Huge amounts were spent on decoration and food. One such feast was given by Rae Durga Prasad to the European residents of Gorakhpur in honour of the District Magistrate's wedding in 1888. No Indians were invited and food prohibited by the Hindu religion was prepared.[53] The gift of a gun to Rana Sir Shankar Baksh Singh by Auckland Colvin overwhelmed the receiver as it was a 'unique mark of distinction conferred on him'. The language papers wondered what a disarmed nobleman would do with a gun—shoot cats and dogs, salute the Lt.-Governors and the Governor-Generals when they visited, or go to the frontier if Russia invaded?[54]

Most taluqdars opposed the National Congress, in disfavour with the British, and while praising the British administrators, expressed their lack of sympathy with the Congress.[55] Pro-Congress papers accused them of 'selfishness and narrow-mindedness' and 'their want of patriotism and sympathy with the people'. It was rumoured that Sir Auckland Colvin disliked the Congress and instigated eminent personages like Sir Syed Ahmad Khan and Munshi Newal Kishore to attempt to check the movement.[56] Raja Jagmohan Singh of Chandapur, Samrotha, went to the extent of labelling the Congress a mischevious movement, calling upon the government to suppress it as the country's peace would be endangered.[57] The language newspapers disgustedly reported the discontinuance by the Maharaja of Varanasi of his subscription to the cow protection society. This seemed to be the effect of Raja Shiva Prasad who was convinced that supporting cows was synonymous with supporting the Congress.[58] The elite tradition in Awadh remained dominant for a long time, and dampened nationalist political activity after it had become extensive elsewhere.[59]

The language papers felt that Indians who wanted to obtain honours from the British had to make efforts to win the goodwill of the authorities by sending them presents and obliging them in various ways. The *Hindi Pradip* of Allahabad of June 1888 remarked that Munshi Newal Kishore had acquired the title of C.I.E. by doing all this, and also by declaring himself against the Congress. Being a newspaper proprietor himself, it was natural that some of his colleagues were happy about the honour bestowed on him, but some newspapers disapproved of it. Bemoaning Newal Kishore's death in 1895, the *Hindustani*, nevertheless wrote that he had come empty-handed to Lucknow had become a millionaire. The praise the *Hindustani* bestowed upon Newal Kishore for having achieved phenomenal success as a press proprietor making his *Oudh Akhbar* the biggest Urdu journal in circulation, seemed to be having an undercurrent of criticism. Sir Syed Ahmad was invested with the K.C.S.I. by the Collector of Aligarh at a public darbar on 14 May 1888. The newspapers were convinced that undeserving men were bestowed with meaningless titles and rewards for sycophancy.[60] Maharaja Pratap Narayan Singh of Ayodhya was allegedly titled because he had remitted arrears of rent amounting to about a lakh of rupees, and granted land worth two lakhs in honour of Her Majesty's Jubilee in 1887, plus Rs. 45,000 to the Lucknow Technical School, Rs. 5,000 to the Female Hospital at Lucknow, and Rs. 6,000 to the Colvin Institute and Library.[61]

These taluqdars were present in all their splendour at the darbars held of the Viceroy and the Lt.-Governor. It was a privilege to be invited, even if the proceedings portrayed the contemptuous and superior attitude of the British towards the supposed elite. The invitees were granted cards of admission and had to give *nazars* to the Viceroy, which he touched and remitted. At one such darbar held at Lucknow on 13 December 1899, Lord Curzon did not hesitate to reaffirm the loyalty of the taluqdars who were 'the real foundation stones of the stable fabric of Her Majesty's Indian Empire'. There was, however, a tinge of warning in his sugar-coated address when he said that the darbar was held at the instance of the taluqdars who, 'recognized in it a compliment to your position as well as a confirmation of your privileges. . .'.[62]

The British kept the taluqdars happy by making them members of the Provincial Legislative Council and the Imperial Legislative Council. The *Hindustani* felt that the Raja of Bhinga had been elevated to the Supreme Legislative Council because of the help of Auckland Colvin. It resented his ridicule of some Hindu customs and did not consider him worthy of his seat. The newspapers were, however, not biased. The election of Raja Rampal Singh to the Provincial Council was considered by the same newspapers as worthy of celebration, as the incumbent was a leading taluqdar and a staunch leader of the Congress. Being a popular newspaper proprietor, his election was regarded as representative of the 'good sense' of the voters.[63] The newspapers were hopeful that the presence of these important personages in these legislative bodies would improve the general condition. Yet the impression one gets is that even as members of the Legislative Council, the taluqdars served only their own selves; and even if a few endeavoured reform, they were defeated being in a minority.[64]

The taluqdars were slighted by the British authorities on several occasions. Considered inferior by the British, they were repeatedly snubbed and ignored. On the occasion of the visit of the Lt.-Governor in 1893 to Sitapur, a dinner was held by Colonel Grigg to which taluqdars were invited. Many over-punctual and over-anxious men arrived at the venue before the time given. They were not allowed to go in and were kept waiting for two hours. They had to leave their carriages outside, and the Colonel did not bother to introduce all of them to the Lt.-Governor.[65] At the Viceroy's evening party on 4 April 1894 at Lucknow, taluqdars were annoyed because at the time of entrance they were asked if they had any arms and were even searched.[66]

Even in matters of administration only crumbs were offered to taluqdars. They had magisterial powers to an extent, but these were further curtailed as a result of government apprehensions about them becoming too powerful. Consequently, their interest flagged and by 1902, from an annual average of 1,350 in the mid-1890s, the total number of cases decided had fallen to 760. The government refused to revive the revenue and civil jurisdiction of the taluqdars, which they claimed had become obsolete through disuse. It curtailed their police powers considerably. Landlords were there only to assist the police in prevention and detection of crime and apprehension of criminals on their estates. So they took no interest, and in fact maintained dacoits in their pay to guard them. For example, the Raja of Mahmudabad kept a bad character of Sitapur on a monthly stipend to preserve his estate from depredations by thieves.[67]

All this deprivation and insult at the hands of the British, engendered feelings of inferiority which the taluqdars tried to hide behind ostentation and grandeur. They incurred unnecessary expenditure as they wanted to impress on people that they were still as important as before. They desisted from educating their children as they would have to go to the same schools as the common people. This false pride was the bane of the Awadh aristocracy. The newspapers gave examples of taluqdars like Raja Odai Pratab Singh and the Raja of Bhinga being contemptuous of the middle classes. The *Hindustani* even went to the extent of saying that many of these high-class land-owners were descendants of butlers or menial servants in service before 1857. It called them 'drunkards, debauchers and liars'.

The Colvin School was established in 1892 in Lucknow for the education of the sons of taluqdars. Colvin, in his speech, encouraged the taluqdars' sense of superiority by warning them that they would be politically supplanted by men 'of no special advantages of either birth or fortune, but endowed with industry and patient resolution', as they had been in education.[68]

Contempt for people of lower status was one way in which the taluqdars tried to establish the myth of their glory. However, educational institutions were established by them. Crosthwaite admired their liberal contributions to establish the Canning College and Technical School, and an Agricultural College at Lucknow.[69] Whether they did this with a genuine desire to encourage education or whether it was just another way of showing off is debatable. The British rewarded them by recruiting their half-educated sons into the Native Civil Service, and appointing them on high posts. The language press resented this and wanted recruitment by a system of examination.[70] When the question of supporting Mr. Paul's resolution on the question of simultaneous Civil Service examination came up, the taluqdars initially supported it, but later revoked their acceptance, probably at the behest of government officers. They were also guarding their self-interest, as many among them were not educated and would not be able to compete successfully with the classes below theirs.[71]

Much time and money were spent in protracted legal tussles over land and property. In the Mehdona and Balarampur estates, for example, legal battles of succession took place. With armed battles prohibited, these men took recourse to legal battles in the courts, visibly affirming to the world their power and position in society. What the litigant lost financially was amply compensated by the prestige victory gave him.[72]

The cow-agitation was decried by a number of taluqdars who took it as an anti-British move. The Raja of Bhinga was a perfect example of the taluqdars decrying this agitation. The Hindu newspapers were in a furore and felt that in order to gain the goodwill of English officers, he would not hesitate 'even to cut his own throat'.[73]

AGRICULTURAL COLONIALISM

The land revenue policy of the government came under fire from the editors of the language newspapers. It affected both landlords and tenants. R.C. Dutt rightly pointed out that excessive land tax was responsible for the travails of the Indian classes. Besides being over-assessed, it was fluctuating and uncertain, and collected rigorously. Dutt felt that the uncertainty of land tax paralyzed agriculture, prevented saving, and kept the tiller of the soil in a state of poverty and indebtedness.[74]

One half of the gross rental was the standard of assessment, but being under the impression that the proprietors did not disclose their full profits, the Settlement Officers sometimes fixed the government demand at more than one half. It was true that landholders often concealed their true incomes by understating rentrolls, but this was only because they were apprehensive about the tendency of Settlement Officers to over-assess the revenue. Even Crosthwaite declared that it was unfortunate that the government did not practice what it preached about holding land revenue as a trust for the people. He felt that the government should increase the revenue at the revision of settlement but the assessments should be just, fair and not severe.[75]

With regard to settlement, the newspapers had different viewpoints. A landowning, sycophantic newspaper like the *Oudh Akhbar* felt that Awadh should emulate NWP in the type of settlement as then there would be no need for future settlement operations. On the other hand when settlement operations were going on in Awadh in 1893, many newspapers hoped that the settlement would not be as severe as it had been in the NWP. Crosthwaite too accepted that,

> The delay which, under our revenue system occurs in giving relief in cases of over-assessment and of deterioration of villages since settlement is one of the faults of our administration, and it is lamentable to see the mischief that has occurred in Etah, Mainpuri and elsewhere from a failure to observe the mischief at work and slowness in applying the proper remedy.[76]

The newspapers felt that even though the intentions of the government might have been honourable, entrusting the entire assessment of revenue to Settlement Officers was wrong. The latter tended to arbitrarily raise revenue. Survey Officials represented inferior lands to be of higher quality, and resultantly revenue was over-assessed. The *Azad* of 4 August 1893 gave the example of Sir Auckland Colvin, who as Settlement Officer, assessed a landowner's estate so severely that he transferred it to Colvin free. The subordinate officers reportedly sucked 'the blood of the landholders'. The newspapers argued that even without arbitrary enhancements, landholders were oppressed. Even when the government had assessed the revenue at a quarter of the gross produce, the landholder had to pay half of his gross profits as revenue, 16 per cent on account of different cases, 5 per cent as the lambardar's fees and another 5 per cent on account of village expenses. He was thus deprived of 76 per cent of his income. Further deductions on account of presents made to the patwari, kanungo and tahsil officials meant that he hardly had anything left for himself.[77]

In the midst of criticism of the government, there were a few examples of benevolent settlement officials. D.C. Baillie, the Deputy Collector and Settlement Officer of Rae Bareli, was reputed to be courteous, benevolent and sympathetic. The newspapers hoped that other civilians would follow his example.[78]

The Landlords

Notwithstanding this sporadic praise bestowed on the government, most papers lamented the condition of the agriculturists. Without resorting to generalizations, it is obvious that newspapers like the *Oudh Akhbar* and *Azad* of Lucknow were owned by landlords themselves, hence definite pro-landlord positions were visible in their writings. The *Hindustan*, also owned by an eminent landlord, Raja Rampal Singh, was however unbiased.

The landholders were in a precarious position where they had to look after the interests of the tenant farmers, and also had to meet the demands of the government. They never regarded zamindari estates as their own property, and realized that on improving them at their own cost, the government would by means of its periodical settlements come in for its share of the additional profits and enhance the revenue at its own sweet will.[79]

A fair idea of the increasing land revenue demand can be had from Table 9.2.

TABLE 9.2: LAND REVENUE DEMAND IN THOUSANDS OF RUPEES[80]

District	*1880-1*	*1890-1*	*1900-1*
Rae Bareli	974	1,244	1,502
Faizabad	1,113	1,127	1,358
Unnao	1,204	1,327	1,650
Pratapgarh	953	996	1,226
Sitapur	1,335	1,300	1,498
Sultanpur	1,068	1,177	1,415
Bahraich	977	904	1,153
Barabanki	1,677	1,558	1,893
Kheri	744	830	903
Lucknow	609	716	848
Gonda	1,509	1,503	1,573
Hardoi	1,329	1,349	1,483

The language newspapers repeatedly objected to the harassment meted out to the landlords. Irrigation officials blackmailed the landlords and oppressed those who did not comply with their unreasonable demands. The method of realizing revenue from joint estates was objectionable. If a co-sharer did not pay his instalment, the revenue authorities at once realized it from the defaulter himself by any of the eight methods provided by the law. When a well-to-do zamindar had to pay several revenue instalments for his co-sharer in this way, he himself became poor. He had to resort to the Civil Courts if he desired recovery from his co-sharer, becoming poorer in the bargain because of the heavy cost of litigation.[81] The *Faryad-i-Hind* of Allahabad of 15 May 1885 went to the extent of saying that cultivators and landholders were 'looked down upon as if they were inferior in position even to shoemakers, blacksmiths and sweepers', though in England the House of Lords was composed of landholders.

What pained the people the most was the rigidity of the land revenue policy. Raja Rampal Singh complained that the government's share of profits had to be paid even when there was a failure of crops.[82] In the Allahabad district in 1895, there was excessive rainfall that damaged the last two crops. Though they were unable to realize rent from the tenants, landholders were asked to pay the revenue instalment. Similarly, in 1894, at Azamgarh, the autumn and the spring harvests failed, but the district officers appeared ignorant of the sufferings, insisted that crops had not been injured, and continued with their revenue collections.[83] The failure of the *kharif* crop at Fatehpur-Sikri, Agra, made the newspapers demand a suspension of the land revenue.[84]

The famine of 1896-7 resulted in several outbursts in the language press. The *Oudh Akhbar*, the predominantly landlord oriented newspaper, said that this famine had affected all classes of people but would tell most heavily on the landowing zamindars and taluqdars. They were sunk in debt, but continued to maintain a show of grandeur in dress and retainers. The newspapers in general reported severe collection of arrears of revenue in famine affected districts in the UP. The fact was that the government was not convinced of the real poverty in which the zamindars were steeped. It still thought that they possessed accumulated wealth and would be able to pay the revenue despite failure of harvests. The reality, according to the language papers, was that not even 20 per cent of the taluqdars possessed abundant wealth. The number of taluqdars who paid the government dues was very small, and even those were either hereditary men or carried on some other business along with the zamindari The Annual Revenue Report of the UP for 1897 stated that of Rs. 6,08,91,991, the total amount due to government, as much as 75 per cent was realized; and of the remaining Rs.1,47,35,518, Rs. 1,01,19,541 was declared irrecoverable, that is to say, could not be realized even if the estates of the landowners concerned had been sold off by auction and the defaulters sent to jail. Government was consequently obliged to grant suspension amounting to Rs. 1,53,64,251 and subsequently remitted Rs. 60,05,691 after the famine was over. Thus government remitted only 10 per cent of the land revenue. Now if the zamindar deducted his share of 5 per cent in the remitted revenue, the tenants obtained relief only to the extent of the remaining 5 per cent. In some places the harvest failed completely, so that a remission of 5 per cent or even 25 per cent on the rent was meagre. Government could not collect more than 45 per cent of the revenue from villages under its direct management in the Allahabad and Lucknow divisions. The obvious conclusion is that severity must have been exercized in realizing 75 per cent from these unfortunate zamindars. As many as 2,056 zamindars were arrested and their property sold, attached or alienated. The newspapers took this as proof of the indigent state of the zamindars as otherwise they would have not willingly submitted to this disgrace.[85]

The press generally blamed the petty government officials for the travails of the landholders. The tahsildars were accused of misusing their unlimited powers of distraining their movable and immovable property, having them arrested, jailed, or otherwise disgraced. The zamindars were reportedly most careful about paying off their revenue excepting those among them who were unable to pay it at all, owing to an unforeseen calamity or over-assessment. Despite this, helpless zamindars were mistreated by the tahsildars. The newspapers more or less seemed to think that the men at the top would be in favour of a lenient dealing with the zamindars. Sir A.P. MacDonnell was, allegedly, bent upon putting a stop to all manner of official high-handedness, and had forbidden tahsildars in UP to ill-treat landholders in realizing revenue.[86]

MacDonnell's policy of favouring landlords was in accordance with that of his predecessors, but more practical. 'I held that the maintenance of the landed proprietaries in dignity and solvency is among the best guarantees of stable government in this country.' His object, however, was 'to improve the condition of the tenant and thereby to save the landlord from those dangers and losses which in the long run, always come from denying justice to the cultivator of the soil'.[87] During the famine of 1896 he felt that the indigence of zamindars had been overexaggerated, but their condition was definitely bad, and so he advised suspension.[88] With the astuteness of an administrator, he denied that land tax was in any way responsible for agricultural distress.[89]

Landlords and Tenants

Some newspapers resented the rights given to tenants at the cost of landlords. The Awadh Tenancy Act of 1886 was considered a blight on the interest of landlords. These newspapers argued that eviction of a tenant did not mean the end of everything for him, as he could obtain land elsewhere. Raja Shiva Prasad was quoted as having observed in his *History of India* that cultivators were 'to be seen almost naked, but their wives wear jewellry'.[90] The smaller landlords were most affected. The government had framed the Act with the aim of 'robbing Peter to pay Paul'. The *Nasim-i-Agra* of December 1887, regretted that landlords in Agra were hard-pressed owing to heavy assessments and bad crops, but government was bent upon extending occupancy rights to cultivators.

Similarly, when the question of the NWP Rent Bill and Revenue Bill came up, the landlords were unhappy,and were supported by a number of newspapers. Granting of occupancy rights to tenants was a disadvantage to the zamindars, as the former sublet their lands at rates higher than what they themselves had to pay. The subtenants could be ousted any time and so had no interest in making improvements on the lands. These newspapers felt that occupancy tenure would diminish the productiveness of the soil. The necessity of granting receipts for payments made by tenants to landlords was resented. These newspapers ominously predicted, 'government will certainly be committing a serious political blunder in offending such a loyal and useful class."[91]

The connection between revenue and rent was stressed on by almost all papers. When government enchanced the revenue, the landholders could only meet the demand by extracting more rent from the tenants. The pro-landlord newspapers complained that while government recovered revenue forcibly from the landholders, the latter had great difficulty in realizing rent from the cultivators. As said earlier, they became penurious because of the extortions of the money-lender and the expenditure of court cases. Suspicion that landlords were trying to conceal rents and understating amounts on the rent rolls led to over-assessment by the government. This met with great opposition from the press, who vouchsafed the honesty of the landlords in preparing rent rolls.[92]

The situation was most peculiar. At times of natural calamity or crop failure government remitted land revenue to the landlords. The latter did not always welcome the idea, as otherwise they would have to remit double the amount as rent to the tenants. Besides, they would have no money to pay back money borrowed to pay government revenue as even in prosperous years they would not be entitled to take arrears of rent from the tenants. The landlords hence preferred suspension of revenue rather than remission, so that in prosperous years they would be able to recover rents to pay the debts incurred in famine years.[93] Similarly, the landlords were disinclined to give advances to their tenants as government never made definite promises regarding the suspension or remission of revenue even in famine years. Historians have stressed this theory of rents being increased because of the increase in revenue. The government repudiated this assertion, but there seems to be more than a grain of truth in it.[94]

The Tenants

The uncertainty and enormity of the land tax resulted in the precarious condition of the tenants.The condition of the tillers of the soil was miserable.They worked from dawn to dusk but could barely manage two square meals a day. Consequently, they were forever steeped in debt.

The Awadh Rent Act of 1886 and the NWP Tenancy Act of 1901 were genuine efforts on the part of the government to improve the condition of the poor tenants. But these were half measures and within a short while of their passage, landlords reverted to evictions or enhancements.

The oppression of the landlords over the tenants formed the topic of discussion of many newspapers who were pro-tenantry. The cultivator worked hard throughout the year, only to encounter either his zamindar or *soukar* with a decree from the court to attach his crops and have them sold by public auction in satisfaction of his demands on the cultivator. Thus the cultivator was ultimately deprived of the fruits of his hard labour. Cultivators paid rent to landholders by selling their best crops like wheat, which they grew only for profit and not for consumption.[95] The *Oudh Punch* of Lucknow of 18 January 1894 contained a picture in which two cultivators, half-clad and barefoot, were represented carrying their landlord in a palanquin. The landlord was a fat man, wearing costly dress and jewelry and also the insignia of the Star of India. The caption was: 'The Cause of Famine'. The cultivator was telling his companion, 'My friend his weight is simply crushing us to death. Why not throw him away?'

Besides extraction, the landlords took advantage of the illiterate tenants and did not grant them receipts for the full amounts paid. Landlords got patwaris to falsify their registers to suit their purposes by means of illegal gratification.[96] The government could ascertain correct accounts by encouraging the use of printed counterfoil receipts for rent. Some newspapers felt that government should realize from landlords an additional rate at 1 per cent or 2 per cent, on revenue assessments, and devote the money collected to providing means of irrigation and supplying improved implements gratis to cultivators.[97]

The landlords were indicted by the press for their oppression of the tenants, but their main grievance was against the government, whose policies were responsible for such meanness. Landlords probably had no alternative but to realize rents from cultivators by fair or foul means, because they had to pay a number of cesses over and above the revenue assessments. The heavy assessments of revenue and the system of periodical settlements were the bane of the country. Until government reduced its demand by 25 per cent or 30 per cent, there was no hope of improvement in the condition of the peasantry.[98]

There were reports of landlords being oppressive at the time of natural calamities like floods and famines. For instance, at Gorakhpur, in the 1896 famine, in spite of acute distress landlords evicted occupancy tenants.[99] At Varanasi, Hindu chiefs had established a large number of charities, which were the main support of no less than half the famine-stricken population of Varanasi. The catch was that those benefiting were mostly Brahmins.[100] However, government was considered the main culprit, and to a large extent the lack of effort of the landlord was attributed to government policies. Floods in the Lucknow district caused the government to issue orders to postpone the collection of rent and to make takavi advances. This was all very well, but what the newspapers complained about was the absence of any government concessions to the zamindars themselves. The latter could not make amends in isolation. Unless the government was prepared to make substantial concessions to them, the zamindars would be considerably constrained.[101]

Government officers, on the other hand, always tried to paint a rosy picture of the condition of the lower rural classes, occupancy tenants, tenants-at-will, agricultural day labourers and artisans. In an enquiry conducted by the provincial government in 1887 on the state of these classes in the various districts, fifteen District Collectors or Commissioners were asked for their opinions. Of them eight, from Meerut, Mathura, Etah, Pilibhit, Kanpur, Ghazipur, Sitapur and Gonda, reported that the condition of the cultivators was satisfactory and there was no lack of food in normal times. Three reports, from Etawah, Shahjahanpur and Rae Bareli, gave the middle view, of the rural people being on the whole well off but suffering in times of calamities. They accepted that a small minority suffered chronic hunger. Only four officers, from Allahabad, Banda, Jhansi and Faizabad, reported that for the majority of the population, there was daily insufficiency of food. The conclusion of the Department of Land Records and Agriculture was that 'there is insufficient ground for the assertion that any considerable portion of the population suffer from chronic insufficiency of food'.[102]

RURAL INDEBTEDNESS

Rural indebtedness affected landlords and cultivators alike. Money was lent very high-handedly by landlords and money-lenders. Cultivators borrowed grain in times of scarcity but when at harvest, they returned it, prices had fallen, and so more grain had to be doled out. The taluqdars had to maintain a large number of old faithful retainers. Besides, the imperative towards conspicuous consumption, which gave them status in society, led them to avail of the increased credit available to them. Running their estates required heavy expenditure, and the easiest way out was to borrow.[103]

The newspapers repeatedly stressed on the cancer of indebtedness spreading in rural society. Cultivators were totally dependent on village usurers, and were caught between the rapacious landlord and the money-lender. The newspapers suggested that the government should take revenue in kind and grant advances to cultivators at moderate rates of interest for agricultural purposes. Advances were generally granted by government only to well-to-do cultivators, who were able to furnish security for the repayment of the money, but the newspapers felt that this benefit should be extended to poorer cultivators who were in need of aid. Similarly, when crops were damaged, government should grant remissions of rent to both classes of tenants.[104] The mahajan or money-lender took high rates of interest and cheated people in various ways. It was government's duty to get cultivators out of the clutches of these men. A thought-provoking cartoon was published in the *Oudh Punch* in November 1887. The cultivator was represented as a very thin man working at his fields, the money-lender a fat man comfortably smoking his *hooka* in his house.[105]

A Bill proposed for the abolition of imprisonment for debt came up in 1886 as an attempt to curb the high-handedness of money-lenders.[106] It received varied responses from the press. Some papers felt that the bill would effectively curtail the arbitrary way in which money-lenders dealt with debtors, and would reduce the number of suits for the recovery of debts.[107] However, most papers did not approve. They said it would ruin trade and commerce. Imprisonment was the only means of recovery of money from recalcitrant debtors of good families, who would never return loans if they did not fear jail sentences. Besides, only 10 per cent of debtors were honest about returning debts, and imprisonment for non-payment was the only way the money-lender could get his due. In the absence of this punishment, the mahajan would think twice before lending to cultivators in general, who would consequently find it difficult to obtain loans in times of need.[108]

By 1897 many taluqdari estates had been sold in execution of the civil court decrees for repayment of loans. The only way out was the advancement of loans by the government. This way the taluqdars would be thankful to the government, and government too would receive forty lakhs a year by way of interest.[109] The newspapers, nevertheless, felt that landlords should give loans to their tenants. In this way big landlords, like Raja Rampal Singh, were more ready to advance money to cultivators than the smaller zamindars, who had no financial security of their own.

The government's duty to solve the crisis of acute indebtedness was considered absolute. The establishment of agricultural banks seemed the panacea for all evils. Taluqdars along with the government had to take the lead. The newspapers cited examples of Seth Raghubar

Dayal and Seth Jaya Dayal, taluqdars of Muizuddinpur, Sitapur district, starting an agricultural bank with a capital of Rs. 25,000 for the benefit of their tenants.[110] When the proposal for agricultural banks was actually mooted, the press in general was dismayed with its actual contents. The *raises* and officers were the main opponents. It was no easy matter to advance money to cultivators at an interest of 10 or 12 *annas* per cent per mensem, instead of Rs.2 at which money was generally lent to them. Besides this, the proposed agricultural banks were not welcomed by smaller zamindars. They borrowed money from the mahajans at an interest rate of 36 per cent per annum for paying government revenue among other expenses. They were willing to take *takavi* advances from government at 6 per cent per annum, by spending 20 per cent of the money to obtain it. They could scarcely be expected to invest money in the proposed banks at 4 per cent. The banks would only succeed if professional money-lenders and well-to-do zamindars were induced to finance them at a low rate of interest, the smaller zamindars being required to lend to their tenants in times of need at a slightly higher rate. The danger of bank officers fleecing the cultivators was also apprehended.[111]

It was believed that the extension of the Permanent Settlement to the whole of NWP and Awadh would improve matters considerably. According to the directive of the Secretary of State in 1862, the Government of India had been asked to extend the Permanent Settlement of land to districts where four-fifths of the land had been brought under cultivation. The NWP and Awadh satisfied this prerequisite in most of its districts, so it was desirable that these districts be permanently settled. The Permanent Settlement would not only relieve the zamindars from the constant anxiety of enhancements of revenue at every periodic revision of land settlement, but also induce them to lay out their capital freely to improve, and thereby increase the products of, their land. Landlords would then readily help their tenants, and the rent demand would not escalate either.[112] The papers accused the government of sabotaging any move towards a Permanent Settlement for selfish reasons. Its expenses were constantly increasing and it could not afford to let go of such a good source of increase in income from time to time. This was short-sighted attitude. Officials could be saved the trouble of making revised settlements which resulted in expensive litigation, and expense involved in settlement operations would also be saved. The pleadings of the language press, however, fell on deaf ears and the government decided that it was not prepared to forgo its share of any future profits on the land.[113]

Government and Indebtedness

Much was written on what the government ought to have done. The government's view regarding this crucial problem is also imperative. The million dollar question was often asked, 'Is it the money-lender who has made an insolvent peasantry? Or, is it an insolvent peasantry which is obliged to go to the money-lender?' The official apologists had their own ideas about the causes of indebtedness: the national character, litigatious and extravagant, was one. Indians spent lavishly on weddings and festivals without bothering about the financial strain. According to the British, another major cause of indebtedness was the 'reproductive instincts' of the Indians, which led to massive population growth. The government argued that the land revenue under the British was the lightest that the peasantry had ever paid.[114] Some leading Indians agreed, whether out of sycophancy or genuine conviction, it is uncertain. Support for government policies was most visible in the Legislative Council debates, where the Indian members were either eager to retain their position, or were greatly outnumbered.[115]

There was, however, a large section of people who refuted this kind of governmental argument. They cited the Census Commissioner's observations that in the matter of density of population, out of twenty-eight countries India came twentieth. Weddings and festivals were only occasional events. The British assertion that land revenue was the lightest in the British period of Indian history fell through if one considered the growing number of famines, the more prosperous cultivators in the 'Native' States, increasing indebtedness, and general agrarian discontent.[116]

The government tried to deal with the problem of indebtedness by the establishment of the Court of Wards, revived in the UP by Auckland Colvin. Those estates which had become centres of mismanagement and insolvency, or where there was no major heir, were taken over by the Court of Wards, and the government would oversee the management of these estates. When all the debts had been repaid, they were handed over to their owners. The Raja of Tiloi was reportedly reformed through the efforts of Babu Ram Singh, the manager of estates under the Court of Wards at Rae Bareli.[117] Sometimes landlords themselves were at fault, and the government was praised for its efforts through the Wards Institute to save them from ruin.

Several agricultural reforms were introduced in some estates and famine relief works were also started. Sometimes agricultural banks were launched on these estates which proved beneficial to cultivators. The press praised the ability of the Court to make a very considerable reduction in the debts of the estates under it.[118] The Court of Wards Act of 1900 enabled landlords to declare the whole or a part of their property inalienable, either for a time period or in perpetuity. Such property, to be called a 'settled estate' could not be sold or transferred either by the owner or by court decree. This was done with a desire to preserve the aristocratic classes, and prevent the divisions of their estates.[119]

However, it is not that the drawbacks of the Court of Wards were not recognized by the language newspapers. According to the latter, on an average the estates under the Court got only 30 to 40 per cent of the gross rental. The question was that when the condition of the estates was such when they were under the Court's management, it would have been worse when they were managed by the proprietors themselves, the amount of unrealized rents being much larger in the latter case. In many estates the revenue exceeded 40 per cent of the gross rental. In the Agra Division, the estates of Abdul Majid Khan and Kalb Ali Khan gave to government as much as 62 and 79 per cent respectively. On the Singhapur estate, gross income was Rs. 2,258, while it paid government Rs. 3,000 as revenue and Rs. 395 as cesses.[120] There were also instances of estates being placed under the management of the Court of Wards as a result of incurring the displeasure of the district authorities.[121] The newspapers complained of the arbitrary way that estates were sometimes taken over, as in the case of the Sisendi estate, leading to grave losses to the Raja. It was only through the interference of Sir Anthony MacDonnell that the estate was released. The *Azad* stated, tongue-in-cheek,

> The taluqdars of Awadh should take lesson from the case of the Sisendi estate and make a point of gaining the goodwill of the powers that be in the best way they can; otherwise they may suffer similar losses.

The inherent problem was that government accepted rural indebtedness as inevitable. In 1888, Crooke, the Collector of Etah, reported, 'Indebtedness is prevalent, but the fact seems to be that with the agricultural classes a normal state of indebtedness is quite consistent with the possibility of passing a life of comparative comfort.'[122]

CONCLUSION

The agrarian societies of Agra and Awadh were thus a conglomeration of diverse elements. The divisions were more social than economic as the taluqdar, at the top of the rung, was as indebted as the tenant and the cultivator. The money-lender, though affluent, did not enjoy a high status in society. The dependence of the lowest in the agrarian hierarchy on the landowners was both economic and social. They had been conditioned to regard their overlords as the ultimate masters whom they both hated and revered.

With the growth of the nationalist awakening, agrarian relations became more complicated and old affiliations more tenuous. This resulted in agrarian unrest, which was as much a natural consequence of an awareness of economic nationalism as that of the colonial manoeuvres. The age-old policy of patronizing landlords and establishing a loyal bloc became more frenetic as political nationalism gained ground. Even as concerns the local language press, those newspapers were encouraged which were either owned by landlords or were pro-landlord in their approach. In no other field were the divisions in the columns of these papers so precise as they were in their stance *vis-a-vis* the landed classes. Thus the economic structure in the UP, which was already based on social divisions, gradually fell victim to blatant politicization.

NOTES

1. *The Cambridge Economic History of India*, Vol. II: 1757-1970. Edited by Dharma Kumar and Tapan Raychaudhari, Hyderabad, 1982; Eric Stokes, *Agrarian Relations: Northern and Central India,* New Delhi, 1978.
2. Eric Stokes, ibid., p. 54.
3. Ibid., p. 61.
4. Ibid., p. 61. Fragmentation of holdings has been exaplained by Stokes. Besides being a result of British policies, it was also because of the clamouring of co-sharers of land to be invididually represented and separately registered.
5. Brass, op.cit.; Eric Stokes, op.cit., p. 53.
6. Brass, op.cit.
7. W. Crooke, *The North West Province of India—their History, Ethnology and Administration,* Delhi, 1897, p. 289.
8. Stokes, op.cit., p. 58. '*Khudkasht*' was land cultivated by the landowner himself.

9. VNR of NWP&O, *Kashshaf*, Muzaffarnagar, 24 Jan. 1895.
10. Ibid.,16 Feb. 1895.
11. The UP and Agra Legislative Council Proceedings, 1900-2, The NWP Tenancy Bill, pp. 61 and 72.
12. Ibid., Meerut district, July 1900, p. 72.
13. VNR of NWP&O, *Nasim-i-Agra*, 7 Sept. 1893, 7 Oct. 1893.
14. The UP and Agra Legislative Council Proceedings, op.cit., pp. 56-80.
15. VNR of NWP&O, *Oudh Akhbar*,.Lucknow, 3 Aug. 1899; *Khairkhawah-i-Am*, Dehradun, 24 Aug. 1899.
16. VNR of NWP&O, *Indian Daily Mail*, Lucknow, 25 Oct. 1901.
17. *Advocate*, Lucknow, 20 Oct. 1901.
18. *Advocate*, ibid., Home Public B, June 1901, No. 6, Memorandum on the Vernacular and Anglo-Vernacular Press of the NWP & Awadh for 1900, pp. 27-8.
19. Home Public B, June 1903, No. 45.
20. Memorandum on the Vernacular Newspapers in UP, 1902, p. 23.
21. VNR of NWP&O, *Zamindar-wa-Kashtkar*, Bijnor, June 1904; *Indian People*, Allahabad, 26 May 1904.
22. *District Gazetteer Allahabad*, 1908, pp. 108 and 121. P.C. Wheeler, *Jaunpur Settlement Report*, Allahabad, 1886, pp. 94-5.
23. Majid Siddiqui, *Agrarian Unrest in Northern India*, New Delhi, 1978, p. 47; '*Khudkasht*' land had to be cultivated by the landowner himself if after 12 years it was to be legally upgraded to '*Sir*' on which no occupancy right would be allowed.
24. GAD Miscellaneous Bound Records, p. 6. Persons to a square mile: Jaunpur 778, Saharanpur 441.
25. Siddiqui, op.cit., pp. 1-5.
26. Kapil Kumar, *Peasants in Revolt: Tenants, Landlords, Congress and the Raj in Oudh 1886-1922,* New Delhi, 1984, pp. 1-10.
27. Erskine Report, File No. 394/1882-3, Part I; Awadh General Files, R.A.D. Rev. A. Prog. 16, April 1884.
28. Between 1881-3, out of 14,012 cases of tenants only 4,095 got their rents reduced. Taken from Awadh Revenue Administration Reviews, 1881-2, 1882-3.
29. VNR of NWP&O, *Prayag Samachar*, Allahabad, 10 June 1885.
30. VNR of NWP&O, *Azad*, Lucknow, 26 Oct. 1886.
31. VNR of NWP&O, ibid., and Siddiqui, op.cit., p. 79, Kapil Kumar, p. 29.
32. *Oudh Revenue Administration Reports*, 1889-90, 1890-1.
33. *Hindustan*, Kalakankar, 8 and 9 March 1892.
34. *Awadh Revenue Administration Report 1888-9*, pp. 30-48.
35. Ibid., *1890-1*. As the Rent Act of 1886 limited the landlord's authority to enhance rents, he would change a formerly cash rented area into a grain rented one. At the end of the tenant's tenure into a cash rent, thus deviously enhancing the rent.

36. Mehta Report, File No. 753/1920. Rev. A., p. 104.
37. Siddiqui, op.cit., pp. 87-8.
38. M. Woodburn to J. LaTouche, 24 Aug. 1902 (demi-official) NWP&O, Rev. Dept. File No. 758 C.
39. Notes by W.H. Moreland of 17 March 1907; S.H. Butler of 6 July 1907 and J.P. Hewett of 3 October 1907, NWP&O, Rev. Deptt. File No. 329, Moreland was Director of Land records and agriculture for UP, Butler was Deputy Commissioner of Lucknow.
40. Siddiqui, op.cit., p. 89.
41. Crooke, op.cit., pp. 288-9. While only 113 people paid revenue above Rs. 5000 in Awadh, 2321 paid above this figure in the NWP. In other categories too, the figures were much less in Awadh.
42. MacDonnell's Papers, No. 735/111-486 C. of 1900, p. 329.
43. This table has been drawn up from: (1) Crooke, op.cit., pp. 37 and 321; (2) GAD Revenue and Agricultural Dept. of GOI, Letter, 17 Aug. 1887.
44. Revenue Scarcity Department, 1888, File No. 16. Economic condition of the Agricultural and Labouring classes in India, p. 4A.
45. Crooke, op.cit., p. 320.
46. Stokes, op.cit., *Cambridge Economic History,* pp. 69-76.
47. VNR of NWP&O, *Advocate,* Lucknow, 1 March 1903.
48. Metcalfe, op.cit.
49. Sec. Chief Commissioner Awadh to Commissioner, Lucknow, 24 April 1860, Wingfield to Barrow, 26 June 1860 (demi-official), and Sec. Chief Commissioner Awadh to Commissioner, Lucknow, 2 July 1860. B.R. Oudh General File, 1964.
50. Metcalfe, op.cit., pp.188-9
51. Harcourt Butler to Dunlop Smith, 1 Dec. 1907, in *Servant of India* by Martin Gilbert, London, 1966.
52. Ibid., pp. 186-7. As L. Barrow said of Hanwant Singh of Kalakankar—'I would make him responsible for the peace in his part of Oudh, and then disarm him with the rest.'
53. VNR of NWP&O, *Prayag Samachar,* Allahabad, 19 Nov. 1888.
54. VNR of NWP&O, *Rahbar,* Moradabad, 9 Aug. 1892.
55. VNR of NWP&O, *Azad,* Lucknow, 19 Jan. 1894.
56. Ibid., 8 and 9 May 1888.
57. VNR of NWP&O, *Anjuman-i-Hind,* Lucknow, 21 July 1888.
58. *Hindustan,* October 1888.
59. Low, op.cit., pp. 7-8.
60. *Aligarh Institute Gazette,* 19 May 1888; VNR of NWP&O, *Jam-i-Jamshed,* Moradabad, 13 May 1888; *Halat-i-Hind,* Allahabad, 28 Feb. 1893.
61. *Bharat Jiwan,* Varanasi, 6 Feb. 1893.
62. *Darbar Book,* Darbars held by H.E. the Viceroy and Governor-General Dec. 1899.

63. VNR of NWP&O, *Hindustani*, Lucknow, 24 May 1893; *Hindustan*, Kalakankar, 26 May 1893.
64. NWP Tenancy Act of 1901 debate. UP and Agra Legislative Council Proceedings 1900-2, Financial Statement.
65. *Hindustani*, Lucknow, 20 Dec. 1893.
66. *Azad*, Lucknow, 6 April 1894.
67. Metcalfe, op.cit., pp. 237-304.
68. *Oudh Punch*, Lucknow, 5 May 1892.
69. VNR of NWP&O, *Hindustani*, Lucknow, 8 March 1893.
70. VNR of NWP&O, *Hindustan*, Kalakankar, Dec. 1887; *Najm-ul-Akhbar*, Etawah, 12 Sept. 1887.
71. VNR of NWP&O, *Hindustani*, Lucknow, 23 Aug. 1893, 4 April 1894; *Hindi Pradip*, Allahabad, April, June 1894.
72. VNR of NWP&O, *Oudh Akhbar*, Feb. 1889; Metcalfe, op.cit., pp. 347-52.
73. *Hindustan*, Lucknow, 25 April 1894.
74. Saxena, op.cit., pp. 44-5.
75. VNR of NWP&O, *Hindustani*, Lucknow, 8 March 1893, *Anis-i-Oudh*, Rae Bareli, 7 Feb. 1893.
76. VNR of NWP&O, *Hindustani*, Lucknow, 12 July 1893.
77. VNR of NWP&O, *Dabdaba-i-Qaisari*, Bareilly, 24 Dec. 1893.
78. VNR of NWP& O. *Anis-i-Oudh*, Rae Bareli, 23 March 1893.
79. VNR of NWP&O, *Hindustani*, Lucknow, 6 Feb. 1895.
80. *Imperial Gazetteer Volumes: district headings.*
81. VNR of NWP&O, *Nasim-i-Agra*, 15 Feb. 1885.
82. VNR of NWP&O, *Riaz-ul-Akhbar*, Gorakhpur, 16 April 1895. The Raja compared the British revenue system to Raja Todar Mal's revenue system in Akbar's time, under which a landholder had to deliver to the king 1/5 of the produce, being exempt from any payment when the crops failed.
83. VNR of NWP&O, *Hindustani*, Lucknow, 3 August 1894.
84. VNR of NWP&O, *Mihr-i-Nimroz*, Bijnor, Feb. 1888.
85. VNR of NWP&O, *Hindustani*, Lucknow, 20 July 1898.
86. *Bharat Jiwan*, Varanasi, 14 Sept. 1896.
87. MacDonnell Papers, MS. Eng. Hist. C. 363, BPD 6368, 6 Feb. 1896—Lucknow Darbar Speech. Quoting poet Sadi he said: 'Raiyyat cho bekhast—O Sultan darakht, Darakht ai pisar, bashad az bekh sakt.' He advised landlords to be thrifty, educate their children, be good to their tenants. He asked them to detect and correct abuses in administration.
88. MacDonnell Papers, MS. Eng. Hist. C 352, BPD 6368. 54 Exp. Letter from MacDonnell to Woodburn, 31 Oct. 1896.
89. VNR of NWP&O, *Indian Daily Mail*, Lucknow, 16 Aug. 1901.
90. VNR of NWP&O, *Rozanah*, Lucknow, 17 May 1886.
91. VNR of NWP&O, *Nizam-ul-Mulk*, Moradabad, 16 March 1900;

Zamindar-wa-Kashtkar, Bijnor, 28 Sept. 1900; *Riaz-ul-Akhbar*, Gorakhpur, 28 May 1900; *Oudh Akhbar*, Lucknow, 15 Jan. 1900.

92. VNR of NWP&O, *Azad*, Lucknow, 3 July 1891.
93. VNR of NWP&O, *Advocate* and *Hindustani*, Lucknow, 7 and 10 May 1905.
94. Stokes, op.cit., pp. 62-7.
95. VNR of NWP&O, *Anis-i-Hind*, Meerut, 5 Jan. 1898, *Hindi Pradip* Allahabad, 1898.
96. VNR of NWP&O, *Sitara-i-Hind*, Moradabad, 28 March 1893.
97. VNR of NWP&O, *Akhbar-i-Alam*, Meerut, December 1887.
98. VNR of NWP&O, *Sanadhyopkarak*, Agra, April, May 1906.
99. VNR of NWP&O, *Riaz-ul-Akhbar*, Gorakhpur, Aug. 1896.
100. *Bharat Jiwan*, Varanasi, 24 Aug. 1896.
101. VNR of NWP&O, *Jubilee Paper*, Lucknow, 16 Nov. 1891.
102. GAD, Letter dt. 17 Aug. 1887, op.cit., pp. 6-11.
103. Metcalfe, op.cit., pp. 229-331.
104. VNR of NWP&O, *Nur-u-Anwar*, Kanpur, 25 Dec. 1886.
105. VNR of NWP&O, *Azad*, Lucknow, 18 Nov. 1887.
106. Home Jud. B, June 1886, Nos. 202-4. The Bill said: 'Notwithstanding anything in the Code of Civil Procedure or any other enactment, a person shall not be liable to arrest or imprisonment for default in compliance with a decree or order of Civil or Revenue Court for "payment of money" except in a few cases'.
107. VNR of NWP&O, *Oudh Akhbar*, Lucknow, 2 July 1886; *Hindustan*, Kalakankar, July 1886.
108. VNR of NWP&O, *Azad*, Lucknow, July and Aug. 1886; *Tamannan*, Lucknow, *Tahzib*, Moradabad, 1886. Though against the system of borrowing which led to indebtedness, the papers were realistic enough to realise that without easy means of getting loans, the small agriculturists would suffer inordinately for lack of money.
109. VNR of NWP&O, *Karnamah*, Lucknow, 10 June 1896; *Azad*, Lucknow, 11 Sept. 1896.
110. *Hindustan*, Kalakankar, 26 April 1892.
111. VNR of NWP&O, *Hindi Pradip*, Allahabad, Nov. 1901; *Zamindar-wa-Kashtakar*, Bijnor, Oct. 1901, *Shahna-i-Hind*, Meerut, 24 July 1901.
112. VNR of NWP&O, *Hindustani*, Lucknow, 8 Nov. 1893; *Khurshed-i-Nanpara*, 16 May 1895; *English Hindustan*, Kalakankar, 10 July 1901.
113. *English Hindustan*, 6 Feb. 1905.
114. GAD, File No. 106 C/772, 1899
115. UP and Agra Legislative Council Proceedings, 1901-2, 1903-4,1904-6, 1896-9. The objections of Munshi Madho Lal, Lala Nihal Chand and Pandit Bishambar Nath to the passage of the NWP Tenancy Act were immaterial as they lost to the supportive majority.
116. GAD, File No. 106 C/772, 1899.

117. VNR of NWP&O, *Oudh Punch*, Lucknow, 26 Jan. 1888; *Anis-i-Hind*, Rae Bareli, 7 Aug. 1892.
118. VNR of NWP&O, 1892-1900: *Hindustan*, Kalakankar; *Hindustani*, Lucknow.
119. Metcalfe, op.cit., p. 235; VNR of NWP&O, *Azad*, Lucknow, 13 June 1900.
120. VNR of NWP&O, *Hindustani*, Lucknow, 2 Oct. 1895.
121. *Bharat Jiwan*, Varanasi, 14 Dec. 1896 gave the example of the Rani of Barhar estate in Mirzapur district.
122. Revenue Scarcity Department, 1888. Economic Condition of the Agricultural and Labouring Classes in India, p. 9.

Conclusion

RETROSPECT AND PROSPECT

The significance and viability of newspapers in Indian languages in Uttar Pradesh during 1885-1914 become obvious after a perusal of the foregoing analysis. Hindi and Urdu newspapers flourished here, and there are instances of some of the editors of the language press also taking out English editions. The language press had come to stay and was showing symptoms of becoming an effective medium of manifesting the sentiments of the Indian intelligentsia, performing the task of keeping a check on irrational government endeavours. It can be regarded as being representative of public opinion on the whole as it went beyond the confines of educated classes and definitely reached out, however indirectly, to the masses. The lack of education or the inability to buy newspapers because of economic constraints of the public did not prevent people from getting to know issues highlighted in the newspapers. Thus, the smallness of their circulation, their tendency to be shortlived or unsatisfactory periodicity cannot be taken as indicative of their ineffectiveness or unpopularity.

Newspapers grew alongwith the growing national consciousness. The new politics which emerged found expression in columns of the press. The growing educated classes were a part and parcel of the nationalism that was evolving. They naturally found in the Hindi and Urdu press an adequate media through which nascent nationalism could attain fruition. The UP was considered the backwaters of nationalist activity and compared to Bengal the province probably lagged behind. However, during this period Congress sessions were held here at regular intervals and national leaders like Madan Mohan Malviya, Ajodhianath, etc., came into the forefront. They organized provincial conferences to instil national consciousness in the UP. Most of them were newspaper proprietors and editors and expressed their innermost beliefs—political or otherwise—in newspaper columns. Though the Gandhian era came later, the eminence and intelligence of these nationalists made considerable contribution to the growth of national awareness.

The rise of radical nationalists changed the course of nationalist activity. Bengal was the centre of revolutionary nationalism yet the rumblings were certainly felt in the UP. The radical Congressmen in the province Shanti Narayan, Nand Gopal, etc., the militant nationalists like Hardayal, Ram Sarup, etc., connected to Shyamji Krishna Verma; the spiritual extremists like Bal Krishna Bhatt were very active. Most of them were also connected to newspapers either as proprietors or editors or both. A branch of one of the main revolutionary organizations in the Bengal, the Anushilan Samiti, was established by Sachin Sanyal at Varanasi. Thus, although not a great centre of extremist activity, the UP was not quiescent or inert, newspaper reportage of these developments was wide and effective.

Seditious and revolutionary pamphlets increased in number and circulation. Newspapers like *Swarajya* and *Karmayogi* wrote in an impassioned way. Their editors were radical nationalists and did not like to mince words. The colonial government found ways and means of muzzling the press. The Press Act of 1910 was considered necessary for the UP. This meant an arbitrary system of warnings, securities being impounded, editors being imprisoned, the system of a press or paper existing only if government gave it a license and considered it fit to be registered. This act completed the colonial stranglehold on Indian pressmen yet they could not be permanently cowed down as punishments only increased their bitterness and defiance.

Nationalist activity was as much political as social and economic. It was influenced by societal, educational, cultural and economic permutations. Simultaneously it affected these different phenomena. Thus the national movement cannot be regarded in isolation. This interdependence came out clearly in the columns of language newspapers. The birth of the Congress in 1885 created a ruffle among the people. The Congress claimed to be representative of all the people without distinction of caste or creed, yet its growing popularity generated a certain watchful tension among different sections of society. The nationwide restlessness thus created was felt in the UP.

Muslims doubted the sincerity behind the unequivocal assertion of the Congress about its non-casteist and secular character. Its stress on Muslim support did not dispel the suspicion of the Muslims that the Congress was primarily a Hindu body. As elsewhere, this affected communal relations in the province. Sir Syed Ahmad Khan, the doyen of education of the Muslims, was averse to the Congress from its inception. He regarded it as a symbol of Hindu hegemony. Unless Muslims became educated they could not become powerful. The new government educational and job recruitment policies created a turmoil in his mind as well as among the Muslims in general. They developed a fear of Hindus outdoing them in all spheres. The introduction of Hindi in Courts seemed to them an example of the growing Hindu domination. Sir Syed established the Aligarh College to further Muslim education so that ultimately the Muslims would get more government jobs. He opposed the Congress demands for simultaneous Civil Service Examinations being held in England and India, and the introduction of the elective principle in the Legislative Councils. He felt this would unfairly affect Muslim interests who lagged behind the Hindus in education and in numbers. Being a newspaper proprietor himself, his views found sufficient means of expression. Realizing the usefulness of Sir Syed, the colonial government encouraged him to unhesitatingly state his views and even subsidized his newspaper.

The period saw a growing communal awareness among the language newspapers: Hindu newspapers, Muslim newspapers, Shia newspapers, etc. They had their own opinions about the religious quarrels that ensued between the two communities. Dussehra and Muharram fell at the same time of the year. Both communities complained of the other trying to purposely impede the progress of their processions or deliberately being mutually irreverent. Disturbances at Bakr-Id occurred periodically. Cow sacrifice by the Muslims was inimical to Hindus who regarded the cow as a holy animal. Many cow protection societies were formed to save the cow. These Gaurakshini Sabhas became centres of Hindu religious sentiments. People flocked around them and very soon they became politicised. A large section of the Hindu press backed them and Muslim newspapers were naturally apprehensive about their true intentions. They were accused of furthering communal feeling. The colonial government played the game of keeping both parties guessing as to its true intentions. The imperialists played one against the other with the balance tilted somewhat in favour of Muslims. The cow protection societies were held responsible for most of the religious discords: the sabhas too could not wholly absolve themselves of the blame.

Muslim and Hindu press became sorely divided at the time of the Partition of Bengal in 1905. Muslims had been fostered by the British. Except for Anthony MacDonnell, the other Lt.-Governors of the UP had favoured them for various reasons, the most important being to encourage divisiveness thus keeping the colonial stranglehold intact. Muslims, already feeling at a disadvantage—regarding education and government jobs—*vis-à-vis* the Hindus did not mind British benevolence. Hindus vehemently rejected the Partition, clubbed boycott and Swadeshi while Muslims did not want this association. They agreed to perpetuate the cause of Swadeshi but did not want to take part in the anti-Partition agitation or actively preach boycott. The Partition thus let off the dual forces of radical nationalism and heightened communal consciousness. The eagerness to gain a political base led to the establishment of the Muslim League in 1906 with a number of provincial branches and headquarters at Aligarh. The League enumerated its objective as loyalty to the British Government.

The passage of the Morley-Minto reforms in 1909 sent shock waves among Hindus as separate electorates had been established for the Muslims: the latter were not happy either as they expected more. The UP newspapers protested,

> the attempt to alienate Musalmans from the Hindus is most insidious and if separate electorates are provided at all stages, the real object of Lord Morley's scheme will be hopelessly defeated, for racial bitterness will continue to grow and the cleavage will become a public danger.

Muslim and Hindu newspapers became mutually suspicious. There were several instances when they accused each other of deriding their particular religions. The more balanced ones pleaded for restraint while the diehard ones did not mince words in the contempt they felt for the religious outpourings of the opponent newspapers. The Muslim press was probably more stringent and resolute than the Hindu press, but this was the result of the general insecurity felt by the Muslims.

The onset of Pan-Islamism influenced Anglo-Muslim camaraderie negatively. Hewett, the Lt.-Governor of the UP, accepted the presence of Pan-Islamic trends. The Turkish Relief Fund was instituted and all classes of Muslims contributed to it. Appeals were made by newspapers like *Al Bashir* of Etawah, *Aligarh Institute Gazette* and *Al Mushir* of Moradabad to all prominent men of UP to raise subscriptions for the fund. Not all Muslims were hit by the Pan-Islamic fever and this was evident in the newspapers which still vouchsafed for cordiality with the British. The Pan-Islamists formed several societies and established funds in the UP for furthering their cause. The Anjuman-i-Khaddam-i-Kaaba was the most prominent one. It was formed by the theologians of the Firangi Mahal in Lucknow in 1913, but the Deoband Ulema disapproved of it. The direct result of Pan-Islamism was the growth of cordiality between Hindus and Muslims, who came together against the common enemy—the British. The

Kanpur Mosque Case in 1913 increased the disillusionment of the Muslims. Almost a newspapers condemned the incident and the government resorted to heavy press prosecutions. With war imminent, the colonial government thought it desirable to effect unity at home. Meston, the Lt.-Governor, convened a conference at Lucknow in 1914 to settle the differences between Hindus and Muslims. Yet mutual suspicion continued though this was the period when Hindu-Muslim camaraderie was at its peak. The Congress and the League held their sessions simultaneously at the same place and a direct result was the Lucknow Pact of 1916. The situation, however, had become quite complicated. So many local organizations like the Provincial Hindu Sabhas, etc., had sprouted that a unified communal thinking was difficult. This trend is clearly seen in the language newspapers of the time.

Newspapers were no less divided in their approach towards social reform. The Arya Samaj, the Brahmo Samaj, the Theosophical Society were some organizations that had sprung up for the purpose of modernizing Hindu society and relieving it of the prevalent social ills. Along with these were present the orthodox socio-religious organizations to whom any change in the set practices was unacceptable. The impact of Western ideas and the imparting of English education had considerably modernized a section of society and had engendered a sincere desire to get rid of age-old regressive social and religious practices. The emergence of societies based on caste had also influenced social thinking. Most of them had their own newspapers, hence the divergence in their reporting.

Yet the prevailing social problems formed topics of animated reporting in columns of the language newspapers. Alcoholism was regarded by all as an avoidable social evil, but the newspapers differed in their approach to the problem. There were some who wanted to avoid interfering as it entailed revenue loss, while others felt that a certain amount of alcoholism was a part of Indian culture . The efforts of the more progressive elements to do away with child marriage, prostitution, oppressive marriage rules, compulsory labour, etc., were not welcomed by the orthodoxy. The latter regarded efforts to encourage widow remarriage as a devious design to change the accepted social norms completely. Enforced widowhood was so deeply entrenched in traditional socio-religious belief that any endeavour to do away with it met with vehement opposition. Progressive newspapers who espoused the cause of social reform were divided in their opinion regarding governmental intervention in doing away with retrogressive social practices. Some found governmental interference unacceptable while others realized the necessity of legislation.

The task of the British of initiating social reform was thus a difficult one. Legislation proved anathema to the public who jealously guarded their established social practices while the rest of their familiar institutions were gradually being eroded as a natural consequence of an alien rule. Caste newspapers complicated the issues by their rigid adherence to practices that synchronized with their own caste interests. They staunchly defended any move to change society and these were a few instances of a particular person being excommunicated from his caste: his crime being a trip overseas. The higher castes were contemptuous of the lower, the latter had minimal influence as newspapers supporting their cause were almost non-existent. It was the later Gandhian period which saw their uplift-ment. Nationalism that was to emerge was a synthesis of political beliefs, communal trends, societal changes and affiliations based on economy. Such diverse elements naturay entailed diversity of views of newspapers.

The dominance of sectional interests in language newspapers is visible in their opinions on the agrarian hierarchy. The divisions in the rural economy of the UP were somewhat irreconciliable. Awadh was the centre of big landlordism where taluqdars enjoyed an enviable position. The north-western part of the province had only small zamindars. There was a difference in the prosperity of the eastern and western parts of the province. Then there were some areas that were permanently settled and enjoyed a certain level of self-sufficiency. The single factor in common with them was the poor condition of the tillers of the soil. The government did make some legislation to improve their plight but these were half-baked measures. The colonial administration fostered the taluqdars to create a class loyal to the government who would act as buffer between the people and the government. Small concessions were made to them arousing an everlasting gratitude in them. The British realized the usefulness of keeping the Awadh aristocracy happy but could not conceal their contempt of taluqdars on social occasions. A rigid stance was maintained in major issues like disarmament and involvement of taluqdars in administration. Language newspapers in general resented the denial of taluqdari interests even if they regarded them as sycophants of the government.

In the duel between taluqdars or zamindars and the tenants or the tillers of the soil, one gets the impression that majority of newspapers had landlord interests at heart. They bemoaned the travails of the occupancy tenants-at-will, constantly appealing to government to do something about giving them more rights. Yet, any infringement on the rights of landlords was frowned upon by most newspapers. Excessive land revenue and improper collection were regarded as the forces responsible for the deteriorating condition of landlords and the tillers-of-the-soil.

Many of the taluqdars and zamindars were newspaper editors or made relevant contributions to newspapers. To name a few—Munshi Newal Kishore, Sir Syed Ahmad Khan, Raja Shiva Prasad. They unswervingly supported government measures. This inflamed the other newspaper editors and proprietors who felt their interests had been compromised. They lamented the precariousness of peasant economy emphasizing that the ryots, artisans and labourers never rose above want in normal times, experiencing near starvation during famines and epidemics. However, most of these newspapers blamed the government for this.

Thus, the political, social, economic, cultural, educational: all matters found their place in the language press of UP. Newspapers had become an effective medium of disseminating information and offering solutions to problems. They may have been divided having different leanings, yet their columns reveal the conditions of the time as no other source does. The efforts of the colonial government to curb them speaks volumes of their importance to the administration. Press censorship led to greater defiance and increased the popularity of the newspapers. As nationalism became more potent, the language press became viable force inalienably entrenched in the political and social scenario of Uttar Pradesh.

Bibliography

PRIMARY SOURCES

Home Department Proceedings: Judicial, Public, Revenue, 1886-1915.

United Provinces of Agra And Oudh

Legislative Council Proceedings: 1900-10, Vernacular Newspaper Reports; 1885-1914; General Administration Department Files, 1885-1914.

Board of Revenue Proceedings, 1885-1914; NWP Gazeteer.

Imperial Gazeteer of India: Provincial Series. United Provinces Acts, 1887-1906.

United Provinces Court of Wards, 1878-1933.

United Provinces, Government Educational Department Report, 1856-1901.

Education Commission (NWP and Oudh). Report of the Director of Public Instruction.

United Provinces Foreign Trade Report, 1877-1924.

Uttar Pradesh Freedom Stuggle. Report of the 4th Indian National Congress at Allahabad, 1888; Kayastha Conference, 1893.

The United Provinces Code, 1887-1916.

Private Papers

(i) Dufferin and Ava Collection, 1884-8.
(ii) Marquis of Landsdowne, 1888-94.
(iii) Lord Curzon of Kedleston, 1899-1905.
(iv) Lord Elgin, 1894-9.
(v) First Viscount Cross, Secretary of State for India, 1886-92.
(vi) Hamilton Correspondence, 1894-1903.
(vii) Minto Papers.
(viii) Hardinge Papers.
(ix) Sir Auckland Colvin, Lt.-Governor of UP.
(x) Sir Anthony MacDonnell, Lt.-Governor of UP.
(xi) Sir James Meston, Lt.-Governor of UP.
(xii) Sir John Hewett, Lt.-Governor of UP.

BRITISH INDIA ASSOCIATION PAPERS
VERNACULAR NEWSPAPERS

Abhyudaya (Hindi), Allahabad, 1907-48.
Advocate (English), Lucknow, 1886.
Aligarh Institute Gazette (Urdu and English), 1886-1941.
Bharat Jiwan (Hindi), Benares, 1884-1903.
Hindi Pradip (Hindi), Allahabad, 1877-1908.
Hindustan (Hindi), Kalakankar, 1884.
Oudh Punch (Urdu), Lucknow, 1878-1918.

SECONDARY SOURCES

BOOKS, JOURNALS, ARTICLES AND SPEECHES

Ahmad, Siddiqui, *Tarikh-i-Anjuman-i-Hind,* Awadh, 3 Vols., Lucknow, 1935.
Andrews, C.F. And G. Mukerji: *The Rise and Growth of the Congress in India,* London, 1938.
Anonymous: *Open Letters to Sir Syed Ahmad Khan, KCSI,* 'By the Son of an Old Follower of His', reprinted from the *Tribune,* Lahore, 1888.
Ansari, G., *Muslim Caste in Uttar Pradesh.*, Lucknow, 1960.
Aziz, K.K., *Britain and Muslim India,* London, 1963.
Baden-Powell, B.H., *The Land Systems of British India,* 3 Vols., Oxford, 1892.
Bahadur, L., *The Muslim League: its History and Achievements,* Agra, 1954.
Bajpayee, Ambika Prasad, *Samachar Patron Ka Itihas,* Benares, 1953.
Baljon, J.M.S., *The Reforms and Religious Ideas of Sir Sayid Ahmad Khan,* 3rd edn., Lahore, 1964.
Bayly, C.A., *The Local Roots of Indian Politics: Allahabad, 1880-1920,* London, 1975.
———, 'Patrons and Politics in Northern India', *Modern Asian Studies,* VIII, 3 (1973).
———, *The Development of Political Organization in the Allahabad Locality, 1880-1925,* Unpublished D.Phil. Thesis, Oxford, 1970.
Beck, T., *Essays on Indian Topics,* Allahabad, 1888.
Bhargava, Prag Narain (ed.), *Who's who in India,* Containing Lives and Portraits of Ruling Chiefs, Nobles, Titled Personages and other Eminent Indians, 2 Vols., Lucknow, 1911.
Bhargava, Moti Lal, *Role of Press in the Freedom Movement,* Delhi, 1987.
Bhatia, B.M., *Famines in India: A study in some aspects of the Economic History of India, 1860-1965,* Delhi, 1967.
Brass, Paul. R., *Language, Religion and Politics in Northern India,* Cambridge, 1974.
———, *Factional Politics in an Indian State: The Congress Party in UP,* Bombay, 1966.

———, *Muslim Separatism in the United Provinces: Social Context and Political Strategy before Partition—Economic and Political Weekly*, Jan. 1970.

Briton-Martin, Jr., *New India 1885, British Official Policy and the Emergence of the Indian National Congress*, Bombay, 1970.

Butler, S. Harcourt, *Oudh Policy, the Policy of Sympathy*, Allahabad, 1906.

Butts, H.H., *Report on the Settlement of Land Revenue in Lucknow District*, Lucknow, 1873.

Chand, Tej Pratap, *The Administration of Avadh (1858-1877)*, Varanasi, 1971.

Chandra, Bipan, *Nationalism and Colonialism in Modern India*, New Delhi, 1979.

———, *The Rise and Growth of Economic Nationalism in India: Economic Policies of Indian National Leadership, 1880-1905*, New Delhi, 1966.

Chandra, Bipan, Amalesh Tripathi and Barun De, *Freedom Struggle*, New Delhi, 1972.

Chandra, Sudhir, *Literature and the Colonial Connection (Occasional Papers on History and Society)*, New Delhi, 1983.

———, *Dependence and Disillusionment: Emergence of National Consciousness in Later 19th Century India*, New Delhi, 1975.

Chew, E.C.T., *Sir Alfred Comyn Lyall: A study of the Anglo-Indian Official Mind* (unpublished Ph.D. Thesis), Cambridge, 1969.

Chintamani, C.Y., *Indian Politics since the Mutiny*, Allahabad, 1947.

Cohn, Bernard, S., 'Recruitment of Elites in India Under British Rule', in *Essays in Comparative Social Stratification*, ed. by Leonard Plotinor and Arthur Tuden, Pittsburgh, 1970.

———, 'The Initial British Impact in India: A case study of the Benaras Region', *The Journal of Asian Studies*, XIX, 4, 1960.

Crooke, W., *The North West Provinces of India—their History, Ethnology and Administration*, Delhi, 1897.

Gallagher, J., G. Johnson, and A. Seal (eds.), *Locality, Province and Nation. Essays on Indian Politics, 1870-1940*, Cambridge, 1973.

Ghose, Hemendra Prasad, *Newspapers in India*, Calcutta, 1952.

Ghosh, P.C., *The Development of the Indian National Congress, 1892-1909*, Calcutta, 1960.

Gopal, R., *Indian Muslims: A Political History (1858-1947)*, Bombay, 1959.

———, *Linguistic Affairs of India*, London, 1966.

Gopal, S., *The Permanent Settlement in Bengal and its Results*, London, 1949.

———, *The Viceroyalty of Lord Ripon 1880-84*, London, 1953.

———, *British Policy in India—1858-1905*, Madras, 1965.

Goyal, O.P., *Studies in Modern Indian Political Thought: The Moderates and the Extremists*, Allahabad, 1964.

Graham, G.F.I., *The Life and Work of Sir Syed Ahmad Khan*, KCSI, new and rev. edn., London, 1909.

Guha, Ranjit (ed.), *Subaltern Studies I and II—Writings of South Asian History and Society,* Delhi and New York, 1983.

Gupta, Raghuraj, *Hindu-Muslim Relations,* Lucknow, 1976.

Hasan, Mushirul, *Communal and Pan-Islamic Trends in Colonial India,* New Delhi, 1981.

Hay, Sidney, *History of Lucknow,* Lucknow, 1939.

Hobsbawn, Eric, *Revolutionaries; Contemporary Essays,* New York, 1973.

Hunter, W.W., *The Indian Musalmans,* rpt. of 3rd edn. (London 1876), Calcutta, 1945.

Irwin, H.C., *The Garden of India or Chapters in Oudh History and Affairs,* 2 Vols., Lucknow, 1880.

Iyengar, Rangaswamy, *Lectures on 'Newspaper Press in India'*, delivered at Bangalore on 26 Nov. 1932, New Delhi.

Jain, M.S., *Aligarh Movement: Its origin and development 1858-1906,* Agra, 1965.

Khan, H.A., *The Vernacular Controversy.* Resolution No. 585/111-343 C-68 of Sir A.P. MacDonnell, 18 April 1900, Lucknow.

Kumar, Dharma, *The Cambridge Economic History of India,* Vol. II: *1757-1970,* Hyderabad, 1982.

Kumar, Kapil, *Peasants in Revolt. Tenants, Landlords, Congress and the Raj in Oudh 1886-1922,* New Delhi, 1984.

Kumar, Ravinder, *Essays in the Social History of Modern India,* Delhi, 1983.

Lal Bahadur, *The Muslim League: Its History, Activities and Achievements,* Agra, 1954.

Lovett, Verney, *A History of the Indian National Movement,* London, 1920.

Low, D.A. (ed.), *Soundings in Modern South Asian History,* Berkeley, 1968.

Lutt, J., *Hindu Nationalism in Uttar Pradesh (1867-1900),* Stuttgart, 1970.

———, 'The Hindi Movement and the Origin of a Cultural Nationalism in Uttar Pradesh', Unpublished papers, Cambridge.

Lyall, A.C., *The Life of the Marquis of Dufferin and Ava.* 2 Vols., London, 1905.

———, *Asiatic Studies.Religious and Social,* London, 1899.

Majumdar, B.B. and B.P. Mazumdar, *Congress and Congressmen in the Pre-Gandhian Era, 1885-1917,* Calcutta, 1967.

Manmohan Kaur, *Role of Women in the Freedom Movement 1857-1947,* Delhi, 1968.

Metcalfe, T.R., *The Aftermath of the Revolt in India: 1857-1870,* Princeton, 1965.

———, *Land Control and Social Structure in Indian History,* ed. by R.E. Frykenberg, Madison, 1969.

———, *Land, Landlords and the British Raj: Northern India in the 19th Century,* Delhi, 1979.

Mihr, Ghulam, *Tabarukat-i-Azad,* Lahore, 1959.

Misra, B.B., *The Indian Political Parties—A Historical Analysis of Political Behaviour upto 1947,* Delhi, 1976.

Morrison, T., *The History of the M.A.O. College, Aligarh,* Allahabad, 1903.

Mukherji, H. and U. Mukherji, *The Growth of Nationalism in India-1857-1905,* Calcutta, 1952.

Musgrave, Peter, J., 'Landlords and Lords of the Land: Estate Management and Social Control in Uttar Pradesh 1860-1920', *Modern Asian Studies* 6, No. 3, 1972.

Narain, Prem, *Press and Politics in India 1885-1905,* New Delhi, 1970.

Natarajan, S., *Rise of Journalism, A History of the Press in India,* Bombay, 1962.

Nesfield, J.C., *A Brief View of the Caste-System of the North West Provinces and Oudh,* Allahabad, 1885.

Nevinson, Henry W., *The New Spirit in India,* London, 1908.

Noman, M., *Muslim—India Rise and Growth of the All-India Muslim League,* Allahabad, 1942.

Padmasha, *Indian National Congress and the Muslims,* New Delhi, 1980.

Pal, B.C., *Memoirs of My Life and Times (1886-1900),* Calcutta, 1951.

Prasad, Ishwari and S.K. Subedar, *Hindu-Muslim Relations,* Allahabad, 1974.

Reeves, P.D. 'The Landlord's response to Political Changes in the United Provinces, 1921-34' (Unpublished thesis), Australian National University, 1963.

Rizvi, S.A.A., and M.L. Bhargava, *Freedom Movement in Uttar Pradesh,* Vol. I, Lucknow, 1957.

Sarkar, Bejoy Kumar, *Study of Indian History,* Calcutta, Auckland, 1915.

Saraswati Aur Rashtriya Jagran (Hindi), New Delhi, 1983.

Saxena, Vinod Kumar, *Indian Reaction to British Policies, 1898-1911,* Delhi, 1978.

Saxena, V.K., *Muslims in the Indian National Congress,* Delhi, 1985.

Seal, Anil, *Emergence of Indian Nationalism: Competition and Collaboration in the later 19th century,* London, 1968.

Sen, S., *Press and Democracy,* Calcutta, 1957.

Sen, S.P., *Historical Writings on the Nationalist Movement in India,* Calcutta, 1977.

Siddiqui, Majid, *Agrarian Unrest in Northern India,* New Delhi, 1978.

Stokes, Eric, *The Peasant and the Raj: Studies in Agrarian Soceity and Peasant Rebellion in Colonial India,* Cambridge, 1978.

Syed Ahmad Khan, *Speech on the Institution of the British India Association,* Aligarh, 1867.

———, *On the Present State of Indian Politics,* Allahabad, 1888.

Temple, Sir R., *Men and Events of My Time in India,* London, 1882.

Tiwari, Arjun, *Swantrata Andolan Aur Hindi Patrakarita* (Hindi), Varanasi, 1982.

Uttar Pradesh Swatantrata Sangram Itihas, Vol. IX., Lucknow, 1885-1909.

Verma, Ganeshilal, *Party Politics in U.P. (1901-1920)*, Delhi, 1978.

Whitcombe, Elizabeth, *Agrarian Conditions in Northern India*, Vol. 1: *The United Provinces under British rule 1860-1900*, Berkeley and Los Angeles, 1972.

Index